Business Intelligence

Practices, Technologies, and Management

RAJIV SABHERWAL
Ph.D., University of Missouri-St. Louis

IRMA BECERRA-FERNANDEZ
Ph.D., Florida International University

WILEY

JOHN WILEY & SONS, INC.

Vice President & Executive Publisher:	Donald Fowley
Executive Editor:	Beth Lang Golub
Editorial Assistant:	Mike Berlin
Marketing Manager:	Christopher Ruel
Designer:	RDC Publishing Group Sdn Bhd
Production Manager:	Janis Soo
Senior Production Editor:	Joyce Poh

Cover credit © Image DJ/Age Fotostock

This book was set in 10/12 Times Roman by Thomson Digital and printed and bound by Courier Westford. The cover was printed by Courier Westford.

This book is printed on acid free paper.

Library of Congress Cataloging-in-Publication Data

Sabherwal, Rajiv.
   Business intelligence/Rajiv Sabherwal, Irma Becerra-Fernandez.
     p. cm.
   Includes index.
   ISBN 978-0-470-46170-9 (pbk.)
  1. Business intelligence. 2. Technological innovations—Management.
I. Becerra-Fernandez, Irma, 1960- II. Title.
   HD38.7.S23 2011
   658.4'72—dc22

                                               2009048002

Printed in the United States of America
10 9 8 7 6 5 4 3 2 1

PREFACE

Business intelligence is a phenomenon of considerable importance to all business professionals. It relies on emerging new technologies and can produce significant business impacts, but it needs to be managed well. Therefore, *Business Intelligence: Practices, Technologies, and Management* is designed to serve as a comprehensive introduction to the various aspects of business intelligence (BI), including the business impacts, technologies, and management and development of BI.

We define business intelligence as the leveraging of a variety of sources of data as well as structured and unstructured information to provide decision makers with valuable information and knowledge. These sources of information and data could reside within or outside the organization, and the information and data could be either quantitative or qualitative.

The book is written for graduate students and for academic as well as professional readers. It seeks to enhance the conventional exposition of BI with an in-depth discussion of the technologies used to facilitate BI in large and small organizations. It includes a complete description of the important capabilities of BI, the technologies that enable them, and the management of BI. We examine BI in terms of both business and technical aspects. However, the focus is on the business aspects, with an attempt to provide clear explanations of capabilities as well as technologies while avoiding excessive technical jargon. The discussion of technology is at a level commensurate with the typical business administration graduate student or corporate executive.

The book utilizes a variety of examples to illustrate BI capabilities, technologies, and impacts. Each chapter also includes a set of Review Exercises and Application Exercises. We hope this book will help our readers acquire the relevant suite of managerial, technical, and theoretical skills for utilizing, developing, and managing BI capabilities, tools, and solutions in the modern business environment.

The book is divided into three parts:

Part I: Introduction to Business Intelligence: Provides a more detailed introduction to BI and differentiates it from other information technologies (e.g., data warehouses). This section also describes the concepts of BI capabilities, tools, and solutions. It also introduces and illustrates the different types of BI capabilities.

Part II: Technologies Enabling Business Intelligence: This section of the book is devoted to a detailed discussion of the four key BI capabilities: organizational memory, information integration, insight creation, and presentation. The various technologies that enable each capability are examined and illustrated.

Part III: Management and Future of Business Intelligence: This section examines the leading BI vendors and the BI tools offered by them. It also examines the development of BI solutions and the management of BI over time. The section concludes by examining some of the emerging directions for BI.

This book may be adapted in several different contexts:

- An elective course for students pursuing a graduate degree in business administration, or majoring in areas such as Finance, Marketing, and International Business. In such a situation, this book could be supplemented with a set of case studies that may be explored alongside the concepts presented here. A list of suggested cases will be provided in the Web site accompanying the book and will be updated regularly.

- A required course for graduate students with a major in Information Systems, Decision Sciences, Accounting Information Systems, Information Science, or Computer Science. In such a situation, this book could be supplemented with some case studies, and with additional technically oriented materials from published articles and online sources. A list of suggested technical materials will also be provided in the Web site accompanying the book and will be updated regularly.

- Either an elective or a required course for undergraduate students. In such a situation, this book could be supplemented using a technical book with a focus on specific technology issues, such as data warehousing, depending on the focus of the course and the instructor's preference. A list of such suggested books will be provided in the Web site accompanying the book and will be updated regularly.

To complement the text and enhance the learning and pedagogical experience, we provide the following support materials through the instructor's Web site:

- An Instructor's Manual
- A suggested list of cases that may be used to supplement each chapter
- A suggested list of technical materials that may be used to supplement the book
- A suggested list of technical books that may be used to supplement the book
- A Test Bank, including multiple-choice questions for each chapter
- Instructor's PowerPoint slides for each chapter
- Links to some demo software related to BI
- Links to Web pages of the leading BI vendors
- Links to teaching materials such as course syllabi, projects, and BI system demos

We look forward to further improving this book in the future, so that it can become even more useful as the field of BI evolves. Therefore, we invite all readers to help us by e-mailing any suggestions or concerns to sabherwal@mac.com and becferi@fiu.edu. We also invite instructors adopting the book to share with us any relevant material that could be included on the Web site to reinforce and enhance the students' experience.

ACKNOWLEDGMENTS

We have so many people to acknowledge! First, we want to recognize the encouragement, support, and patience of our families during the time we spent in conceptualizing, discussing, and writing this book.

We also thank our administrators, who were very understanding when our other academic commitments could not be completed in time. These include Keith Womer, Tom Eyssell, and Ashok Subramanian at the University of Missouri-St. Louis, and Joyce Elam and Christos Koulamas at Florida International University. We are also grateful to our graduate students who provided valuable comments on the draft of the book. Rajiv also wishes to thank Shaji Khan, Stan Solomon, and Kathy Ntalaja for research assistance, and the Cutter Consortium, with which his research on BI first started. Irma also wishes to thank Jose Rocha, Frank Andollo, Lauren Suarez and Karyne Bury for their assistance.

We are also deeply indebted to many individuals at John Wiley & Sons, who have helped make this book possible. We are especially grateful to our editor, Beth Golub, who has guided us through the development of this book. We are also grateful to the anonymous reviewers who have provided numerous insightful and constructive suggestions to improve the manuscript. Finally, we are grateful to Michael Berlin for coordinating the reviews.

▶ ABOUT THE AUTHORS

Dr. Rajiv Sabherwal is University of Missouri System Curators' Professor, Emery C. Turner Professor of Information Systems, and the Director of Ph.D. Program in Business Administration at University of Missouri, St. Louis. He is serving as the Fulbright-Queen's School of Business Research Chair of knowledge management at Queen's School of Business in 2009–2010. He conducts research on business intelligence; knowledge management; and management, adoption, and success of information systems. His papers appear in numerous journals, including Management Science, Information Systems Research, MIS Quarterly, California Management Review, Organization Science, Journal of MIS, IEEE Transactions on Engineering Management, and Information Systems Journal. He is currently Senior Editor for a special issue at Information Systems Research, and serves on the editorial board for Journal of MIS. He has previously served as Departmental

Editor of IEEE Transactions on Engineering Management, Senior Editor of MIS Quarterly, and editorial board member of Management Science, Information Systems Research, and Journal of AIS. He is Conference Co-chair for the 2010 International Conference on Information Systems, to be held in St. Louis, and will serve as the Editor-in-Chief of IEEE Transactions of Engineering Management from June 1, 2010. Dr. Sabherwal is a Fellow of the Association for Information Systems.

Dr. Irma Becerra-Fernandez is Director and Fellow of the Pino Global Entrepreneurship Center and the Knight Ridder Research Professor of Management Information Systems at Florida International University College of Business Administration. She was the MIT Sloan Visiting Scholar with the Center for Information Systems Research last spring. Also she's the 2007 Kauffman Entrepreneurship Professor. Her research focuses on knowledge management (KM), KM systems, enterprise systems, disaster management, and IT entrepreneurship. She has studied and advised organizations, in particular NASA, about KM practices. She founded the FIU Knowledge Management Lab ten years ago, and has obtained funding as principal investigator for over $1.8 M from the National Science Foundation, NASA (Kennedy, Ames, and Goddard Space Flight Center), and the Air Force Research Lab to develop innovative KM systems. She has published extensively in leading journals including the Journal of MIS, Decision Sciences, Communications of the ACM, European Journal of Operational Research, IEEE Transactions on Engineering Management, ACM Transactions on Internet Technology, Knowledge Based Systems, International Journal of Expert Systems Research & Applications, and others. Dr. Becerra-Fernandez is an author of the book Knowledge Management: Challenges, Solutions, and Technologies (Prentice Hall, 2004) and co-editor of the monograph Knowledge Management: An Evolutionary View of the Field (M.E. Sharpe, 2008). She has delivered many invited presentations at many NASA Centers, the NAVY Research Lab, universities around the world, and many international conferences with both an academic and a practitioner focus. Dr. Becerra-Fernandez was the recipient of the 2004 Outstanding Faculty Torch Award, presented by the FIU Alumni Association, the 2006 FIU Faculty Teaching Award and the 2001 FIU Faculty Research Award. She is currently the Americas Region representative to the Association for Information Systems Executive Council. She has served as the faculty director for the Masters in MIS and the director of the MIS Ph.D. Program. She serves in the editorial boards of the International Journal of Knowledge Management, the International Journal of Knowledge and Learning, the International Journal of Mobile Learning and Organisation, the International Journal of Doctoral Studies, the International Journal of Computers (IJoC), and the International Journal of Interdisciplinary Telecommunications and Networking (IJITN).

CONTENTS

CONTENTS

PART I

INTRODUCTION TO BUSINESS INTELLIGENCE

CHAPTER 1

BUSINESS INTELLIGENCE AND ITS IMPACTS

▶ 1.1 INTRODUCTION

Business intelligence is a highly important field for organizations across all industries. A number of organizations have derived, and continue to obtain, significant benefits through the careful use of business intelligence. The following examples illustrate this emerging trend:

▶ EXAMPLE 1.1

At Northern Europe's largest hospital—Sahlgrenska University Hospital in Gothenburg, Sweden—business intelligence is used to provide doctors with a simple, easy, and, fast way to sift through test results and evaluate whether a patient recovering from brain surgery has meningitis (which is a common likely consequence of brain surgery) and how it should be treated. The business intelligence solution takes data from a number of different places, including physical examination, tests, and other factors, and thereby precludes the need for doctors to manually go through numerous sheets of paper with details of patient histories and test results, do computations, and then reach their conclusions. (*Computerworld*, 2007) ∎

▶ EXAMPLE 1.2

SkyTel, a pager company, wanted to tackle a major cause of dissatisfaction among its clients: when they exceeded the minutes on their billing plan, they would only find out about it upon receiving their monthly bill. SkyTel decided to try to contact these clients before the bill went out and offer to move them to the right payment plan. They achieved this by setting up a business intelligence system where they could see how many pages customers were allowed, and how many they received, and then advise them. Through the use of this system, the company was able to increase customer satisfaction. (Grossman, 2007) ∎

▶ EXAMPLE 1.3

The Michigan Department of Human Services (DHS) annually grants about $5 billion in public assistance to some 1.2 million Michigan residents, which includes some individuals who misrepresent their situation in their applications. The information that investigators need to help expose fraud was stored across different agencies' information

3

systems. But in 2004, DHS implemented a business intelligence initiative that integrated data from multiple repositories into a single data warehouse, and business intelligence query tools and reports were made available to hundreds of investigators and staffers. As a result, DHS identified instances of fraud that added up to $9.2 million in 2005 and $8.7 million in 2006, up from $3.3 million in 2004. Indeed, publicity about this business intelligence solution and the subsequent prosecutions may have contributed to subsequent reduced occurrences of fraud from then on. (Mitchell, 2007)   ■

The above three examples summarize the benefits that three very different kinds of organizations have obtained through the use of business intelligence. Indeed, business intelligence plays a crucial role in the effective management and deployment of intellectual capital (including data, information, and insights), which is widely recognized as a potential source of sustainable competitive advantage for contemporary organizations. According to one estimate, the market for business intelligence applications is over $13 billion annually (Blokdijk, 2008), and is expected to grow considerably due to the generation of vast amounts of data through technologies such as Radio Frequency Identification Devices (RFID). Business intelligence is a phenomenon of considerable importance to all business professionals. It relies on emerging new technologies and can produce significant business impacts, but these efforts need to be managed well.

In this text, we hope to provide a comprehensive introduction to the various aspects of business intelligence (BI) while incorporating related business and technical aspects. In doing so, we describe the important capabilities of BI, the technologies that enable them, and how BI should be planned, developed, and managed to enhance its benefits while reducing associated costs. Examples drawn from a variety of organizations are used to illustrate and explain these aspects.

In this chapter, we first distinguish among three important concepts: data, information, and knowledge. We then explain and illustrate the concept of business intelligence, and examine the factors driving the importance of BI, including the huge growth in the volumes of structured and unstructured data. BI is then distinguished from some other related technologies: decision support systems, knowledge management, data mining, and data warehousing. Subsequently, we discuss the relevance of BI to modern organizations, examining the ways in which BI can benefit organizations, such as by improving business operations, enhancing customer service, and identifying new opportunities. This is followed by a discussion of the obstacles encountered in designing, developing, and utilizing BI. Finally, we discuss how the rest of the book is organized.

▶ 1.2 DATA, INFORMATION, AND KNOWLEDGE

Data comprises facts, observations, or perceptions, which may or may not be correct. By itself, data represents raw numbers or assertions, and may therefore be devoid of meaning, context, or intent. That a sales order at a restaurant included three large burgers and two medium-sized vanilla milkshakes is one simple example of data.

Information is a subset of data, including only those data that possess context, relevance, and purpose. Information typically involves the manipulation of raw data to obtain a more meaningful indication of trends or patterns in the data. For the manager of the restaurant, the numbers indicating the daily sales (in dollars, quantity, or percentage of daily sales) of burgers, vanilla milkshakes, and other products are information. The manager can use such information to make decisions regarding pricing and raw material purchases.

Knowledge is intrinsically different from information. Instead of simply being a richer or more detailed set of facts, knowledge in an area is justified beliefs about relationships among concepts relevant to that particular area. The daily sales of burgers can be used, along with other information (e.g., information on the quantity of bread in the inventory), to compute the amount of bread to buy. An example of knowledge is the relationship between the quantity of bread that should be ordered, the quantity of bread currently in the inventory, and the daily sales of burgers (and other products that use bread). Understanding of this relationship (which could be stated as a mathematical formula) helps to use the information (on quantity of bread in the inventory and daily sales of burgers, etc.) to compute the quantity of bread to be purchased. However, the quantity of bread to be ordered should itself be considered information. Thus, knowledge focuses on beliefs about relationships among concepts, with the beliefs being justified in some way, such as through logic (including mathematical proofs) or empirical observations.

Figure 1.1 summarizes the above difference among data, information, and knowledge. Although decisions could be made directly from data or information,

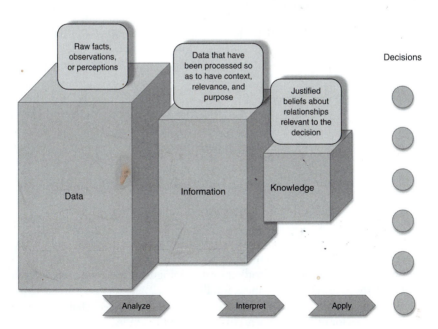

FIGURE 1.1 Data, Information, Knowledge, and Decisions

the value or reliability of decisions increases when they are based on knowledge rather than data or information.

▶ 1.3 WHAT IS BUSINESS INTELLIGENCE?

We define **business intelligence (BI)** as providing decision makers with valuable information and knowledge by leveraging a variety of sources of data as well as structured and unstructured information (Sabherwal 2007, 2008). The information and data could reside within or outside the organization, could be obtained from multiple sources, could be structured in different ways, and could be either quantitative or qualitative.

The key intellectual output of BI is knowledge that enables decision making, with information and data being the inputs. Thus, BI utilizes data, which could be internal or external, and obtained from a variety of sources, including a data warehouse, and information, which is produced through appropriate analytics and then presented in a friendly fashion, such as through scorecards and dashboards. The knowledge could relate to such diverse aspects as understanding customer preferences, coping with competition, identifying growth opportunities, and enhancing internal efficiency.

The term "business intelligence" has been used in two different ways. It is sometimes used to refer to the **product** of this process, or the information and knowledge that are useful to organizations for their business activities and decision making. On other occasions, BI is used to refer to the **process** through which an organization obtains, analyzes, and distributes such information and knowledge.

We distinguish between **BI tools** developed by BI vendors and **BI solution** deployed within organizations. BI solutions utilize the BI tools acquired by the organization, and draw upon the vast amounts of data from existing data warehouses and transaction processing systems, as well as structured and unstructured information from these and other sources (such as e-mail messages) to provide information and knowledge that facilitate decision making. These data and information could relate to such diverse aspects as understanding customer preferences, coping with competition, identifying growth opportunities, and enhancing internal efficiency (Sabherwal, 2007). BI enables managers to make better decisions by providing them with the ability to formulate the necessary questions, interactive access to the data and information, and the tools needed to appropriately manipulate them in order to find the required solutions.

Thus, BI tools are used in BI solutions, and BI solutions support the BI process through which valuable information and knowledge are provided. BI tools can also directly help in obtaining data and information (such as through extraction, transformation, and loading of data). Figure 1.2 depicts this relationship among these aspects of business intelligence.

Let us consider an example of the use of BI. Tesco, a grocery chain in the UK, employs BI tools for effective data access and analytics (McAfee and Brynjolfsson,

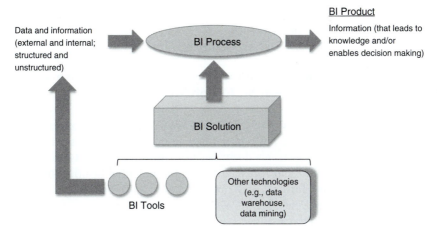

FIGURE 1.2 BI Product, Process, Solution, and Tools

2008). It collects detailed data on purchases by using customer-rewards cards, and then uses a BI solution to categorize customers and to develop knowledge on how offers should be customized. The BI process thus benefits from the BI solution, but it is broader in nature, and includes Tesco's tracking redemption rates in detail. This application of BI to generate useful information (about customer categories) and knowledge (about potentially beneficial changes in internal processes) has enabled Tesco to modify its business processes to obtain better response from customers. Consequently, Tesco has been able to raise the redemption rate for its direct-marketing initiatives to about 20%, which is much greater than the industry norm of about 2%, and has thereby increased its sales.

Some variants of business intelligence have been discussed in the literature. The most notable of these is "real-time business intelligence." We define real-time BI[1] as the kind of business intelligence that provides the required inputs to decision makers whenever needed, so that business processes are not slowed down in any perceptible fashion due to waiting for information or knowledge from the BI solution. For simplicity, we assume all "business intelligence" to be "real-time" in nature, unless otherwise stated. "Operational business intelligence" is another term that has been used to qualify a specific type of BI—that is, BI that focuses specifically on operations rather than planning or generating insights.

---

[1] We consider "real time" to be synonymous with "right time," which is a term that is now used by some IT professionals (White, 2004). This view is consistent with much of the prior literature in information systems, as exemplified by the following quote from a paper on real-time BI states: "For many people, "real time" is synonymous with "instantaneous." Is this incorrect when applied to data warehousing? Data only need to be as fresh as the business requirements. For these reasons, some people prefer the term "right time" (White, 2004). We use the terms simultaneously and recognize that real-time does not always mean instantaneous" (Watson, Wixom, Hoffer, Anderson-Lehman, and Reynolds, 2006, p. 8).

Business Intelligence in Practice 1.1 illustrates the role BI technologies are playing in contemporary organizations.

Business Intelligence in Practice 1.1: BI Helps Improve Health Care at St. Joseph Medical Center

St. Joseph Medical Center, a 364-bed, nonprofit regional medical center in Towson, Maryland, is using business intelligence to analyze patient data from lab reports and other electronic documents to improve care (McGee, 2008). The BI tools help filter and sort data to identify potential health problems before they escalate further, and provide authorized users, such as the director of diabetic patients, secure Web-based access to information needed to provide better health care.

According to an applications analyst at St. Joseph's, "For a cardiac surgeon, glucose isn't the first thing that comes to mind." However, following the surgery, glucose problems in a patient who had not previously been diagnosed as diabetic can cause major complications. BI tools help go through reports to identify patterns of high glucose readings in lab tests or finger-prick tests of patients who may not have been previously considered diabetic. This helps provide diabetic treatment to these patients in a more timely way, and facilitates appropriate postsurgical care to avoid blood-sugar-related complications.

Another health care manager at St. Joseph's was able to use BI tools to extract data from a 4,000 page report in a PDF file to analyze how long it takes for nurses to respond to patients when they push their bedside call button. In addition to providing the insight that helps improve patient care, it helps from a business perspective, especially in situations where insurers financially reward health care providers that meet important quality criteria, such as "avoiding postsurgical complications." (McGee, 2008)

In the next section we discuss the factors that have contributed to the increasing importance of BI.

▶ 1.4 FACTORS DRIVING BUSINESS INTELLIGENCE

The increasing prominence of BI is driven by a number of factors, which can be classified into the four sets discussed below.

Exploding Data Volumes: The confluence of technological progress (improved data storage capabilities as well as the tremendous increase in electronic connections through the Internet and intranets) and regulatory changes (e.g., the Sarbanes Oxley act of 2002, which requires senior executives in publicly traded firms to be actively involved in their firm's information assets) has led to a dramatic increase in the data collected and stored by organizations. Moreover, organizations have been storing electronic data in operational systems for years, and have consequently accumulated large data volumes about aspects such as sales, customers, product defects, and complaints. Consequently, managers encounter enormously greater amounts of data (collected in finer detail and at greater frequency) than before. Although the availability of more and better data should enable better decisions, this can only happen if managers are able to utilize the data. Otherwise, the larger data volumes could make decision making *more* difficult. It is worth noting that: "The average manager spends two hours a day simply looking for data, and half the information found is later deemed useless" (Howson, 2007, p. 11). BI solutions provide managers the ability to more effectively utilize these larger data volumes. According to Kim Stanick, vice president of marketing at ParAccel, "The amount of enterprise data being generated is skyrocketing, and companies are being challenged to deliver information expediently, pervasively and efficiently. They need not only performance, but also tools to help them rapidly develop and flexibly deploy business intelligence capabilities throughout the enterprise."

Increasingly Complicated Decisions: With increasing competition from across industries and across countries, decision making in organizations has become increasingly complicated, at least in terms of the variety of factors that need to be considered. Many organizations operate globally, in multiple industries, and round the clock, with competitors in one arena being collaborators in another. The intricacy of internal and external processes and the availability of greater information also contribute to the increased complexity of organizational decision making. Consequently, the diversity of factors that need to be considered and the diversity of information required to make decisions have increased tremendously. Moreover, decisions need to be made based on not only information obtained from structured transactional data, but also unstructured information available from Web sites, e-mail messages, news media, internal documents, and so on. BI solutions provide managers the ability to make decisions that incorporate all the important factors and are based on integration across these structured and unstructured sources of information.

Need for Quick Reflexes: The pace of change, or volatility, within each market domain has increased rapidly in the past decade. For example, market and environmental influences can result in overnight changes in an organization. Corporate announcements of a missed financial quarterly target could send a company's capitalization, and perhaps that of a whole industry, in a downward spiral. Due to the acceleration in the pace at which the global economy operates, the time available for organizations to respond to environmental changes has been decreasing. This makes it critical that managers be able to quickly access actionable information, so that decisions can be made and implemented before the window of opportunity closes. Three kinds of delays constrain such quick reflexes: delays in converting data from a variety of sources into information, delays in integrating information across these various sources, and delays in making the resulting information and knowledge available to the decision makers. Effective BI solutions help address each of these three types of delays, as we discuss and illustrate in this book.

Technological Progress: The above factors make it imperative for managers to make decisions that utilize the large volumes of data and information, incorporate all the important factors affecting the decision, and do so at the accelerated pace required in contemporary environments. The fourth factor relates to the progress that has been made in information technology over the past two decades. The utilization of BI in contemporary organizations is made possible by the developments in decision support systems, enterprise resource planning systems, data warehousing, data mining, and text mining. As a result of these developments, BI vendors have the necessary inputs for developing effective BI tools, and organizations adopting these BI tools have the needed platform so that the BI solutions can be most effective.

▶ 1.5 BUSINESS INTELLIGENCE AND RELATED TECHNOLOGIES

Business intelligence is distinct from knowledge management and the other information technologies that are used in contemporary organizations. We discuss these differences next. The earlier distinction among data, information, and knowledge is relevant in this regard.

Knowledge management (KM) refers to doing what is needed to get the most out of knowledge resources. KM focuses on creating, sharing, and applying knowledge. The traditional emphasis in KM has been on explicit knowledge (i.e., knowledge that is recognized and is already articulated in some form), but, increasingly, KM has also incorporated managing important tacit knowledge (knowledge that is difficult to articulate and formalize, including insights, intuitions, and hunches).

BI differs from KM in several respects. BI starts with data and information as inputs, whereas KM begins with information and knowledge as inputs. The direct results of BI are information (which is produced through appropriate analytics and then presented in a friendly fashion, such as through scorecards and dashboards) and new knowledge or insight, obtained by revealing previously unknown connections or patterns. The direct result of KM is the creation of new knowledge (from other types of knowledge), the conversion to another form of knowledge (i.e., from tacit to explicit or vice versa), or the application of knowledge in making a decision. Thus, KM is not directly concerned with data for the most part (with the exception of knowledge discovery, which focuses on discovering knowledge from data and information using techniques such as data mining, and which represents an area of overlap between KM and BI), unlike BI, for which data is critical. However, the results of BI can be, and often are, useful inputs to KM. Figures 1.3 and 1.4 depict these inputs and outputs for BI and KM, respectively. In addition,

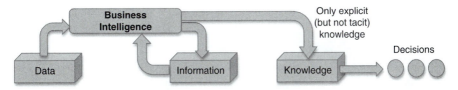

FIGURE 1.3   Roles of Data, Information, and Knowledge in Business Intelligence

FIGURE 1.4   Roles of Data, Information, and Knowledge in Knowledge Management

KM involves using social aspects as well as information technology, whereas BI as well as data warehousing, data mining, and decision support systems are technical in nature. Moreover, the connection between BI and knowledge is limited to knowledge creation (although BI deals with the whole aspect of knowledge discovery, discovering patterns based on existing explicit data and information), whereas KM incorporates knowledge capture, sharing, and application in addition to creation. Finally, only explicit knowledge can directly result from BI, whereas KM produces both explicit and tacit knowledge.

BI also differs from three other information technologies: data warehousing, data mining, and decision support systems. Two of these technologies—data warehousing and data mining—focus on data. A **data warehouse** is a single logical repository for an organization's data, with the data in the data warehouse being obtained from multiple operational systems such as a point-of-sale system, a customer relationship management system, and so on, using tools to extract, transform (to make the data consistent), and load (ETL) data. **Data mining**, on the other hand, refers to the process of discovering hidden patterns from data stored in electronic form (usually in a data warehouse). Thus, data warehousing starts with data stored in different systems and often with inconsistencies (in terminology, formats, and so on), and converts it into data stored in a single logical repository, although not necessarily at a single physical location. Data mining starts with data and produces information (i.e., patterns or relationships). **Decision support systems**, and more recently, automated decision systems (Davenport and Harris, 2005), focus on support or automation of decision making in organizations. They use data (from a date warehouse or operational systems) as input along with

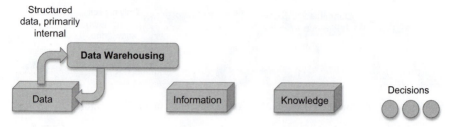

FIGURE 1.5 Roles of Data, Information, and Knowledge in Data Warehousing

FIGURE 1.6 Roles of Data, Information, and Knowledge in Data Mining

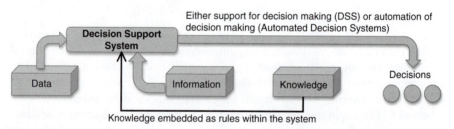

FIGURE 1.7 Roles of Data, Information, and Knowledge in Decision Support Systems

prior knowledge (used to create rules that guide the decisions). Figures 1.5, 1.6, and 1.7 depict these inputs and outputs for data warehousing, data mining, and decision support systems, respectively.

BI also differs from data warehousing, data mining, and decision support systems in some other important aspects. BI incorporates internal as well as external data and information, whereas these other data-centric information technologies (i.e., data warehouse, data mining, DSS) focus primarily on internal data. Moreover, BI incorporates structured as well as unstructured data and information as inputs, whereas these other technologies focus primarily on structured data. These distinctions are important because important information about the organization's competitors, customers, and industry is often not available in internal systems, and considerable important data exist in unstructured form, such as in e-mail messages, letters, news items, presentations, Web pages, and so on. Indeed, according to one estimate, about 80% of business information is available in unstructured form

Table 1.1 Distinctions between BI and Other Related Technologies

	Business Intelligence	Knowledge Management	Data Warehousing	Data Mining	Decision Support Systems (DSS) or Automated Decision Systems (ADS)
Inputs	Data, information	Data, information, knowledge	Data (from multiple systems)	Data	Data, information, knowledge
Nature of Inputs	Internal or external, structured or unstructured	Internal or external, structured or unstructured	Internal, structured	Internal, structured	Internal or external, structured
Outputs	Information and explicit knowledge	Tacit knowledge and explicit knowledge	Data (in a single logical repository)	Information	Decision recommendation (in case of DSS) or automated decision (in case of ADS)
Components	Information technologies	Information technologies, social mechanisms, structural arrangements	Information technologies	Information technologies	Information technologies
Users	Across the organization	Across the organization	IT personnel	IT personnel, others trained in IT	Specific, targeted users

(Herschel and Jones, 2005). Whereas BI solutions are explicitly geared toward incorporating both unstructured and external information, data warehouse, data mining, and decision support systems usually focus on structured and internal data. BI also differs from data warehouse, data mining, and decision support systems in that BI explicitly focuses on presenting information to individuals with little technical expertise, unlike the usual focus on individuals who are more technically skilled or have received training in the specific technology.

Table 1.1 summarizes the above differences among BI, KM, data warehousing, data mining, and decision support systems. It highlights the differences in terms of the inputs and their nature, the outputs, the components, and the users.

▶ 1.6 BUSINESS INTELLIGENCE IN CONTEMPORARY ORGANIZATIONS

Contemporary organizations operate in environments that are in a continual state of flux. Sales patterns change over time and from one place to another. Products evolve over time as competitors innovate and add new features. Customers become more demanding as they become accustomed to current offerings. Suppliers change prices and delivery schedules. Currency valuations vary over time. In such environments, managers need to make a variety of decisions to improve performance in the short term as well as the long term. Should the organization increase or decrease the size of its workforce? What kind of individuals should be hired or fired? What kind of products and markets should the organization focus on? How much should the organization invest in research and development? How should the organization serve its customers to maximize their satisfaction? How should the organization negotiate with its suppliers? And so on.

Information technologies have long facilitated reporting of information about the past and providing information that could be used for making decisions about the present or planning for the future. BI solutions help organizations by enabling the dissemination of real-time information in user-friendly fashion. This incorporates providing users a single-point access to important information, while using a consistent format and a dynamic classification scheme (Weiss, Capozzi, and Prusak, 2004). BI solutions also contribute by enabling the creation of new knowledge based on information about the past. They also help organizations to be more responsive and anticipative when making decisions that are based more closely on all the latest information and also incorporate predictions regarding the future. Moreover, BI solutions facilitate better planning for the future through the more effective use of information, through the use of past data for predictions about the future, and through the development of knowledge based on information about the past. These four contributions of BI—dissemination of real-time information, creation of new knowledge based on the past, responsive and anticipative decisions, and improved planning for the future—produce a variety of benefits in terms of organizational success. These benefits can be grouped into three broad categories, discussed next.

Improvement in Operational Performance

By enabling the decision makers to make more responsive and anticipative decisions using both real-time and historical data and information, BI solutions help improve the operational performance of the organization. BI solutions also provide real-time information on how the organization is performing while adopting an end-to-end view of processes, thereby helping managers to identify aspects that need improvement (Coetzer, 2007). They enable managers to detect events (such as a delay in reaching the desired production level for a new product or flight delays from an airport due to poor weather) and monitor trends in the business environment as well as within the organization, and thereby respond faster and more efficiently to the changes in conditions affecting the organization. For example, BI tools helped an oil and gas company, which was facing cash flow problems, to recognize that although it was delivering gas to customers on time, it was sending the invoices a week too late. Identification of this underlying problem led to the company taking measures to institute a new rule requiring invoicing within a day of delivery (Howson, 2008).

BI solutions enable managers to use these trends to anticipate what might happen in the future and make sound decisions (using analytical tools such as consideration of alternative "what if" scenarios) that lead to improved organizational performance. By utilizing data generated through the organization's operations in a real-time fashion, BI solutions facilitate decisions that recognize the latest trends.

BI solutions also help make organizations more efficient. For example, a BI solution enabled a paint-manufacturing firm to increase production by 30% while using existing resources and existing information (*Industry Week*, 2008). BI solutions help reduce inefficiencies that arise from inadequate access to latest information or from managers spending time in extracting information or manipulating spreadsheets rather than understanding and interpreting information. Furthermore, when they are effectively developed and implemented, BI solutions provide these improved abilities to access and analyze information to individuals across the organization. The information being provided is no longer limited to IT personnel, users with excellent IT skills, top managers, or individuals at a particular location. BI facilitates quick corrective actions by all individuals by enabling them to directly obtain the information they require, without the need for time-consuming third-party intermediaries, such as when one individual must depend on a group of programmers to deliver the information necessary to make decisions.

Business Intelligence in Practice 1.2 illustrates the role BI technologies are playing in improving operational performance at contemporary organizations.

Improvement in Customer Service

By enabling decision makers to make more responsive and anticipative decisions related to customer requests and needs using both real-time and historical data and information, BI solutions also help improve the quality of customer service provided by the organization. Through the use of the latest information and analyzing alternative "what if" scenarios, BI solutions can help organizations to anticipate the consequences of changes in customer-oriented processes, such as the effects of introducing an additional channel for interaction with customers or assigning more people to work on a customer-oriented process. For example, an insurance company could use the information provided by a BI solution to analyze and reengineer the claim process, from the submission of the claim to the payment to the customer (Coetzer, 2007).

Business Intelligence in Practice 1.2: BI Helps Virginia Police Fight Crime

The police department in Richmond, Virginia, a city of about 200,000, started using business intelligence in 2002 by first adopting predictive business analytics. This enabled the police department to identify the areas of the city that were more prone to gunfire, and thereby enable more officers to be placed in those locations to prevent incidents. This led the Richmond police to being able to reduce the number of "shots-fired" complaints by 45% on New Year's Eve and by 26% on New Year's Day.

An increasing challenge faced by the police department is the increasing amounts of information flowing into the police as a result of homeland security alerts and improved data collection. Moreover, Richmond police have been dealing with data from a diverse set of sources, including legacy reports written in a narrative style. BI tools enabled the department to do much of its querying on an ad hoc basis, without having to wait for someone to write programs enabling those queries, according to Colleen McCue, program manager with the department's crime analysis unit. It also allowed them to identify motives and flag incidents where crimes are likely to escalate. For example, analytical and operational groups within the department collaborated to identify the illegal drug markets, ascertain when the activity was set to spike, and then share that information with officers.

In just a few years, BI has become a normal way of life for the Richmond police department. It has extended the initial analytics implementation into a near real-time BI system, with a four-hour data update cycle, according to Rodney Monroe, the Richmond police chief. The department can therefore use the results of its analysis quickly to mitigate developing problems, such as identifying crime patterns and deploying officers to potential hot spots. The data sources include thousands of crime reports from the preceding five years, the results of emergency phone calls, and information about weather patterns and special events.

Recently, the department added more granularity to its reports. Instead of grouping all violent crimes together, police now are able to look at crimes such as robberies and homicides independently, which enables them to zero in on patterns relevant to a specific kind of crime.

Commanders, supervisors, and officers have embraced the BI system because it helps them do their jobs better on a daily basis. Police at every level in the force now receive daily BI reports, rather than wait until the end of the month, as they used to do. Officers receive a BI report at the start of their shifts, indicating problem areas and describing activities to concentrate on. Shift supervisors receive a similar report, along with real-time notifications if the system detects a crime pattern in some area. Commanders, who have 24/7 responsibility for their assigned sectors, receive even more detailed reports.

The return on investment from BI efforts at the Richmond police department is measured in lives and safety, not dollars. According to Monroe, the system helped facilitate the arrests of 16 fugitives and the confiscation of 18 guns last year. BI has enhanced public safety, reduced emergency calls, and enabled better use of its 750 officers as there is better data about where certain kinds of crimes may occur. The success of BI at the Richmond police department is well recognized, and the department received the Gartner BI Excellence Award in 2007.

(Compiled from Beal, 2004, and Smalltree, 2007)

BI solutions also help improve customer service by identifying frequent problems with each product and identifying potential solutions, so that when one of these problems occurs, the appropriate solution can be more quickly identified. For example, Whirlpool uses BI to track its warranty program to identify the fundamental causes of warranty problems and improve customer satisfaction with products (Howson, 2008).

BI solutions also help reduce the concerns about customer service that often result from interacting with the customer based on incomplete, incorrect, or old information. They can also help improve customer retention through the creation of loyalty programs for the most valuable customers and preventive marketing campaigns. For example, mobile operators could use BI solutions to identify customers that are likely to move to another carrier, by analyzing their airtime usage patterns and other behavior, and target these customers for efforts intended to prevent them from defecting.

Business Intelligence in Practice 1.3 illustrates the role BI technologies are playing in improving customer service at contemporary organizations.

Identification of New Opportunities in Contemporary Organizations

By enabling the decision makers to make more responsive decisions using both real-time and historical data and information, BI solutions help identify new opportunities for the organization. BI facilitates new insights and knowledge through the discovery of previously unknown patterns, correlations, and trends. It also enables better understanding of the market based on latest information, and the anticipation of future market trends. Moreover, by making these insights and knowledge available to individuals across the organization, BI helps organizations to prepare better for the future, by providing support for the identification of new products and services. Through better insight into market trends and the buying behavior of current customers, BI solutions can enable managers to anticipate the kind of new product features that would appeal to the organization's current customers, as well as identify the profile of potential new customers. The new information obtained through BI solutions about the products that are selling well

Business Intelligence in Practice 1.3: BI Helps eCourier Seek Customer Happiness

Business intelligence has given eCourier.co.uk, a Web- and London-based courier service firm, the ability to keep tabs on its service as well as its customer satisfaction. The company was founded by Tom Allason and Jay Bregman, in response to the appalling service they received from a courier company in May 2004. According to Tom: "A courier company lost a set of tickets that we had bought. The courier who was meant to be delivering them was eventually tracked down in a pub. We just thought it was a bad way to do business."

Before implementing business intelligence, eCourier's founders discarded the notion of phone dispatchers and instead provided GPS-enabled handhelds to their couriers, so that they could be tracked and orders could be electronically communicated. They also focused on developing user-friendly applications to make online booking easy and rewarding. Customers can track online exactly where their courier is, eliminating the need for guesswork on package delivery.

The company's initial attempt at BI involved the use of Business Object's Crystal Reports, which indicated, on a weekly basis, average bookings for clients over the preceding couple of weeks. This helped eCourier to determine patterns and identify any bookings that were problematic. However, going through reports on eCourier's over 2,000 clients was difficult. Also, even when problems were identified, they could be more than a week old.

To remedy the situation, eCourier implemented SeeWhy, a real-time, event-driven business intelligence system that tracks customers' booking behaviors, creates their unique profiles, and provides users with the ability to do real-time monitoring. eCourier still uses Crystal Reports for analyzing higher-level information—for example, the growth and spending of each account.

The SeeWhy software is designed so that a "normal" client booking pattern is developed from the first use and is subsequently deepened with each booking. Changes in the rate of bookings for an account generates an alert, which is sent to that client's account manager, who can take appropriate action. Such alerts have provided the ability to keep and grow customers through timely attention.

BI tools allow eCourier, whose couriers carry 2,000 packages around London daily, to keep real-time tabs on customer satisfaction. This is a critical distinctive competence in London's competitive same-day courier market, where clients are likely to switch to another company instead of reporting a problem to their current courier. Indeed, the online directory London Online[2] lists more than 350 courier services.

---

[2] See: See: http://www.londononline.co.uk/local/Transport_and_Logistics/Couriers/

Consistent with the company's emphasis on customer service, most of the company's Web pages[3] include the phrase "happiness delivered" after the company name. BI is the key for the company in achieving this customer happiness. According to Jay Bregman, who, in addition to being the company's cofounder, is its chief technology officer: "It allows us to provide an individualized account management service by using technology rather than people."
(Compiled from Gilmore, 2006; Daniel, 2007; Prevett, 2008)

and products that encounter complaints also helps organizations to create new products that are less likely to face these problems and therefore perform well in the market. For example, faced with increasing competition and rising consumer demands in northern Europe, one bank used BI to distinguish customers by their needs, better understand the preferences and needs of its high-value customers (i.e., the 27% customers who generated 80% percent of its income), and improve customer service by targeting their specific needs (Rogalski, 2005).

The information BI solutions provide about the market, such as sales of various products in different geographic regions, also helps managers to identify opportunities for geographic expansion or growth through partnerships. For example, Dow Chemical Company utilizes BI to develop a better understanding of the value proposition associated with joint ventures (Howson, 2008).

By identifying and disseminating information on relationships discovered from data and information, BI solutions also lead to the development of new insights and knowledge. Such knowledge is especially important when it is based not just on structured internal data but incorporates unstructured and external information as well. This new knowledge can help enhance managers' effectiveness when identifying new product opportunities, especially in an environment that involves increasing levels of economic and political uncertainty. BI solutions further encourage innovation by enabling innovative projects to be tracked more effectively using real-time information.

Business Intelligence in Practice 1.4 illustrates the role BI technologies are playing in identifying new opportunities in contemporary organizations.

Figure 1.8 summarizes these impacts of BI on organizational performance and relates them to BI's direct outcomes.

▶ 1.7 OBSTACLES TO BUSINESS INTELLIGENCE

Business intelligence can provide several benefits, as discussed above. However, the path to success with BI is not straightforward. Several obstacles could be encountered in designing, developing, and utilizing BI. Two of the most important obstacles include business events not being consistently defined throughout the

---

[3] See: See: http://www.ecourier.co.uk/justme_home.php

Business Intelligence in Practice 1.4: BI Helps Dunkin' Donuts Expand Globally

Dunkin' Donuts has been using BI to seek the best franchise operators and locations. A large proportion of Dunkin' Donut's more than 5,000 U.S. franchises are located in areas such as Boston, New York, and other Northeast locales, but Dunkin Donuts is planning a major worldwide expansion, aiming to move from about 8,000 to 15,000 franchises worldwide. Its main competitor is Starbucks, which has 12,000 stores worldwide, including 8,800 in the United States.

To help it win this race for global expansion, Dunkin' Donuts is using a new system that helps it more quickly close franchising deals. This is especially important in the competition with Starbucks because Starbucks does not franchise, and its growth is therefore not inhibited by difficulties in finding, and signing up, appropriate and willing franchise operators.

Dunkin' Donuts salespeople and managers use a dashboard-type BI system, developed within six weeks by Oco Inc., to manage information about franchise operators, including the stage of each potential deal and how their financing is going. They can identify any problem areas so they can keep deals on track. They can obtain a geographic view of regions where deals are facing problems, and then drill down into a specific account to determine the underlying causes. They can also identify potential deals that are too close in proximity. Some of the key metrics tracked by the managers include the average cycle time for getting a franchise deal done, the size of deals, and average cycle time for different types of deal.

Such analysis depends on access to the clean data obtained from a data warehouse. Oco used proprietary technology based on an artificial intelligence engine that takes data from multiple sources, and then cleans and organizes it into an intelligent data schema, to extract customer data from Dunkin Donut's various systems and clean it up in a data warehouse. Updated information is fed daily into the data warehouse.

Dunkin' Donuts' CIO Dan Sheehan compares the system to a customer resource management system along with a scorecard. "It's a huge win in terms of instant access to who and what is in the pipeline," says Sheehan. "When you look at the a.m. market, we've been a leader in the Northeast. Now we'll take that leadership and go across the country and the world."

(Compiled from *Business Wire*, 2007, and Weier, 2007)

---

organization, which makes it difficult to utilize organization-wide BI, and BI solutions frequently requiring large initial investment. When BI vendors argue that BI solutions are expensive (for example, Jeff Raikes, president of the Microsoft Business Division stated: "The bad news is, we feel people are paying far too

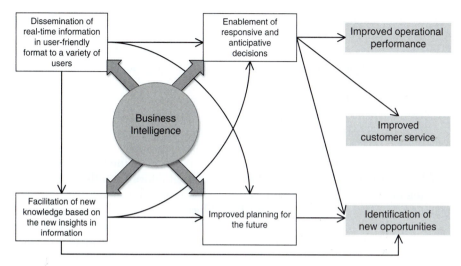

FIGURE 1.8 Impacts of Business Intelligence

much for BI and not getting enough. The promise of BI is unfulfilled"), possibly in an attempt to position their own emergent solutions as a relative bargain, it reinforces the belief that BI is overly expensive. The concern about BI expenses is exacerbated by the fact that traditional ROI assessment is difficult for BI because its benefits are often intangible or long term in nature.

The obstacles encountered with respect to BI can be divided into two broad categories (Sabherwal, 2007): technological obstacles and organizational obstacles. Technological obstacles include the following: BI tools are difficult to use; BI training is expensive; BI requires large initial investment; BI requires substantial ongoing costs; BI return-on-investment is difficult to justify; BI needs of business users are difficult to identify; managers are too busy to use BI; and BI tools are difficult to customize for specific types of users. In contrast, organizational constraints include four obstacles related to the organization's lack of preparation for BI: business events are not consistently defined throughout the enterprise; BI makes business information too transparent; users don't recognize the power of BI; and a single BI solution for all the BI needs of the organization is difficult to find.

▶ 1.8 TEXT OVERVIEW

This book is composed of 10 chapters, divided into three parts.

Part I: Introduction to Business Intelligence: This section of the book provides an introductory discussion of BI and its impacts and underlying capabilities. This section begins with an overview of BI, presented in Chapter 1, including a discussion of BI and its differences from other technologies, the role that BI plays in organizations, and the factors driving the importance of BI. Chapter 2 describes the four major kinds of capabilities associated with BI: organizational memory, which is the storage of information in a form that can be later accessed and used; information integration, which is the ability to link structured and unstructured data from a variety of sources; business analytics, which is the ability to create new insights and use them, in the short term or long term, to make better decisions; and presentation, which is the ability to use appropriate reporting and balanced scorecards tools to make BI more valuable to concerned users.

Part II: Technologies Enabling Business Intelligence: This section includes four chapters that describe the technologies enabling the four important BI capabilities discussed in Chapter 2. Chapter 3 focuses on the technologies that enable organizational memory by storing structured information that is used for BI. Relevant technologies, including data warehouses and enterprise resource planning (ERP) systems, are described and illustrated. Chapter 4 focuses on the technologies that enable the integration of structured information from data warehouses and ERP systems with unstructured information and information from other sources, including public information, interorganizational information, and information from Web sites, e-mail messages, and so on. Relevant technologies, including environmental scanning, text mining, Web mining, and radio-frequency identification (RFID), are discussed along with illustrative examples. Chapter 5 focuses on technologies that help create new insights from information and help use insights to make better decisions. Relevant technologies, including data mining, business analytics, and real-time decision support, are described and illustrated. Chapter 6 focuses on the dissemination of information so as to make BI more valuable to concerned users. Relevant technologies, including online analytical processing (OLAP), visualization, digital dashboards, and balanced scorecards, are examined. Digital dashboards are also connected to a discussion of corporate performance management and scorecards.

Part III: Management and Future of Business Intelligence: This section includes chapters on BI tools and vendors, development of BI, various aspects of management of BI, and future directions of BI. Chapter 7 summarizes BI tools and classifies them into four types based on the four kinds of BI capabilities. It describes the selection of BI tools by an organization. It also summarizes some leading BI vendors and their major BI products. Chapter 8 focuses on the development of BI. It describes the important considerations in developing BI solutions, including agile design of BI, integration across BI tools, customization versus standardization of BI tools, BI vendors and products, and design considerations for digital dashboards. Chapter 9 focuses on the management of BI. Specific topics include cultural changes associated with BI, BI centers of excellence, BI governance, centralized/decentralized approach to managing BI, building a business case for BI, building organizational support for BI, and evaluation of BI impacts. Finally, Chapter 10 examines the future directions for BI, due to factors such as the safeguards needed for insuring the security of internal and external information, the progress in information technology and the increased use of streaming data, mobile-computing devices, and technology-based audio and video communications.

▶ 1.9 SUMMARY

In this chapter we discussed some of the basics of business intelligence. The chapter distinguished among data, information, and information. This distinction was useful in explaining business intelligence and also in comparing it with some other important information technologies—knowledge management, data warehousing, data mining, and decision support systems. The factors driving the emerging importance of BI were also discussed. Moreover, in this chapter we examined some direct effects of BI and discussed some of the consequent impacts on organizational performance. BI and its effects were illustrated using some short examples as well as some more detailed illustrations of BI in practice.

▶ KEY TERMS

business intelligence (BI)	data warehouse	knowledge
data	decision support system	knowledge management
data mining	information	(KM)

▶ REVIEW QUESTIONS

1. Distinguish between information and knowledge.

2. Identify and illustrate any two important benefits of business intelligence.

3. Briefly explain, and illustrate using an example, your understanding of the term "business intelligence."

4. Distinguish between business intelligence and knowledge management.

5. Explain how business intelligence differs from each of the following: (a) data warehousing, (b) data mining, and (c) decision support systems.

6. Identify and briefly explain any two factors that have led to the increasing importance of business intelligence.

7. Briefly explain the relationship between BI tools and BI solutions.

8. Discuss how BI could be viewed as a "product" or as a "process."

▶ APPLICATION EXERCISES

1. Consider the four forces driving BI described in this chapter. Provide one example (other than those mentioned in the book) that illustrates each of these forces.

2. Select any one of the four Business Intelligence in Practice examples presented in this chapter. Use the Web to obtain additional information about the organization and its BI efforts. Then explain the effects BI has had on this organization in terms of Figure 1.4.

3. Select any one of the three examples discussed at the start of this chapter. Use the Web to obtain additional information about the organization and its BI efforts. Then explain the effects BI has had on this organization in terms of Figure 1.4.

4. Construct a hypothetical example to show how BI can lead to improved operational performance of the organization. For the organizational context, use any one of the three organizations in the Business Intelligence in Practice examples other than the Richmond police (i.e., Business Intelligence in Practice 1.2), the three examples presented at the start of this chapter, or an organization that you work at or have worked at in the past.

5. Construct a hypothetical example to show how BI can lead to improved customer service in an organization. For the organizational context, use any one of the three organizations in the Business Intelligence in Practice examples other than eCourier (i.e., Business Intelligence in Practice 1.3), the three examples presented at the start of this chapter, or an organization that you work at or have worked at in the past.

6. Construct a hypothetical example to show how BI can lead to improved customer service in an organization. For the organizational context, use any one of the three organizations in the Business Intelligence in Practice examples other than Dunkin' Donuts (i.e., Business Intelligence in Practice 1.4), the three examples presented at the start of this chapter, or an organization that you work at or have worked at in the past.

▶ REFERENCES

Beal, B. 2004. Analytics Take a Bite Out of Crime. SearchCRM.com, January 16. http://searchdatamanagement.techtarget.com/news/article/0,289142,sid91_gci1137769,00.html

Blokdijk, G. 2008. *Business Intelligence: 100 Success Secrets*. Emereo Pty Ltd., United States.

Business Wire, 2007. "Oco Deploys Business Intelligence Solution for Dunkin' Donuts in Six Weeks," April 9.

Coetzer, J. 2007. "Tools For a Powerful Solution." *Business Day*, March 28.

Computerworld. 2007. "Honors Program: QlikTech International," August 22.

Daniel, D. 2007. "Delivering Customer Happiness through Operational Business Intelligence." *CIO*, December 6.

Davenport, T. H., and Harris, J. G. 2005. "Automated Decision Making Comes of Age." *Sloan Management Review*, 46(4), 83–89.

Gilmore, G. 2006. "Whiz-Kids on the Right Track." *The Times*, April 29.

Grossman, N. 2007. "How To Mine All That Customer Data." *Forbes*, September 21.

Herschel, R. T., and Jones, N. E. 2005. "Knowledge Management and Business Intelligence: The Importance of Integration." *Journal of Knowledge Management*, 9(4): 45–55.

Howson, C. 2007. *Successful Business Intelligence: Secrets to Making BI a Killer App* (McGraw-Hill Osborne).

Howson, C. 2008. *Successful Business Intelligence: Secrets to Making BI a Killer App* (McGraw-Hill Osborne).

Industry Week, 2008. "Meeting the Challenge of Today's Global Manufacturing Imperatives," August: 53.

McAfee, A., and Brynjolfsson, E. 2008. "Investing in the IT that Makes a Competitive Difference." *Harvard Business Review*, July–August: 98–107.

McGee, M. K. 2008. "Mount Sinai Medical Center's Latest Surgical Tool: Data Mining." *Information Week*, October 29.

Mitchell, R. 2007. "Best in Class 2007: State of Michigan." *Computerworld*, August 14.

Prevett, H. 2008. "In Profile: eCourier." *Growing Business*, September 29.

Rogalski, S. 2005. "Top Companies View Business Intelligence (BI) as Key to Future Growth." *DM Review Special Report*, June. http://www.dmreview.com/specialreports/20050621/1030269-1.html

Sabherwal, R. 2007. "Succeeding with Business Intelligence: Some Insights and Recommendations." *Cutter Benchmark Review*, 7(9): 5–15.

Sabherwal, R. 2008. "KM and BI: From Mutual Isolation to Complementarity and Synergy." *Cutter Consortium Executive Report*, 8(8): 1–18.

Smalltree, H. 2007. "Business Intelligence Case Study: Gartner Lauds Police for Crime-Fighting BI." *SearchDataManagement.com,* April 5. http://searchdatamanagement.techtarget.com/news/article0,289142,sid91_gci1250435,00.html

Watson, H. J., Wixom, B. H., Hoffer, J. A., Anderson-Lehman, R., and Reynolds, A. M. 2006. "Real-Time Business Intelligence: Best Practices at Continental Airlines." *Information Systems Management*, 23(1): 7–18.

Weier, M. H. 2007. "Dunkin' Donuts Managers Are Using a Dashboard-Type Software Application to Fend Off Advances by Its Nemesis." *Information Week*, April 16.

Weiss, L. M., Capozzi, M. M., and Prusak, L. 2004. "Learning from the Internet Giants." Summer, 45(4).

White, C. 2004. "Now Is the Right Time for Real-Time BI." *Information Management*, September 1.

Whiting, R. 2006. "BPM Gets Smarter with a Little Help from BI." *Information Week*, November 6.

CHAPTER 2

BUSINESS INTELLIGENCE CAPABILITIES

▶ 2.1 INTRODUCTION

In Chapter 1, we explained and illustrated the concept of business intelligence (BI) and differentiated BI from some other related technologies. We also distinguished between BI tools and solutions, examined some of the factors driving the importance of BI, and discussed the ways in which BI can benefit contemporary organizations.

In this chapter, we introduce four key capabilities of BI solutions, which are subsequently discussed in detail in the next four chapters: organizational memory capability (Chapter 3), information integration capability (Chapter 4), insight creation capability (Chapter 5), and presentation capability (Chapter 6). We summarize the four capabilities in the next section, and then examine and illustrate them in Sections 2.3 to 2.6. Finally, the chapter is summarized in Section 2.7.

▶ 2.2 FOUR SYNERGISTIC CAPABILITIES

In Chapter 1, we distinguished between BI tools developed by BI vendors and BI solutions deployed within organizations. A BI solution has BI capabilities that are supported through BI tools acquired by the organization and other ITs. These BI capabilities are used in the BI process.

We focus on four key capabilities of BI solutions, which are shown in Figure 2.1. The foundational BI capability is **organizational memory**—that is, the storage of information and knowledge (especially explicit knowledge) in such a form that they can be later accessed and used. It benefits the second BI capability, **information integration**, which is the ability to link structured and unstructured data from a variety of sources. Information integration, in turn, facilitates **insight creation**, which is the ability to develop new insights and use them, in the short term or long term, to make better decisions. Finally, insight creation capability provides inputs to **presentation capability**, the ability to use appropriate reporting and balanced scorecards tools, and thereby make BI more valuable to its users. Thus, the capabilities are different, and can be considered hierarchical as depicted

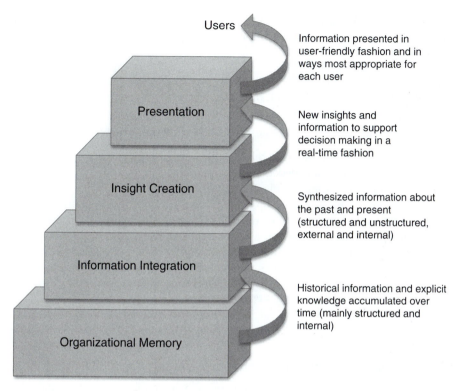

Users

Information presented in user-friendly fashion and in ways most appropriate for each user

Presentation

New insights and information to support decision making in a real-time fashion

Insight Creation

Synthesized information about the past and present (structured and unstructured, external and internal)

Information Integration

Historical information and explicit knowledge accumulated over time (mainly structured and internal)

Organizational Memory

FIGURE 2.1 Four Synergistic Business Intelligence Capabilities

in Figure 2.1: organizational memory collects quantitative data from within; information integration also takes external and nonquantitative data; insight applies analytics to the data; and presentation is dissemination of results in visual and user-friendly formats. For simplicity, these four capabilities are presented below as being completely distinct, and the technologies are discussed in Chapters 3 to 6 along with the capability that they most directly support and those they overlap to some extent. Some technologies could support more than one capability.

These four BI capabilities are distinct and important, although they are mutually synergistic in nature, and are all present to varying extents in each BI solution. They provide inputs to each other as shown in Figure 2.1. Organizational memory provides information and knowledge from the past, and thus provides important inputs for information integration. Information integration capability, in turn, produces synthesized information about past and present, based on both structured and unstructured information as well as external and internal information, which serves as the basis for insight creation. Insight creation capability leads to new insights and information that enable decision making. Presentation capability then disseminates these insights in a user-friendly fashion and in ways most appropriate for each user.

The BI capabilities support what are sometimes considered "features" of BI solutions. The features of a BI solution are classified into three broad categories (Sabherwal, 2007):

i. benchmarking relative to competition and industry trends;

ii. intelligence in terms of the ability to search and utilize data across disparate sources; and

iii. convenience in terms of customization and connectivity.

These three types of features relate to the four BI capabilities. Organizational memory provides the data needed for benchmarking. Information integration and insight creation together enable intelligence through the use of data from disparate sources for the development of new insights. Finally, presentation capability is directly related to convenience features, as it focuses on providing BI outputs in an appropriate and user-friendly fashion.

We examine the four capabilities in Sections 2.3 to 2.6. We also identify, for each capability, the factors necessitating it and the related enabling technologies. We also provide an illustrative example for each capability.

▶ 2.3 ORGANIZATIONAL MEMORY

2.3.1 Factors Necessitating Organizational Memory Capability

Several factors lead to organizational memory being an important BI capability. First, as discussed in Chapter 1, technological progress and plummeting data storage costs have led to a sharp increase in data volumes as organizations store large amounts of data and keep them over long periods of time. Therefore, large amounts of data and information exist in transactional systems, enterprise resource planning systems, and databases and data warehouses. At any point in time, organizations have large amounts of accumulated data and information, which comprise an important component of organizational memory (Ferguson, Mathur, and Shah, 2005).

Second, the pervasiveness of computers for creating and modifying documents and presentations, and the increased use of electronic mail and other electronic communication media (e.g., chats and posts on discussion groups and social media such as Facebook), imply that unstructured information and explicit knowledge are stored in electronic form. As a result, at any point in time, organizations have large amounts of unstructured information and knowledge in documents, presentations, and communication contents from the past. Retention of this unstructured content so it can be subsequently browsed and searched through is an important aspect of organizational memory (Weiss, Capozzi, and Prusak, 2004).

Third, improvements in knowledge management technologies have led to considerable organizational knowledge being stored in explicit form in knowledge repositories. Such knowledge repositories include best practices databases, lessons-learned systems, and incident report databases, and they represent an important component of organizational memory.

2.3.2 Organizational Memory Capability

Organizational memory capability represents an organization's accumulated history, including data, information, and explicit knowledge. Data, information, or explicit knowledge stored in the organizational memory may be either structured or unstructured. Structured data or information could reside, for example, in database records. Structured explicit knowledge could reside in knowledge repositories and answers to frequently asked questions (FAQs). Unstructured data and information, on the other hand, do not have an associated data model or metadata. Unstructured data, information, and knowledge, reside in various forms including e-mail messages stored over time, audio and video files, and historical versions of sites, as well as prior presentations, memos, and other documents.

Organizational memory focuses on the storage of intellectual resources (data, information, and explicit knowledge) in such a form that they can be later accessed and used. Thus, the inputs for organizational memory capability are data, information, and explicit knowledge that are stored in individual systems as events occur. At any point in time, the outputs from organizational memory capability are the accumulated (but not necessarily integrated) information and explicit knowledge about the past. Although the importance of storing data in an accurate and consistent fashion is clear, data inaccuracy and inconsistency are two of the most important problems with organizational memory (Swartz, 2007).

Organizational memory capability focuses primarily on internal and structured content. Moreover, organizational memory capability is most beneficial when it is associated with the ability to conduct enterprise-wide content search across multiple disparate databases. Finally, organizational memory capability is a foundational capability, in that the other three BI capabilities directly or indirectly depend on it; organizational memory capability helps store data, information, and explicit knowledge over time, so that they can subsequently be integrated and used along with the emergent, real-time content to create insights and make decisions.

2.3.3 Technologies Enabling Organizational Memory Capability

Several important technologies that enable organizational memory capability do so by storing structured data and information. These include:

- **Transactional systems**, which are also called operational systems, transaction process systems, or source systems (Howson, 2007).
- **Enterprise resource planning (ERP) systems**, which lead to consistency with standardized processes and are broader in scope than traditional transactional systems.
- **Data warehouses** (DWs), "the collection of data *extracted* from various operational systems, *transformed* to make the data consistent, and *loaded*

for analysis" (Howson, 2007, p. 28). As discussed in Chapter 1, a DW is different from BI, but represents an important technology that enables BI.

• Technologies that support the capture of unstructured information (e.g., **document management systems**), retaining explicit knowledge (i.e., **knowledge repositories**), and archiving audio and video files. (i.e., **digital content management systems**).

Although ERP systems and DWs facilitate organizational memory capability, they are not necessary for organizational memory. It is possible to use transactional or operational systems as organizational memory for BI, and BI solutions at some organizations do operate directly through information integration across transactional systems (Howson, 2007). However, the performance of BI is improved by the existence of an efficient DW and the presence of an ERP system.

Indeed, two recent surveys have found that organizations encountering problems with respect to BI are concerned about the quality of their DWs. In one survey of 741 managers by Data Warehouse Institute (Preston, 2007), 81% of the respondents complained about inaccurate data reporting, 78% about arguments concerning which data is appropriate for "master data" repositories, and 51% about poor decisions due to incorrect definitions. Another survey of 72 organizations (Sabherwal, 2007) found organizations to be least prepared for BI in terms of having been successful in DW efforts and having accurate data in their DWs. It is therefore no surprise that most organizations—for example, Cardinal Health (Carte, Schwarzkopf, Shaft, and Zmud, 2005) and Continental Airlines (Anderson-Lehman, Watson, Wixom, and Hoffer, 2004; Watson, Wixom, Hoffer, and Anderson-Lehman, 2006)—first improve the quality of the data in their DWs before embarking upon BI solutions. BI needs to be linked directly to DW in organizations that have a DW, with the DW incorporating data from ERP and transactional systems. Thus, organizational memory capability depends directly on DW, but its dependence on ERP is less direct—that is, through DW.

Chapter 3 describes the various technologies enabling organizational capability in greater detail. Business Intelligence in Practice 2.1 illustrates the role organizational memory as a BI capability plays in contemporary organizations. In this example, the BI solution does not utilize only organizational memory; instead, it benefits from all four BI capabilities as discussed in this chapter and subsequently in Chapters 3 through 6.

► 2.4 INFORMATION INTEGRATION

2.4.1 Factors Necessitating Information Integration Capability

Four main factors make information integration a critical BI capability. First, structured data and information often exist in a number of transactional systems that are mutually disconnected and often incompatible. For example, in 2003, before Canadian Tire Corporation started to focus on a data warehouse, its IT

Business Intelligence in Practice 2.1: Organizational Memory Helps Bahamas' Tourism Industry

Searching for a reporting tool that would enable more effective use of its advertising dollars, Bahamas' Ministry of Tourism contracted with Indusa Global to help select and implement a business intelligence solution. Indusa built the BI system using an SQL server database and an Enterprise Reporting Application Platform from Actuate Corporation to provide reports and cubes, or drill-down tools, to all users. Indusa developed the system over a few years, phasing in such features as analysis cubes, enhanced reporting, and dashboards.

The Ministry of Tourism has been collecting prearrival information, which is obtained via immigration cards on arrival, and postvisit satisfaction data, which is obtained at departure. The collection and storage of immigration data started with the Bahamas government's decision to improve national security through faster processing of immigration cards, enabling immigration officers to extract and cross-reference prior information on travelers. However, the increase in organizational memory through the collection and storage of this data has also provided the country with intelligence in predicting future visitor trends and helping it to develop visitor programs through incentive-based, personalized, multichannel marketing.

From the immigration cards, specific data are provided to the immigration department and aggregate data are provided to the Ministry of Tourism. The data are fed into a back-office system, and then moved to data warehousing, before being used for business intelligence. According to Jo Ram, the chief operating officer and vice president of product development of Indusa, "We get data feeds from a lot of different sources—U.S. postal code data, census data, and Nielsen data," Ram said. "All this data goes into one database from which you can pull reports as to where a person is coming [from], where they're staying, age group, income level."

The organizational memory capability of BI serves as the basis for several reports for industry partners. For example, hotels are now able to access information on how tourists perceive their travel experience. They can examine how tourists view what they are doing and also where the destination appears with respect to the entire country. A system called Visiconnect enables the analysis and helps in identifying customers who match a specific profile, so that marketing campaigns can be targeted directly at them. It also enables the government to track how changes such as the Western Hemisphere Travel Initiative might affect travel to the Bahamas.

According to the Hon. Obie Wilchcombe, Minister of Tourism of the Bahamas: "Technology is transforming the tourism industry and the Ministry of Tourism intends to be in the forefront of that transformation. We can now

(continued)

improve our productivity because we have accurate information readily available to make intelligent business decisions. One benefit of this information is that we are able to implement better structured programs that bring about the convergence of innovative thinking, people, and technology." Gary Young, senior director of research and statistics at the Ministry of Tourism, remarked: "We're able to tell how many U.S. citizens who visited us last year had passports. We have been able to do a lot of analysis showing that, based on various segments, around 20%–30% of the people who came here last year did not have passports. That kind of information helps us to make an estimate of the economic impact in terms of lost jobs if people don't come." He further remarked: "You can do so much with this data. Hotels can view their top-producing ZIP code and plan marketing activities around that."

Prior to BI, even though the Bahamas had a lot of tourist data from the required visitor immigration cards, it was not very accessible. But BI has enabled the government and hoteliers to better understand visitors and develop unique marketing programs to increase tourism. Indeed, the new BI system is helping the Bahamas break tourism records. More than 5 million individuals visited the country in 2005, and spent over $2 billion—two new records for Bahamas' Ministry of Tourism.

(Compiled from *Pensions Management*, 2007; Smalltree, 2006; *Business Wire*, 2004; Bailor, 2004)

group "supported, operated, and managed over 100 different mainframe, server and desktop development and integration tools, 10 different hardware platforms, 14 operating systems, seven database management systems, and over 450 different production applications and desktop-based applications and tools" (Haggerty and Meister, 2003). For effective BI, and to avoid inconsistent and inaccurate information outputs, it is crucial to integrate information across such silos.

Second, considerable amounts of data, information, and explicit knowledge exist outside operational systems and DWs, such as in e-mail messages, presentations, internal company documents, audio and video files, and so on. In order to maximize benefits from organizational memory, it is important to integrate unstructured information and explicit knowledge from these sources with structured data and information from operational systems. According to Preston (2007, p. 1): "But even if all your data is clean, up to date, and easily accessible in a central repository, then there's the matter of all that unstructured content hidden away in Word files, PDFs, spreadsheets, and other electronic documents—the oft-forgotten 90% of a company's information. If you think data warehousing is hard, try [wrapping] your arms around enterprise content management."

Third, a considerable amount of data, information, and knowledge is available from external sources, such as in Web sites, public media, industry reports, and expert opinions. It is important to integrate this external content with the internal content and with content available from organizational memory.

Fourth, as discussed in Chapter 1, increasing decision complexity implies that the diversity of factors that should be considered to make decisions has increased tremendously. Integration of relevant content about these diverse factors, which is available from different sources including organizational memory, is needed to enable managers to develop insights and make appropriate decisions.

2.4.2 Information Integration Capability

Organizational memory focuses on the past. In addition, BI depends on the latest data, information, and knowledge based on the ongoing current events. Moreover, content from diverse sources needs to be synthesized before using it to produce insights. The second important business intelligence capability plays an important role here. It represents the ability to link the past structured and unstructured content (i.e., data, information, or knowledge) from a variety of sources that comprise organizational memory with the new, real-time, content. In doing so, it is important to integrate the following: (a) structured information and knowledge from ERP, transactional systems, and knowledge repositories; (b) external information and knowledge from environmental scanning and Web mining; and (c) unstructured information and knowledge from text mining, Web mining and digital content management systems. Figure 2.2 summarizes these aspects of information integration.

The input for information integration capability is the past content, stored over time, from organizational memory, and real-time content based on emerging events.

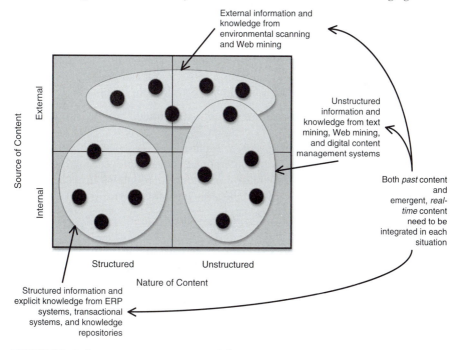

FIGURE 2.2 Information Integration Capability

Individually, and without being mutually integrated, these types of content would be difficult to use for creating new insights. Information integration capability helps address this problem by producing synthesized content about the past and present, which can be used more effectively and efficiently to create new insights.

Information integration capability relates to several features of BI (Sabherwal 2007, 2008). These include: monitoring of business trends; competitive benchmarking; ability to conduct enterprise-wide content search across different types of content (e.g., Word documents, e-mails, databases, and XML/HTML); the ability to incorporate nonquantitative data; text mining, or extracting relevant information from unstructured text; and integration with Web portals.

2.4.3 Technologies Enabling Information Integration Capability

Several technologies enable information integration capability, including the following:

- **Environmental scanning** refers to "the acquisition and use of information about events, trends, and relationships in an organization's external environment, the knowledge of which would assist management in planning the organization's future course of action" (Choo, 2001a, 2001b).

- **Text mining** refers to mining the content of unstructured data, by automatically "reading" large documents of text written in natural language (like the English language).

- **Web mining** focuses on searching the Web and mining online text (Zanasi, 2000).

- **Radio frequency identification devices** help obtain information regarding the location of goods, and transmit it so that it can be stored and used along with other relevant information regarding the item being tracked.

These technologies, and their roles in information integration, are discussed in detail in Chapter 4.

Business Intelligence in Practice 2.2 illustrates the contribution of the information integration capability to contemporary organizations using the example of the Swiss cable network operator, Cablecom. Although we focus below on information integration, the BI solution benefits from the other three BI capabilities as well, especially insight creation.

Business Intelligence in Practice 2.2: Information Integration Helps Cablecom Improve Client Satisfaction

A division of Liberty Global, Cablecom is the largest cable network operator in Switzerland, with 1,500 employees. The Zurich-based company provides cable television, broadband Internet access, and telephone services to its

(continued)

---

customers. Seventy percent of its television service contracts are with apartment building landlords, who bill the eventual users.

Despite being a market leader, Cablecom faced challenges. Before 2005, its marketing efforts focused on acquiring customers, but paid little attention to customer retention. As the market became saturated, the company sought to focus on ways to reduce customer turnover. Federico Cesconi, Cablecom's director of business intelligence, remarked: "It's very difficult to win back customers after they've left you. And in Europe, the win-back rate is only about 10% to 15%. So, our intent was to assess the satisfaction of every single customer."

Industry statistics reveal that dissatisfied customers start complaining about nine months into their contracts and leave their contracts after about 12 to 14 months. Recognizing this, Cesconi wanted to analyze customer attitudes at the seven-month mark. However, the assessment of the customers' real sentiment from about 40,000 feedback responses received each month was difficult, especially because many of these responses were open ended and occasionally rambling.

After going through an extensive software evaluation process, Cablecom's customer insight and retention team shortlisted two candidates, and then selected software from the Chicago-based SPSS, Inc., due to its ability to integrate the various customer data sources. Moreover, SPSS allowed Cablecom to make a small initial investment that could later be scaled up (e.g., Cablecom began with one workstation license that grew to two server licenses and 15 clients). In addition to the SPSS Base statistics and Clementine data mining products, Cablecom also acquired the SPSS Dimensions product for customer survey research as well as SPSS's text-mining product.

The SPSS customer analytics software accesses behavioral data from multiple sources managed within Cablecom's Oracle data warehouse, including data from the call center, call detail record data, demographic data, and externally bought data. More than 60 criteria are used to analyze customers. In addition to the Oracle data warehouse, managed by Cablecom's IT department, the marketing department has its own data mart based on the Microsoft SQL server. The marketing group utilizes the SPSS software to access the key standardized data from the central Oracle data warehouse, and supplement it using marketing-specific data (e.g., attitudinal data from customer surveys) from both and Microsoft SQL server databases.

These structured data sources are supplemented by unstructured data sources, including free-format text data in the form of customer views, obtained through the Web, help desks, call centers, automated phone surveys, sales, and other points of contact with the customer. Moreover, the SPSS tool is also used to analyze audio content obtained through the company's interactive voice response systems after transforming the MP3 audio files into text.

(continued)

> To evaluate the success of text mining, Cesconi performed an experiment using a control group and a test group of end users. The test group's feedback was analyzed via text mining, whereas this was not done for the control group. The control group's turnover was 14%, whereas the test group, with customer-service follow-up, had a turnover of only 2%. After this experiment, the BI solution was utilized broadly. Cesconi indicated that after six months of use, Cablecom's new approach successfully identified dissatisfied customers and increased satisfaction in 53% of all cases. Cablecom's excellent customer service was recognized in September 2008, when the company received the "Gartner & 1to1 Gold Award for Excellence in Customer Strategy."
> (Compiled from: *CRM Today*, 2008; Hosford, 2008; Vesset and McDonough, 2007)

▶ 2.5 INSIGHT CREATION

2.5.1 Factors Necessitating Insight Creation Capability

Two of the factors discussed in Chapter 1—the need for quick reflexes and increasing domain complexity—lead to insight creation being an important BI capability. The need for quick reflexes implies that decisions need to be made quickly, whereas increasing domain complexity requires consideration of information from diverse arenas. Therefore, even after content has been integrated across time (past content from organizational memory with real-time content related to emergent events), across sources (internal and external, and across various types of systems and technologies), and across various types (e.g., structured and unstructured, textual and nontextual, quantitative and nonquantitative), managers would not be able to spend considerable time in using the integrated content to make decisions and develop insights. The insight creation capability of BI can help them by identifying patterns, trends, relationships, and so on.

Technological progress, also discussed in Chapter 1, has led to the availability of tools that can enable the quick use of vast amounts of information and complicated models in making decisions (Davenport and Harris, 2005). Consequently, an organization that does not have insight creation capability runs the risk of falling behind its competitors. This is especially important because: "The number of people who can spend the time to deeply analyze data are shockingly few, even in large organizations." (Kellen, 2007, p. 16)

2.5.2 Insight Creation Capability

Together, the first two BI capabilities, organizational memory and information integration, provide the integrated data, information, and knowledge that constitute the raw materials needed for insight and decision making. The third BI capability, insight creation, focuses on the utilization of these raw materials to produce valuable new insights and enable effective decision making based on continual rather than periodic analysis (Prahalad and Krishnan, 2008).

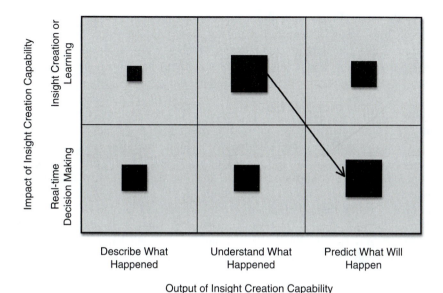

<table>
<tr><td></td><td>Describe What
Happened</td><td>Understand What
Happened</td><td>Predict What Will
Happen</td></tr>
</table>

Output of Insight Creation Capability

Note: The relative sizes of the boxes in the above cells represent the relative magnitudes of impact of insight creation capability on real-time decision making and insight creation or learning.

FIGURE 2.3 Insight Creation Capability

As shown in Figure 2.3, insight creation capability produces three kinds of outputs (Scheps, 2008):

a. A description of what happened, which focuses on identifying trends or patterns in prior events and actions or classification of customers based on their past buying behavior;

b. An understanding of what happened, which focuses on identifying the underlying causes, based on considerations such as correlations over time, thereby gaining insights into inherent relationships so that a model (e.g., a cause-and-effect model) could be developed; and

c. A prediction of future behavior, which could depend on a model that is developed based on an understanding of the past, and then tested and refined using additional information or over time.

The desire to use insight creation capability for prediction is evident, for example, in the case of SYSCO (which we will discuss in detail in Chapter 8), which focused its BI efforts on seeking answers to two questions (McAfee and Wagonfeld, 2004): "What additional products could we be selling to each of our customers?" (p. 8) and "Which of our current customers are we most likely to lose?" (p. 9).

As shown in Figure 2.3, description of what happened in the past has relatively little effect on learning or the creation of new insights, but it enables real-time decision making to some extent, which is achieved through the use of existing information about how decisions seem to have been made to build systems that make similar decisions. Understanding of what happened has a similar effect on real-time decision making, but it also contributes to the development of insights and models, based on the co-occurrences and correlations. These models can then be used to predict what will happen, as shown using the arrow in Figure 2.3, and thereby facilitate real-time decision making, such as in responding quickly to shortage of a product or a price change by a competitor. Such real-time decision making depends on real-time data (Anderson-Lehman, Watson, Wixom, and Hoffer, 2004), which is analyzed continually rather than periodically or in an ad hoc fashion (Prahalad and Krishnan, 2008), and could be automated through the use of models and rules (Davenport and Harris, 2005). Predictions of what will happen also provide additional insights to some extent. These aspects are discussed in greater detail in Chapter 5.

2.5.3 Technologies Enabling Insight Creation Capability

Technologies that enable insight creation include data mining, business analytics, and real-time decision support systems.

- **Data mining**, or **knowledge discovery in databases**, refers to extraction of useful knowledge from the identification of previously unknown relationships among variables (Grossman, 2007).

- **Business analytics** is sometimes considered to be distinct from data mining, but some authors (e.g., Kohavi, Rothleder, and Simoudis, 2002) view the two as similar. As we discuss in Chapter 4, which examines the technologies enabling insight creation in detail, we view data mining and business analytics as similar, while acknowledging the more user-friendly nature of business analytics and the historically somewhat more technical nature of data mining.

- **Real-time decision support** is the use of models based on data mining or business analytics to support operational decisions in a real-time fashion. For example, as discussed in Business Intelligence in Practice 2.4, Continental Airlines uses real-time decision support, along with presentation capability, to make decisions aimed at keeping flight arrivals and departures on schedule.

The above technologies enabling insight creation are discussed in greater detail in Chapter 5. Business Intelligence in Practice 2.3 illustrates the benefits of BI's insight creation capability for contemporary organizations. Although we focus below on insight creation, the BI solution benefits from all four BI capabilities.

Business Intelligence in Practice 2.3: Insight Creation Capability at PhoneWorks

PhoneWorks is a professional services firm that assists organizations in developing and implementing sales strategies through the creation of new inside sales teams or the optimization of existing inside sales groups. It has considerably enhanced its insight creation capability through the use of a sales analytics-as-a-service solution from LucidEra.

Prior to the use of LucidEra's sales analytics solution, PhoneWorks' use of Salesforce.com to manage customer relations and sales process was constrained due to its inability to analyze historical data. Salesforce.com provided a comprehensive view of the current business situation through static reports, but did not help PhoneWorks to examine its inner workings to determine trends and manage the progress of the sales cycle. Phone-Works needed the ability to access historical data along with current data and analyze the information to obtain better insights into its overall performance.

PhoneWorks selected LucidEra's sales analytics solution to complement and extend its internal use of Salesforce.com. Through the use of the sales analytics solution, Phone Works has developed the ability to establish and track key sales metrics, such as average deal size and average days to close, and also to analyze historical sales performance trends.

PhoneWorks discovered new insights into its business through the BI solution, especially with respect to how the sales cycle process was progressing from stage to stage. Earlier, PhoneWorks had tracked the average time to complete the sales cycle, but with LucidEra, the company was able to see the progression from each stage of the sales cycle to the next, and thereby identify, for example, gaps and any bottleneck within an individual stage or in the overall process.

Sally Duby, the president and chief operating officer of PhoneWorks, remarked: "Before using LucidEra, we struggled with a fairly static view of our sales pipeline, which meant limited visibility and limited ability to find ways to improve our sales productivity. Now we are able to easily see how opportunities are progressing at every stage of the sales cycle and how this compares to previous quarters. In a competitive and increasingly challenging economic climate, increasing sales productivity is the key to growth and survival. LucidEra has given us insight into our internal sales process in a simple way that avoids the prohibitive cost, complex deployment cycle, and extensive data warehousing effort that a traditional approach to business intelligence would have required."

(Compiled from: dssresources.com, 2008; Wise, 2008)

▶ **2.6 PRESENTATION**

2.6.1 Factors Necessitating Presentation Capability

The results of insight creation capability, whether they are intended to facilitate real-time decision making or learning, need to be provided to the users in such a fashion that they can be best utilized. However, several factors lead to differences in what is being presented in terms of both the content (e.g., level of aggregation, time period, comparison points) and the format (e.g., level of interactivity, and the extent of use of text, tables, graphs, pictures, sound, and videos). Three key factors that affect content and format are role, task, and preference.

First, the presentation would differ depending on the role of the intended user. For example, the content of information would be different for the CEO, CFO, middle managers, and operational-level workers. Top executives might be interested in firm-level performance scorecards, middle managers might be interested in productivity reports for their subordinate employees, and customer-support personnel might benefit most from displays that support real-time response to customer concerns (Blokdijk, 2008). Due to the differences in the individuals' roles as well as the relevant information, the appropriate format for presenting the information would differ as well.

Second, differences across the specific task being performed would also lead to differences in the content and format of the information being presented. For example, a customer-support specialist would use different kinds of information for each task, and benefit from different presentation formats for each task.

Third, even for the same role and the same task, individuals differ in their preferences with respect to information and format. Some users prefer a big-picture view to understand the situation, whereas others like to see the details first. Some users may prefer tables or text, and others may prefer graphs or pictures.

Figure 2.4 summarizes the factors affecting presentation. A good BI solution should have the capability to present different contents and formats according to the situation (i.e., role, task, and preference). In addition to these factors that lead to differences in the content and format of presentation, quick reflexes (discussed in Chapter 1) also require presentation capability so that managers can make real-time decisions quickly and without having to read through extensive reports or numerous screens.

2.6.2 Presentation Capability

Presentation capability is the point of contact between the BI solution and the user. It focuses on presenting appropriate information in a user-friendly fashion based on the user's role, the specific task, and the user's inputs regarding the nature of the presentation. The objective is to deliver the results of insight creation capability to the users such that the users can make their best possible use in terms of learning as well as decision making. Presentation capability relates to convenience features of the BI solution (Sabherwal, 2007, 2008), including presenting results in a customized and user-friendly form for various users; enabling users to

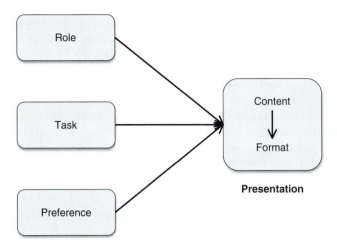

FIGURE 2.4 Factors Affecting Presentation

easily create customized presentation formats; and providing a visual interface for accessing and navigating through data.

Some of the recent developments in presentation capability, especially the use of visualization, are also a result of the earlier use of executive information systems (which have especially contributed to the development of dashboards and interactive controls) and balanced scorecards. The development in presentation capability also benefits from the considerable research on human-computer interfaces, especially on the relative benefits of using tables and graphs to display information. According to one author (Lozovsky, 2009): "If your message requires the precision of numbers and text labels to identify what they are, you should use a table. When you want to show the relationship of the data, use a graph."

2.6.3 Technologies Enabling Presentation Capability

Several technologies enable presentation capability. They are summarized below, and discussed in greater detail in Chapter 6.

- **Online analytical processing (OLAP)** focuses on exploring and analyzing multidimensional data in a highly interactive fashion and with varying levels of aggregation.
- **Visualization** acknowledges the adage "a picture is worth a thousand words," and involves the use of advanced graphics to present information so that it is easier to understand and interpret.
- **Digital dashboards** display metrics in various ways (e.g., tables, charts, graphs, maps, colors, and speedometers) in a customizable interface and a navigable layout, so that users can interactively obtain pertinent

information about the current state (Howson, 2008; Scheps, 2008). For example, as discussed in Chapter 1 (Business Intelligence in Practice 1.4), salespeople and managers at Dunkin' Donuts use a BI solution that relies on dashboards to manage information about franchise operators, including the stage of each potential deal and how its financing is progressing. By monitoring metrics such as the average cycle time for getting a franchise deal done, the size of deals, and average cycle time for different types of deal, they can identify any problem areas so they can keep deals on track. They can obtain a geographic view of regions where deals are facing problems, and then drill down into a specific account to determine the underlying causes. They can also identify potential franchises that are too close in proximity.

- **Scorecards** are also graphical displays similar to dashboards but different in nature. Whereas dashboards present a variety of information, scorecards monitor and show performance by focusing on certain metrics and comparing them to a target, threshold, or forecast (Howson, 2007). One of the most commonly used managerial approaches for scorecards is the "balanced scorecard," which focuses on four perspectives: financial, customer, internal business process, and learning and growth (Kaplan and Norton, 1992).

- **Corporate performance management**, or **business performance management**, focuses on the monitoring and managing of organizational performance using certain carefully selected key performance indicators (KPIs) such as a revenue, operational cost, or a measure of customer loyalty (Whiting, 2006; Scheps, 2008).

Business Intelligence in Practice 2.4 illustrates the benefits of BI's presentation capability using the example of Continental Airlines. Although we focus on presentation, BI at Continental also benefits from the other three BI capabilities. Indeed, we will revisit Continental Airlines' use of BI in Chapter 4, where Business Intelligence in Practice 4.1 will examine Continental's use of information integration capability.

▶ 2.7 SUMMARY

In this chapter we summarized the four main capabilities of BI solutions: organizational memory, information integration, insight creation, and presentation. We discussed each capability and the factors necessitating it. We also examined the interrelationships among these four capabilities, as summarized in Figure 2.5.

We also identified and briefly discussed the technologies facilitating each capability. These technologies are summarized in Figure 2.6. Moreover, we illustrated each of the four capabilities using a concrete example. Overall, this chapter has provided an introduction to the four BI capabilities, which we will discuss in greater detail in Chapters 3 through 6.

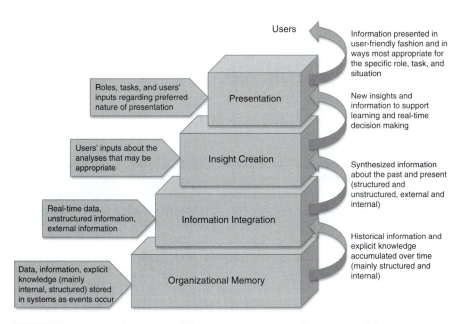

FIGURE 2.5 Inputs and Outputs of the Four Business Intelligence Capabilities

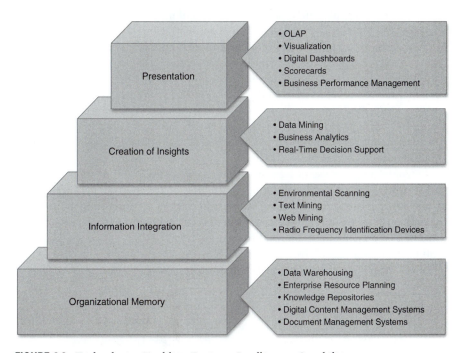

FIGURE 2.6 Technologies Enabling Business Intelligence Capabilities

---

Business Intelligence in Practice 2.4: Continental Airlines' Use of Digital Dashboards

Continental Airlines is a large airline with more than 250 destinations worldwide and over 69 million passengers enplaned in 2007. It has received a number of awards over the years, and was named the Best Airline for North American Travel in Business Traveler magazine's 2008 Best in Business Travel Survey.

Continental Airlines has made excellent use of BI's presentation capability. One such use is in the Flight Management Dashboard. This is a set of interactive graphical displays, which together enable the operations staff to quickly identify issues in the Continental flight network and thereby manage flights to enhance customer satisfaction and airline profitability.

Convenient access to critical information is accomplished in this BI solution through the use of well-designed graphics tools. For example, a graphical depiction of a concourse shows, for each delayed flight, the number of high-value customers who might need assistance in making their connections to each gate, and the time available for them to catch their flights. If necessary, these customers are ushered to their connections to help them avoid missing flights.

On-time arrival is an important operational measure for airlines. In the United States, the Federal Aviation Administration requires airlines to report arrival times and publicly share summary statistics. Therefore, another display depicts the traffic from each of the three Continental hubs, including the flight volumes, the number of late flights, and the ratio of the number of late flights to the total number of flights. This dashboard assists Operations in keeping keep flight arrivals and departures on schedule. By drilling down on this display, staff can see information about individual flights. Operations and resources are adjusted accordingly to handle anticipated problem areas.

Continuing the use of BI's presentation capability, Continental signed a deal with MicroStrategy in February 2009 that is intended to help improve insight into passenger purchasing habits. MicroStrategy's reporting tools and dashboards are expected to help Continental's marketing staff to analyze data and spot trends that can be used to develop appropriately timed marketing campaigns.

(Compiled from: Anderson-Lehman et al., 2004; Watson et al., 2006; Weier, 2009)

▶ KEY TERMS

business analytics
business performance
  management
content
data
data mining
data warehousing
digital content
  management system
digital dashboard
document management
  system

enterprise resource
  planning system
environmental scanning
information
information integration
  capability
insight creation capability
knowledge
knowledge repository
learning
online analytical
  processing (OLAP)

organizational memory
  capability
presentation capability
radio frequency
  identification device
real-time decision
  support
scorecard
text mining
transactional system
visualization
Web mining

▶ REVIEW QUESTIONS

1. Identify and briefly explain the four business intelligence capabilities.

2. Discuss the ways in which the four business intelligence capabilities are interrelated.

3. Briefly explain your understanding of the term "insight creation capability", and illustrate using an example.

4. What are the technologies that facilitate organizational memory capability? Briefly explain.

5. Identify and briefly explain any two factors that necessitate information integration capability.

6. Briefly explain the difference between organizational memory capability and information integration capability.

7. In what aspects do business intelligence solutions improve upon traditional information systems?

8. How does information integration capability facilitate insight creation capability? Briefly explain.

9. What is presentation capability? How does it relate to roles, tasks, and preferences?

10. In terms of the four business intelligence capabilities, explain how business intelligence produces the benefits explained in Chapter 1.

▶ APPLICATION EXERCISES

1. Enter http://academicprograms.teradata.com/tun/ (your course instructor will provide the needed registration information). Click the link (near the top of the screen) titled "Software" and then access "MicroStrategy BI". Then go to "MicroStrategy Application Modules" and select the "Customer Analysis Module". In the resulting screen, under "View", click on "Shared Reports". Next select "Scorecards", and download the PDF file for "Quarterly Customer Analysis". Examine this PDF and describe: (a) how this scorecard could be useful, and (b) how this scorecard could be improved.

2. Download the case titled "Real-Time Dashboards at Western Digital" (complete citation: Houghton, R., O. A. El Sawy, P. Gray, C. Donegan, and A. Joshi, "Vigilant Information Systems for Managing Enterprises in Dynamic Supply Chains: Real-Time Dashboards at Western Digital," *MISQ Executive*, 3:1, March 2004, pp. 19–36.) Read this case, and then compare the following types of dashboards discussed in this case: EIS Business Performance Dashboard, Operations Control Dashboard, Business Process Dashboard, and Collaborative Dashboard.

3. Read the Business Intelligence in Practice example on Continental Airlines. Use the Web and the citations mentioned in this chapter to obtain additional information about the organization and the specific BI effort described here. Then evaluate how the four BI capabilities work together to make this BI effort successful.

4. Read the Business Intelligence in Practice example on Cablecom. Use the Web and the citations mentioned in this chapter to obtain additional information about the organization and the specific BI effort described here. Then evaluate how the four BI capabilities work together to make this BI effort successful.

5. Read Business Intelligence in Practice 1.3 "BI Helps eCourier Seek Customer Happiness" from Chapter 1. Which business capabilities seem to be the important ones in the case of eCourier, and why?

6. Access http://www.cognos.com/performance-management/. Click on the links to Measuring and monitoring, Reporting and analysis, and Planning, budgets, and forecasts. Based on this exercise, what do you understand about performance management, scorecards, and dashboards?

7. Identify any one organization you know well. How can this organization benefit from the four business intelligence capabilities? Identify the specific benefits, and describe how the four capabilities contribute to them.

▶ REFERENCES

Anderson-Lehman, R., Watson, H. J., Wixom, B. H., and Hoffer, J. A. 2004. "Continental Airlines Flies High with Real-Time Business Intelligence." *MIS Quarterly Executive*, December.

Bailor, C. 2004. The Bahamas Ministry of Tourism Checks in with Targeted Marketing. destinationCRM.com, December 27.

Beal, B. 2004. Analytics Take a Bite out of Crime. SearchCRM.com, January 16.

Blokdijk, G. 2008. *Business Intelligence: 100 Success Secrets*. Emereo Pty Ltd., United States.

Business Wire, 2004. "Actuate and Indusa Global Collaborate on a Tourism Reporting Solution for Government of the Bahamas," November 15.

Business Wire, 2007. "Oco Deploys Business Intelligence Solution for Dunkin' Donuts in Six Weeks," April 9.

Carte, T. A., Schwarzkopf, A. B., Shaft, T. M., and Zmud, R. W. 2005. "Advanced Business Intelligence at Cardinal Health." *MIS Quarterly Executive*, December.

Choo, C. 2001a. *Information Management for the Intelligent Organization: The Art of Scanning the Environment*, 3rd ed. (Medford, N.J.: Information Today/Learning Information).

Choo, C. 2001b. "Environmental Scanning as Information Seeding and Organizational Learning." *Information Research*, 7(1).

CRM Today, 2008. "SPSS Customer Cablecom Wins Gartner & 1to1 Gold Award for Excellence in Customer Strategy," September 19.

Davenport, T. H., and Harris, J. G. 2005. "Automated Decision Making Comes of Age." *Sloan Management Review*, 46(4), 83–89.

dssresources.com, 2008. LucidEra's On-Demand Sales Analytics Allow Phone Works to Track Pipeline Progression throughout the Sales Cycle, April 2.

Ferguson, G., Mathur, S., and Shah, B. 2005. "Evolving from Information to Insight." *Sloan Management Review*, 46(2), 51–58.

Grossman, N. 2007. "How To Mine All That Customer Data." *Forbes*, September 21.

Guruprasad, R., and Nikam, K. 2006. "Initiatives in Digital Content Management: A Case Study on Saras (India's First Civil Aircraft Programme)." *Journal of Information Management and Scientometrics*, 3(1), 40–53.

Haggerty, N., and Meister, D. 2003. Business Intelligence Strategy at Canadian Tire. Richard Ivey School of Business, The University of Western Ontario, Canada.

Hosford, C. 2008. "Cablecom Mines Text to Satisfy Clients." *B to B Magazine*, July 14.

Howson, C. 2007. *Successful Business Intelligence: Secrets to Making BI a Killer App* (McGraw-Hill Osborne).

Howson, C. 2008. "Beyond metrics & dashboards." *Teradata Magazine*, June.

Kaplan, R., and Norton, D. 1992. "The Balanced Scorecard: Measures that Drive Performance." *Harvard Business Review*, 70(1), 71–79.

Kellen, V. 2007. "The State of BI: An RV Parked in a Cule-de-Sac." *Cutter Benchmark Review*, September, pp. 16–22.

Kohavi, R., Rothleder, N., and Simoudis, E. 2002. "Emerging Trends in Business Analytics." *Communication of the ACM*, 45(8), 45–48.

Lozovsky, V. 2009. Table vs. Graph. http://www.informationbuilders.com/new/newsletter/9-2/05_lozovsky.html. Accessed April 18, 2009.

McAfee, A., and Wagonfeld, A. B. 2004. *Business Intelligence Software at SYSCO*. Harvard Business School Publishing, 9-604-080.

Pensions Management, 2007. "Bahamas: Tourism–Tracking Tourists," June 1.

Prahalad, C. K., and Krishnan, M. S. 2008. *The New Age of Innovation: Driving Cocreated Value through Global Networks* (New York: McGraw Hill).

Preston, R. 2007. "Down to Business: Business Intelligence Still in Its Infancy." *InformationWeek*, January 6.

Sabherwal, R. 2007. "Succeeding with Business Intelligence: Some Insights and Recommendations." *Cutter Benchmark Review*, 7(9), 5–15.

Sabherwal, R. 2008. "KM and BI: From Mutual Isolation to Complementarity and Synergy." *Cutter Consortium Executive Report*, 8(8), 1–18.

Scheps, S. 2008. *Business Intelligence for Dummies* (Indianapolis, Ind.: Wiley).

Smalltree, H. 2006. Business Intelligence Hits the Beach. SearchDataManagement.com, May 18.

Swartz, N. 2007. "Gartner Warns Firms of 'Dirty Data,'" *Information Management Journal*, May/June, 41(3), 6.

Vesset, D., and McDonough, B. 2007. Cablecom Delivers Unique Customer Experience Through Its Innovative Use of Business Analytics, *IDC*. http://www.spss.com/success/pdf/Cablecom%20-%20IDC%20version.pdf. Accessed April 14, 2009.

Watson, H., Wixom, B. H., Hoffer, J. A., Anderson-Lehman, R., and Reynolds, A. M. 2006. "Real-Time Business Intelligence: Best Practices at Continental Airlines," *Information Systems Management*, Winter, pp. 7–18.

Weier, M. H. 2009. "MicroStrategy Lands Business Intelligence Deal with Continental." *InformationWeek*, February 11.

Weiss, L. M., Capozzi, M. M., and Prusak, L. 2004. "Learning from the Internet Giants." *Sloan Management Review*, 45(4), 79–84.

Whiting, R. 2006. "BPM Gets Smarter with a Little Help from BI," *Information Week*, November 6.

Wise, L. 2008. "Using a Software as a Service (SaaS) Model to Deploy Analytics: LucidEra Answers the Call for Phone Works." *Dashboard Insight*, July 7.

Zanasi, A. 2000. Web Mining through the Online Analyst. In Proceedings of the 1st Data Mining Conference. Cambridge University, Cambridge, UK.

PART II

TECHNOLOGIES ENABLING BUSINESS INTELLIGENCE

CHAPTER 3

TECHNOLOGIES ENABLING ORGANIZATIONAL MEMORY

▶ 3.1 INTRODUCTION

In Chapter 2 we described the capabilities associated with BI—namely, organizational memory, information integration, business analytics, and presentation. We will present the details about these capabilities in the next four chapters. In this chapter we describe the topic of *organizational memory*, which refers to the storage of information in such a form that it can be later accessed and used for BI. Thus this chapter focuses on the technologies that enable organizational memory by storing structured information that is used for BI.

Organizational memory (which is related to aspects such as corporate memory, knowledge repository, and institutional memory) represents the aggregate intellectual assets of an organization. These include data, information, and explicit knowledge which may be either structured or unstructured. Structured data or information could reside, for example, in database records or transactional systems. Structured data is said to be organized according to a data model (also data structure), which is how a computer program can easily use that data. A data model describes how the data is represented and accessed, by providing the definition and format of the data. For example, a database model is a type of data model used to describe how a database is structured and used. Structured explicit knowledge could reside in knowledge repositories and answers to frequently asked questions (FAQs). Unstructured data and information, on the other hand, do not have an associated data model or metadata. Unstructured data, information, and knowledge reside in various forms, including e-mail messages stored over time, audio and video files, historical versions of Web sites, as well as prior presentations, memos, and other documents.

BI focuses on how to create value by discovering knowledge from explicit organizational memory. In Chapter 4 we discuss how BI can drive value from information integration capability, including the integration of structured as well as unstructured data, through text and Web mining, whereas our discussion in Chapter 5 focuses on how BI enables the creation of new insights through the use of analytics and data mining.

Two relevant technologies for the organizational memory capability—enterprise resource planning (ERP) systems and data warehouses—are discussed and illustrated in this chapter. ERP systems refer to transactional systems that capture organizational memory related to all the business processes that the organization engages in. One of these business processes is for example, order-to-cash, which captures all the transactions involved in the organization from the moment the customer places an order to the moment the organization receives payment for the product or service (cash). Transaction systems typically capture all the relevant information for one accounting period, which is a month, quarter, or year depending on the organization. Because organizations typically want to see how these figures evolve over time, data warehouses capture these data over time, providing the source of data and information for the BI analysis.

In addition, the chapter includes a discussion of the topic of enterprise architecture (EA). Finally, we present a case study that describes the ERP implementation at the IBM Personal Systems Group, together with a summary of some of the critical success factors in ERP implementations.

We begin with a description of ERP systems.

▶ 3.2 ENTERPRISE RESOURCE PLANNING SYSTEMS

This section describes **enterprise resource planning systems (ERP)** or, for short, enterprise systems. ERP systems are "software packages composed of several modules, such as human resources, sales, finance, and production, providing cross-organization integration of data through embedded business processes" (Esteves and Pastor, 2001, 2007). ERP systems originate from **manufacturing resource planning or material requirements planning (MRP) systems**. MRP systems were developed to control the aspects around manufacturing, including procurement of materials, production, delivery, and inventory control (Wailgum, 2007). ERP systems include software modules that support all aspects of the enterprise including finance, human resources, manufacturing, supply chain, and inventory. ERP systems are transactional, in the sense that they store data for the current accounting period, which is a month, quarter, or year depending on the organization. In addition, some ERP systems also offer customer relationship management, sales management, and an integrated data warehouse. In order to use the data in an ERP system to do trend analysis, the data will need to be stored in a data warehouse as described in the next section. A number of companies were propelled to implement ERP systems as a measure to bring their enterprise infrastructure to Y2K[1]

---

[1] Also known as the Year 2000 problem, Y2K problem, or the millennium bug.

compliance, as ERP systems would replace the legacy systems that faced the Y2K shortcoming.[2]

ERP systems offer organizations many benefits, including integrated business processes across the enterprise, a single database for the enterprise, access to real-time transaction data, and the elimination of costly legacy stand-alone systems plagued by maintenance complexities, including outdated spaghetti code used to artificially interconnect them. ERP systems provide the infrastructure to improve the way the organization manages the order fulfillment process, from the moment it takes a customer order, processes it, delivers it, and collects the associated revenue. The order fulfillment process effectively integrates the different departments involved in this process, from sales, to finance, to manufacturing, to the logistics department that delivers the product. The last few years have seen substantial consolidation on the vendors offering ERP solutions, and the top four vendors to date include: SAP,[3] Oracle,[4] Sage,[5] and Microsoft Dynamics.[6] There are also open source versions of ERP systems, including OpenERP,[7] GNU Enterprise,[8] and WebERP,[9] among others.

However, implementation of an ERP does not come without significant technical challenges, including large monetary investments and a great deal of organizational change. These technical challenges have resulted in a number of well-published failed ERP implementations. For example, operational problems at Hershey Foods, Whirlpool, FoxMeyer Drugs, and Hewlett Packard were all blamed on poorly implemented ERP solutions (Davenport, 1998; Songini, 2004; Wheatley, 2000).

ERP systems are typically configured to tailor the different software modules to a specific way an organization goes about its business. ERP systems are configured through the use of configuration tables, although the organization also has the option to customize the system by rewriting the software code or integrate the ERP system to other existing legacy systems. Typically users are encouraged to minimize the amount of code customization or integration to

---

[2] In the early days of computers, computer memory was scarce and expensive. Thus, saving the two digits associated with the date field was significant. Any calculations involving estimating time lapse would essentially work properly as long as the dates involved were before the year 2000 (e.g., 99 – 90 = 9 years). The problem essentially would arrive as the year 2000 rolled in, as time lapse would result in a negative number (00 – 90 = –90), which would crash the legacy systems involved. In order to prevent a system crash, legacy systems would need to be modified—for example, by expanding the date field to be four characters. But some organizations adopted a different approach, which involved replacing the legacy systems altogether—say, with ERP systems that would already be Y2K compliant.

[3] www.sap.com

[4] www.oracle.com

[5] http://www.sagenorthamerica.com

[6] http://www.microsoft.com/dynamics

[7] http://www.openerp.com/

[8] http://www.gnu.org/software/gnue/project/what.html

[9] http://www.weberp.org/

existing legacy systems because that increases the complexity of the ERP implementation.

Due to their scope and complexity, ERP implementations have been and will continue to be a challenge. Clearly, the well-published failures indicate that not all organizations have been up to this challenge. The factors that are critical for the success of ERP implementations have been broadly studied in a number of areas within IS research (Rockart, 1979) and specifically within the realm of ERP system implementation (Becerra-Fernandez, Murphy, and Elam, 2005; Markus, Axline, Petrie, and Tanis, 2000). A review of the literature on ERP projects identifies the number of critical factors as varying between 10 and 20 for any project. A careful analysis of this list reveals that many of these factors can be consolidated, leaving six unique, critical success factors for large-scale ERP project implementations:

1. *Top management commitment* includes: top management support, project champion, and business plan and vision.

2. *Strong project management* includes: project management, business process redesign, software development testing and troubleshooting, and monitoring and evaluation of performance.

3. *Team member skills* include: ERP teamwork and composition and appropriate business and IT legacy systems.

4. *Team member motivation and dedication*

5. *Effective communication with users* which refers to how the organization communicates with all those affected by the ERP system implementation, including the employees and customers.

6. *Effective change management* which refers to how the organization manages the changes associated with the new IS infrastructure, including how organizational business processes must change in order to adapt to the new methodologies imposed by the ERP system.

The case that we describe in Section 3.5 describes how all of these critical success factors were present at IBM's Personal Systems Group realization of one of the largest ERP implementations to date.

Some critics of ERP systems point out that in recent years, ERP project spending at organizations has absorbed the attention, budgets, and energy of information technology professionals worldwide. ERP projects represent the single largest investment in an IT project in the histories of these companies and, in many cases, the largest single investment in any corporate-wide project (Sumner, 2000). In addition, implementing ERP software, which aims to consolidate most of the disparate systems in an organization, requires a huge amount of business process and cultural change, resulting in a smooth implementation in only 10% to 15% of the cases (Rutherford, 2001). Actually, midmarket companies or those that wish to minimize their risks are left with no other alternative than to stick to "plain vanilla," meaning out-of-the-box, minimally customized and fast-track ERP implementations, with their absolute lack of process customizability (Pender, 2001). Even in the best situations, ERP may not provide the level of integration expected, often requiring the integration of applications that were not, and will not be, replaced by the implemented systems (Pender, 2000). Furthermore, it is expected that critical knowledge-based systems—for example, actuarial repositories for insurance companies—will not be replaced by standard ERP systems, because the former represent organizational core competencies less likely to be substituted by standard ERP offerings.

ERP critics are also quick to point out that enterprise systems do not drive innovation. The more change in the organizational environment, the more the business requires business agility. The tie between ERP and BI is that a standardized integrated enterprise infrastructure environment creates better opportunities for the organization to be more agile and adopt innovation. ERP standardization focuses on commoditization of the business processes that are not the source of competitive advantage, so that the organization can focus its differentiation efforts on BI and innovation. By first building a standardized enterprise infrastructure, the organization can then focus its attention on using BI to respond with agility to environmental signals.

Another technology that can be used to create an enterprise system, without the use of ERP systems, is through **enterprise application integration (EAI)**. EAI is **middleware** (software that interconnects applications) that can parse, duplicate, or transform data from an application to present it in an acceptable format for each application that needs to receive the data (Slater, 2000). There are different types of systems integration, spanning from business architecture, to application architecture, to inter-organizational process integration (Hasselbring, 2000). EAI technology deals with data integration, sometimes from legacy systems, that facilitates repurposing of old systems into new ways of doing business. In contrast to ERP implementations, which require organizations to adapt their own business processes to ERP prescribed "best practices," EAI technology allows application integration without redefining business practices.

In Business Intelligence in Practice 3.1 we discuss the role of ERP systems in small and medium-size businesses (**SMBs**), some of the specific features they may provide for that market segment, and an example of an SMB success story.

We next discuss the role of data warehouses on preparing the enterprise data for BI.

▶ 3.3 DATA WAREHOUSE

The concept of the data warehouse (DW) was first described by IBM researchers Devlin and Murphy (Hayes, 2002). The practical application of the concept of DW is credited to Inmon (2005). A **data warehouse** can be defined as "a subject-oriented, integrated, nonvolatile, and time-variant collection of data in support of management's decisions" (Inmon, 2005) or "a copy of transaction

---

Business Intelligence in Practice 3.1: Is ERP Applicable for Small and Medium-Sized Businesses?

By now, most Fortune 500 companies have implemented some form of ERP system in order to support an integrated business strategy for their organization (Bingi et al., 1999; Davenport, 1998). But primarily due to the high costs and risks associated with their implementation, many small and medium-size businesses (SMBs) have avoided getting on the ERP bandwagon altogether. Since SMBs are a largely untapped marked segment for most ERP vendors, many of them have announced strategies specifically designed to boost sales to SMBs, including referral and incentive programs.

For example, as a strategy to become more attractive to the SMB sector, Microsoft has suited their Dynamics products with functionality specifically designed to appeal to this market segment. One such example is the Dynamics Environmental Sustainability Dashboard that will enable users to measure their energy consumption and greenhouse gas emissions at their organizations, in order to reduce their energy consumption or carbon footprint (Microsoft, 2009). The dashboard is intended to serve as a detailed guide to enable customers to collect the necessary data to create a greenhouse gas inventory, and setup the dashboard to depict accurate, auditable, and actionable environmental data.

An example of an SMB that has implemented SAP is Artisan Hardwood Floors. Artisan is an SMB that purchased SAP in order to support the operations of its 37 employees in the family-owned company. With no in-house IT staff, the implementation team at Artisan was just three people. Following a successful ERP implementation, Artisan is now able to have a much clearer financial and operational picture than it had prior to having SAP (Wailgum, 2008).

However, the jury is still out to determine whether ERP systems will be able to take a significant "byte" out of the SMB market.

---

data specifically structured for querying and reporting" (Kimball et al., 2008). A more comprehensive definition describes a data warehouse as "an environment—not a single technology—comprising a data store and multiple software products . . . includes tools for data extraction, loading, storage, access, query, and reporting . . . to support decision-oriented management queries" (Bashein and Markus, 2000, p. 3). The four characteristics of a DW environment are (Inmon, 2005):

1. Subject-oriented, which means that depending on the type of company, the major subject areas will be unique. For example, for an insurance company,

the subjects may be auto, life, health, and casualty; for a retailer the major subject areas may be SKU, sale, and vendor.

2. Integrated, so that data is fed into the DW from multiple, disparate sources, including the operational databases, data archives, legacy databases, and even external data. In the process of integrating the data into the DW, it gets converted, reformatted, resequenced, and summarized into a single physical corporate image. As the data is integrated into a single image, issues must be resolved in order to overcome inconsistencies, regarding, for example, naming conventions, data encoding rules, and physical and measurement attributes of the data.

3. Nonvolatile, which means that the DW must be loaded as a snapshot of the operational data, therefore it must be updated with a new snapshot in order to reflect the subsequent changes in the operational dataset.

4. Time-variant, so that every unit of data in the DW is stamped with a date that records the moment of time during which the record was accurate, therefore enabling the time-series analysis of the data. For example, operational data usually reflects a time period of 60 to 90 days, while DW typically contains more historical data and reflects a time horizon of 5 to 10 years. DW may be seen as a series of snapshots of data taken at a set period of time.

Data warehousing is considered to be a prerequisite for BI, since it helps the organization obtain value from its data sources by preparing and storing the enterprise data into a repository designed to support decision making. DW stores data and information in a way that it can be efficiently accessed later by the BI solutions. Data warehouse vendors include Oracle and NCR Teradata,[10] and open source versions like MySQL.[11]

A data warehouse is an architecture that describes the atomic level in the enterprise's data model, which consists of four levels (Inmon, 2005). The first level is the operational level, consisting of the enterprise resource planning systems, which we described in the previous section, and other legacy applications that serve the core transaction processes. The operational level holds the application-oriented raw data (also known as primitive data, as opposed to the derived data stored in the other levels) and serves the needs of all the organization's transaction data. The data warehouse level of data holds integrated historical primitive data as well as some derived data. The **data mart** is considered to be synonymous with the departmental level, and holds data in a specific format that serves the needs of a functional department—say, for example, the marketing or manufacturing department. Data marts are described in more detail in Chapter 6, when we explore the concept of online analytical processing (OLAP). Finally, the individual data is

[10] www.teradata.com

[11] http://www.mysql.com/

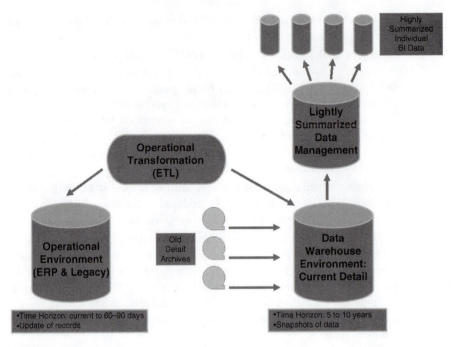

FIGURE 3.1 Four Levels of the Enterprise Data Model (Adapted from Inmon, 2005)

used by organization's individuals to serve specific needs—such as, for example, BI. Figure 3.1 illustrates the four levels of the enterprise data model.

In principle, there are two reasons why an enterprise needs to create a data warehouse (Jukic, 2006):

1. If operational queries running against the operational database (for example, the ERP system) had to compete with the analytical queries (for example, needed to run a BI process), the performance of the operational queries would degrade.

2. It is not possible to structure a database that can be queried for both operational and analytical purposes.

For these reasons, data warehouses are developed specifically to support analytical queries and are designed for the continuous retrieval of data from the operational data sources. A key step in the development of the data warehouse is to extract and integrate the operational data through the use of extract/transform (or transfer)/load (ETL) software tools. Typically, 50% to 70% of the data warehouse project development time is spent on ETL activities (Ponniah, 2001). The data warehouse implementation activities include data sourcing, data staging (or ETL), and the development of BI or decision support end-user applications.

Organizations must choose the appropriate modeling technique based on their analytical needs. Two data modeling techniques are the most popular for data warehousing, and both approaches offer a workable alternative for modeling and creating data warehouses (Sen and Sinha, 2005):

1. The **entity-relational (ER) modeling** technique, proposed by Inmon (2005), describes the data warehouse as an integrated database modeled using traditional ER database modeling techniques. This technique first requires the creation of a centralized DW. Then the central DW serves as the data source for data marts. Data marts are dimensionally modeled. The integration and consolidation of the operational data sources is effected through the ETL process. Once it is completed and populated with the data, the data is extracted into the various data marts that will support the OLAP queries. The process of integrating this process with other data extractions from all sorts of data sources—including, for example, legacy flat files—is known as the Corporate Information Factory (CIF) (Inmon et al., 2001). The Inmon approach requires creating a data warehouse ER model as a first step, which can be used as a basis for modeling dimensional and nondimensional extracts (Jukic, 2006). The Inmon approach could take longer to develop than Kimball's, but could provide a more powerful method by providing a data repository that could be used as a basis for extracts into other data stores structured in multiple ways.

2. The **dimensional modeling** technique, proposed by Kimball (2004), views the DW as a collection of dimensionally modeled data marts, and uses the operational data sources and ETL much like the Inmon approach does. The difference is that in this approach, common dimensions across data sources are modeled first, and then fact tables are added, which are connected to multiple dimensions that may be shared by more than one fact table. As a result, the resulting DW is nothing but a collection of intertwined dimensionally modeled data marts (Chenoweth et al., 2003; Jukic, 2006). In the Kimball approach, dimensionally modeled structures are created without creating an underlying ER model, therefore it could be a quicker and simpler way to create a data warehouse (Jukic, 2006). This methodology is often criticized as it is seen to lack an enterprise focus, but this may be an inaccurate perception. Figure 3.2 depicts the dimensional model process flow diagram.

The two above-mentioned approaches to building the data warehouse have also been described as the enterprise or centralized solution and the evolutionary or data mart approach, respectively. A third approach is the package approach, which employs a vendor's data warehousing solution, specifically designed to work with the corresponding ERP system and operational databases (Bashein and Markus, 2000). Deploying a data warehouse is not an insignificant endeavor by any

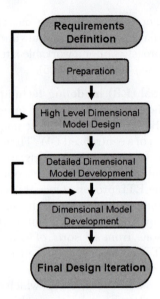

FIGURE 3.2 Dimensional Modeling Process Flow Diagram (Adapted from Kimball, 2004)

means, and presents a series of both technical and sourcing challenges (Bashein and Markus, 2000):

1. *Abundant technical options* which means that each stage (extract, storing, accessing, and analyzing data) offer a number of technical options, including for OLAP, modeling, and so on. These options add significant complexity to the DW project.

2. *Changes in technologies and vendors* which are due to ongoing consolidations in the software industry, that may result in expensive conversions from one vendor to another.

3. *Integration requirements* required, since data warehousing tools may not necessarily integrate seamlessly across vendors or even software versions from the same vendor.

4. *Knowledge transfer challenges* which are due to expertise gaps resulting from the lack of experience about how to successfully implement this type of project.

In addition there may be challenges around the data, caused by uncertain information requirements, large volumes of historical data, uncertain data quality particularly from legacy systems, lack of consistency in data names and definitions, and lack of access to all the data that the organization may require (Bashein and Markus, 2000). Finally, issues around organizational leadership, politics, and human factors may also interfere with the successful deployment of data warehouses. More recently, data warehouses have also been equipped with the ability to extend the users' decision making from historical analysis via an active data warehouse, which supports interactive tactical decision support.

Because DW projects are ongoing, it has been said that data warehousing is more of a journey than a destination (Wixom et al., 2008). A series of characteristics distinguish a mature data warehouse (Watson, Ariyachandra, and Matyska, 2001; Wixom et al., 2008):

1. *Data*, which includes the number of subject areas, the data models used, and the quantity of data stored. In a mature DW, the data reflect the enterprise and are well integrated, over multiple time periods.

2. *Architecture*, which is the structure of the DW and data marts. For a mature DW, there is a clearly defined structure with dependent data marts.

3. *Stability of the production environment*, which refers to the existence of established processes for maintaining and growing the DW. For a mature DW, the procedures involved are routine and documented.

4. *Warehouse staff*, which includes the experience, skills, and specialization of the staff involved with the DW. For a mature DW, the staff includes experienced in-house personnel with well-defined roles and responsibilities.

5. *Users*, which includes the types, numbers, and locations of users of the DW. For a mature DW, users are organization-wide, including suppliers and customers.

6. *Impact on users' skills and jobs* refers to the ways users' jobs and required skills may need to change due to the DW. For a mature DW, users throughout the organization need improved computer skills to perform their jobs.

7. *Applications* refers to the kinds of applications that use the DW. For a mature DW, this includes reports, predefined queries, ad hoc queries, DSS, EIS, BI, and integration with operational systems.

8. *Costs and benefits*, which are those linked to the DW. For a mature DW, benefits include time saving, new and better information, improved decision making, redesigned business processes, and support for corporate objectives.

9. *Organizational Impact* refers to how much impact the DW has on the performance of the organization. For a mature DW, the impact is organization-wide and often strategic, tactical, and operational.

Even when a data warehouse reaches maturity, it continues to change to become the foundation for organization-wide BI and decision making, performance management (such as a balanced scorecard as described in Chapter 6), e-commerce, and customer relationship management (Watson et al., 2001). Business Intelligence in Practice 3.2 describes the development of a small data warehouse used to integrate funded research data across universities, to be used as the source for an interorganizational repository for an expertise locator system.

Business Intelligence in Practice 3.2: A Data Warehouse of University Experts—The Searchable Answer Generating Environment (SAGE)

The goal of SAGE was to enable researchers at the National Aeronautics and Space Administration (NASA) to partner with experts, via the creation of a searchable repository of university researchers in the State of Florida. Each university in Florida kept a database of funded research for internal use, but these databases were disparate and dissimilar. The SAGE Expert Finder created a single funded research data warehouse by incorporating a distributed database scheme, which could be searched by a variety of fields, including research topic, investigator name, funding agency, or university. Figure 3.3 represents the SAGE architecture. In this figure, the canisters in the Florida map represent the disparate databases at each of the Florida universities.

The content of each database was extracted, transformed, and loaded into the SAGE database. The extraction software used a file transfer protocol (FTP) client application that automatically obtained and transferred the database contents of each participating university. The file transfer took place according to a prescheduled transfer rule, to the SAGE database represented by the canister DATABASE. The FTP client was customized to each university, and it's marked by the abbreviations that represent each university (UWF, FAMU, UNF, FSU, UF, UCF, FAU, FIU,

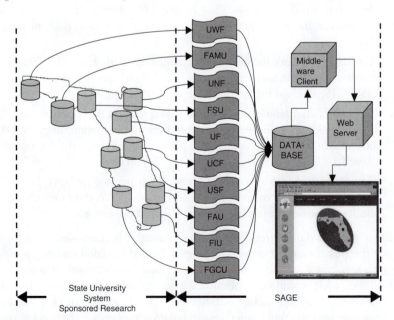

FIGURE 3.3 SAGE Architecture (Becerra-Fernandez, 2006)

(continued)

and FGCU). After the information was in the SAGE server, the next steps involved the migration of the data to the SQL Server format, followed by cleansing and transforming the data to a relational format. This methodology provided flexibility to users and the database administrator, regardless of the type of program used to collect the information at the source. The development of SAGE was marked by two design requirements: to minimize the impact on each of the universities' offices of sponsored research that collect most of the required data, and to validate the data used to identify experts.

One of the technical challenges faced during the design and implementation of this project was that the source databases of funded research from the various universities were dissimilar in design and file format. The manipulation of the source data was one of the most important issues, because the credibility of the system would ultimately depend on the consistency and accuracy of the information. Manipulating the data included the process of cleansing the data, followed by the data transformation into the relational model, and ultimately the databases' migration to a consistent format. One of the most important research contributions of SAGE was the merging of interorganizational database systems.

The next section describes how organizations go about designing the enterprise architecture.

▶ 3.4 DESIGNING THE ENTERPRISE ARCHITECTURE

The preceding sections have described the concepts of enterprise resource planning systems and the data warehouse. When companies face decisions about how to design their underlying IT infrastructure, they seek to align their IT with their business strategy. Most firms understand that it's necessary to do this in order to maximize the value they obtain from their IT investments. But how far they should pursue both their business process standardization as well as the integration of their business process across their business units may not necessarily be a straightforward decision. What complicates matters further when seeking this alignment between business strategy and IT is that the firm's business strategy is typically complex, encompasses many markets, requires different capabilities, and must respond to shifting priorities due to competitive pressures (Ross, 2005). This section describes how firms define their underlying enterprise architecture by making two important choices about their business operations units (Ross, Weill, and Robertson, 2006):

1. How standardized their business processes should be across operational units (meaning departments, regions, market segments, etc.)

2. How integrated their business processes should be across those units

None of the operating models should be considered as "the right one," as the dimensions of standardization and integration pose both benefits and challenges for the organization.

Standardization refers to "defining exactly how a process will be executed regardless of who is performing the process or where it is completed" (Ross et al., 2006, p. 27). In order to decide the level of standardization at your organization, you need to respond to the question: To what extent does the company benefit by having business units run their operations in the same way? (Ross et al., 2006, p.30). Standardization offers both efficiency and predictability across the organization, yet it limits local innovation and often requires the replacement of existing systems by standard, even perhaps inferior, systems. *Integration* "links the efforts of organizational units through shared data . . . between processes to enable end-to-end transaction processing, or across processes to allow the company to present a single face to customers (Ross et al., 2006, pp. 27–28). In order to decide the relevant level of integration for your firm, you should respond to the question: To what extent is the successful completion of one business unit's transactions dependent on the availability, accuracy, and timeliness of other business unit's data? (Ross et al., 2006, p. 30). Similarly, integration increases efficiency, coordination, transparency, and agility throughout the organization, but it poses challenges around the development of standard definitions and formats for the data shared across business units, which can be difficult and time consuming.

Based on these two choices of business process—standardization and integration—organizations will be seen to operate in one of the four possible **operating models** as depicted in Figure 3.4 (Ross, 2005; Ross et al., 2006):

1. The **diversification** model (low standardization, low integration) is used by organizations that follow a decentralized organizational design, pursuing different markets with different products and services, and that benefit from local autonomy. One example of a company that excels in the diversification quadrant is JM Family Enterprises (JMFE) consisting of four strongly interrelated businesses: a Toyota distributor serving 160 dealers, financial services, insurance products, and a Lexus dealership. These business units generate business for each other, and while JMFE may offer some centralized services to its businesses, the company has grown largely through the success of its individual units.

2. The **coordination** model (low standardization, high integration) is used by firms that have high levels of integration through the sharing of customers, products, suppliers, and partners. At the same time, they have little standardization of processes, and business unit leaders are given the

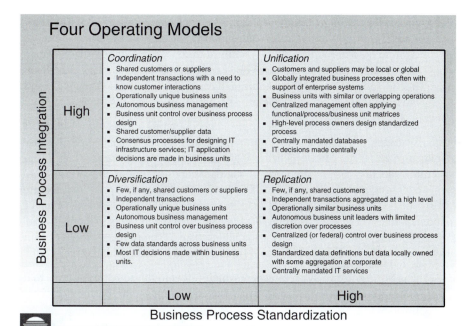

Four Operating Models

		Low	High
Business Process Integration	**High**	**Coordination** • Shared customers or suppliers • Independent transactions with a need to know customer interactions • Operationally unique business units • Autonomous business management • Business unit control over business process design • Shared customer/supplier data • Consensus processes for designing IT infrastructure services; IT application decisions are made in business units	**Unification** • Customers and suppliers may be local or global • Globally integrated business processes often with support of enterprise systems • Business units with similar or overlapping operations • Centralized management often applying functional/process/business unit matrices • High-level process owners design standardized process • Centrally mandated databases • IT decisions made centrally
	Low	**Diversification** • Few, if any, shared customers or suppliers • Independent transactions • Operationally unique business units • Autonomous business management • Business unit control over business process design • Few data standards across business units • Most IT decisions made within business units.	**Replication** • Few, if any, shared customers • Independent transactions aggregated at a high level • Operationally similar business units • Autonomous business unit leaders with limited discretion over processes • Centralized (or federal) control over business process design • Standardized data definitions but data locally owned with some aggregation at corporate • Centrally mandated IT services
		Low	High

Business Process Standardization

Center for Information Systems Research
©2005 MIT Sloan CISR –Ross

Enterprise Architecture as Strategy: Building a Foundation for Business Execution, J. Ross, P. Weill, and D. Robertson, Harvard Business School Press, forthcoming June 2006.

FIGURE 3.4 Characteristics of Four Operating Models (Ross et al., 2006)

autonomy to define their individualistic business processes in order to best serve their customers. One example of a firm in the coordination quadrant is Merrill Lynch,[12] composed of the global investment and banking group, the investment managers, and global private client (GPC) group. In order for GPC to meet the financial needs of its high-value customers, it must be able to deliver customized solutions (low standardization) to its target customers while providing access to integrated data across products and customers (high integration).

3. The **replication** model (high standardization, low integration) is used by firms that provide their units with the autonomy to run independently following highly standardized business processes. For firms in this model, their units do not depend on each other's transactions or data, and their success depends on their ability to innovate globally while implementing highly standardized and optimized business processes. Firms in this company include, for example, Mc Donald's and other similar franchises.

4. The **unification** model (high standardization, high integration) is used by organizations that are highly integrated around standardized business

---

[12] The company announced its acquisition by Bank of America in September 2008.

processes, through integrated supply chains that share transaction, customer, and supplier data. An example firm in this model is Dow Chemical. Around 60% of the firm's core chemical processes are standardized, which drives out inefficiencies and leverages economies of scale. Typically, firms in the unification model quadrant have highly centralized management environments, such as a single instantiation of an ERP system.

Once a firm has identified the appropriate operating model that reflects its business strategy, it is ready to define the *enterprise architecture*. Enterprise architecture refers to "the organizing logic for business processes and IT infrastructure reflecting the integration and standardization requirements of the company's operating model" (Ross et al., 2006, p. 47). The firm's enterprise architecture will serve as the blueprint that will lead its efforts for the development of an IT foundation that will support its future business initiatives, and refers to the high-level logic for business processes and IT capabilities. The IT unit typically defines four levels of architecture below the enterprise architecture (Ross et al., 2006):

1. The *business process architecture* which refers to the activities or tasks that comprise the major business processes identified by the business process owners.

2. The *data or information architecture* which includes the shared data definitions.

3. The *applications architecture* which refers to the individual application systems and their interfaces.

4. The *technology architecture* which includes the infrastructure services and the technology standards they are built on.

The enterprise architecture is typically depicted in a one-page picture called the *core diagram*, which synthesizes a high-level view of the processes, data, and technologies that comprise the organization's *digitized platform* for execution. The organization's core diagram is relevant to its operating model. Therefore, companies that select a specific operating model will have similar core diagrams. As an example, consider the core diagram for Delta Airlines (Ross, 2004), depicted in Figure 3.5. Delta Airlines follows a unification model. We use this example to describe the four elements of the enterprise architecture core diagram:

1. *Core business processes* specifies the set of company-wide capabilities the company requires to respond to its customers according to its operating model. These capabilities are those business processes that don't change for the organization. In the case of Delta, the core processes include the customer experience (Delta's customer touch points), the operational pipeline (loading, moving, unloading, and maintaining planes), the business reflexes (scheduling, pricing, and financial processes), and the employee relationship management (workforce scheduling, compensation, and development).

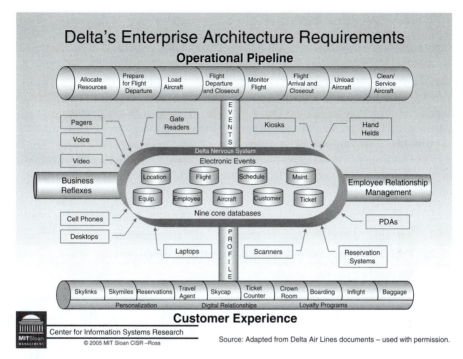

FIGURE 3.5 Delta's Operating Model (Ross et al., 2006)

2. *Sharing of data driving core processes* refers to the customer files shared across the product lines. In the case of Delta, the nine databases that are critical to process execution are depicted in the center of the core diagram: location, flight, schedule, maintenance, equipment, employee, aircraft, customer, and ticket.

3. *Key linking and automation technologies* refers to all the technologies that enable the integration of applications and access to the shared data, including ERP systems, software application packages, and middleware. It also includes those technologies, such as portals, that provide access to the systems, data, and interfaces. Referring to Figure 3.5, the Delta nervous system enables customers, employees, and the company's core processes to access the shared data.

4. *Key customers* include the major customer groups, including channels and segments that are supported by this foundation for execution.

For examples depicting the remaining three operational models, refer to Ross et al., 2006.

The next section describes the component of the organizational memory that deals with unstructured information—that is, the knowledge repository.

▶ 3.5 KNOWLEDGE REPOSITORIES

Increasingly, organizations are integrating knowledge repositories, also known as knowledge sharing systems, into their organizational memories. In general, knowledge repositories include technologies that support the capture of unstructured information and knowledge (**document management systems**), and the archiving of audio and video files (*digital content management systems*). Other related terms include **enterprise content management systems** and **Web content management systems**.

For knowledge repositories to be effective, they must attract a critical volume of knowledge seekers and knowledge owners (Dignum, 2002), so that knowledge owners:

1. Will seek to share their knowledge with a trusted and controllable group
2. Are able to decide when to share and the conditions for sharing
3. Feel reciprocity or receive a fair exchange or reward for sharing their knowledge

By the same token, knowledge seekers:

1. May not be aware of all the possibilities for sharing, thus the knowledge repository will typically help them explore these possibilities through searching and ranking
2. May require contextual information that will help them decide on the applicability of the explicit knowledge to the particular situation

A knowledge-sharing system is said to define a **learning organization**, which supports the sharing and reuse of individual, group, and organizational knowledge. As discussed above, the technologies that support knowledge repositories are document management systems and digital content management systems. Many vendors provide software offerings with these capabilities, including Microsoft (Sharepoint), OpenText (Hummingbird, Livelink), and EMC (Documentum). Furthermore, there are a number of open source offerings as well—as, for example, OpenKM, Alfresco, and KnowledgeTree, among others.

At the core of a document management system is a repository, an electronic storage medium with a primary storage location that affords multiple access points. The document management system essentially stores unstructured information. This repository can be centralized or it can be distributed. Document management builds upon the repository by adding support to the classification and organization of information, unifying the actions of storage and retrieval of unstructured data (such as documents, pictures, video, etc.) over a platform-independent system. A document management system aggregates relevant information through a common, typically Web-based interface. The document management collaborative application increases communication, thus allowing the sharing of organizational knowledge.

The document management application increases the sharing of documentation across the organization, thus assisting the sharing of organizational knowledge. Unstructured data are typically organized or *indexed* following a standard hierarchical structure or classification taxonomy, much like the index catalog is used to organize the books in a library. Frequently, *portal* technologies are used to build a common entry into multiple distributed knowledge repositories, using the analogy of a "door" as a common entry into the organization's knowledge resources. Portals provide a common user interface, which can often be customized to the user's preferences, such as local news, weather, and so on.

Knowledge repositories can be classified according to their attributes or the specific purpose they serve for the organization. Some examples of specific types of knowledge repositories include (Becerra-Fernandez and Sabherwal, 2009):

1. **Incident report databases** are used to disseminate information related to incidents or malfunctions—for example, of field equipment (like sensing equipment outages) or software (like bug reports). Incident reports typically describe the incident together with explanations of the incident, although they may not suggest any recommendations. Incident reports are typically used in the context of safety and accident investigations.

2. **Alert systems** were originally intended to disseminate information about a negative experience that has occurred or is expected to occur. However, recent applications also include increasing exposure to positive experiences. Alert systems could be used to report problems experienced with a technology, such as an alert system that issues recalls for consumer products. Alert systems could also be used to share more positive experiences. Alert systems may be applicable to a single organization or to a set of related organizations that share the same technology and suppliers.

3. **Best practices databases** describe successful efforts, typically from the reengineering of business processes, that could be applicable to organizational processes. Best practices differ from lessons learned in that they capture only successful events, which may not be derived from experience. Best practices are expected to represent business practices that are applicable to multiple organizations in the same sector, and are sometimes used to benchmark organizational processes.

4. **Lessons learned systems (LLS)** The goal of LLS is "to capture and provide lessons that can benefit employees who encounter situations that closely resemble a previous experience in a similar situation" (Weber, Aha, and Becerra-Fernandez, 2001). LLS could be pure repositories of lessons or sometimes could be intermixed with other sources of information (e.g., reports). In many instances, enhanced document management systems are supporting distributed project collaborations and their knowledge sources, while actively seeking to capture and reuse lessons from project report archives.

5. **Expertise locator systems** The goal of expertise locator systems (ELS) is to help locate intellectual capital—in other words, to find an expert who can be a source of information and who can perform a given organizational or social function (Becerra-Fernandez, 2006). The intent when developing these systems is to catalog knowledge competencies, including information not typically captured by human resources systems, in a way that could be queried later across the organization.

The differences among these types of knowledge repositories are based upon (Becerra-Fernandez and Sabherwal, 2009):

1. Content Origin: Does the content originate from experience like in lessons learned systems, or from industry standards and technical documentation as in best practice databases?

2. Application: Do they describe a complete process, or perhaps a task or a decision?

3. Results: Do they describe failures, like in incident report databases or alert systems, or successes, like in best practices databases?

4. Orientation: Do they support an organization or a whole industry?

Table 3.1 contrasts these knowledge repositories based on these attributes.

In summary, knowledge repositories are increasingly gaining the attention of IT leaders as an important source of intelligence that can be mined to improve decision making within the organization as the firm seeks to become a learning organization. In the next section we describe a case study that outlines the implementation of an ERP system at the IBM Personal Systems Group.

Table 3.1 Types of Knowledge Repositories (Adapted from Becerra-Fernandez, 2006, and Weber et al., 2001)

Knowledge Sharing System	Originates from experiences?	Describes a complete process?	Describes failures?	Describes successes?	Orientation
Incident Reports	Yes	No	Yes	No	Organization
Alerts	Yes	No	Yes	No	Industry
Lessons Learned System	Yes	No	Yes	Yes	Organization
Best Practices Databases	Possibly	Yes	No	Yes	Industry
Expertise Locator System	Yes	No	No	Yes	Organization and Industry

THE SAP IMPLEMENTATION AT IBM PERSONAL SYSTEMS GROUP[13]

In the spring of 1993, Lou Gerstner became the CEO of IBM, on a year that the company lost $8 billion dollars, capping a three-year loss of nearly $16 billion (Becerra-Fernandez et al., 2005). Big Blue was plagued with high expenses, too many employees, and redundancies in manufacturing and R&D. Whether IBM would be able to make the changes necessary to survive was very much in doubt. The strategic imperative for IBM in 1993 called for reducing costs, speeding up product development cycles, going to market as one IBM, becoming one integrated global organization, and making it easier for customers to do business with IBM. To accomplish this strategic imperative, IBM set out to transform the way it did business by adopting five major, common, end-to-end business processes: integrated product development, integrated supply chain (procurement, production, fulfillment), customer relationship management, human resources, and finance.

The need to transform the way IBM did business was evident in the Personal Systems Group (PSG). The PSG manufactured personal computers, including the ThinkPad™, Personal System/1™, Personal System/2™, Value Point™, and Ambra™. In 1993, in anticipation of strong PC sales, senior PSG management convinced the business to authorize a significant expenditure to buy more PC components, in order to avoid being out of stock of their most popular product. In the past, this had been one of the more frequent complaints from their dealers, and PSG management wanted to avoid this situation and provide high availability of its PC brands to meet market demand. Around the world, each manufacturing plant had its own application systems and technologies for supporting the various parts of the supply chain. This made it next to impossible to coordinate a PSG-wide response to this problem. By year's end, the PSG had missed their forecast "by several hundred million of dollars" and had over $3 billion remaining in inventory. The net loss was estimated to be $1 billion.

As a result, a new management team was brought to the PSG in 1994. A massive reengineering effort was launched to straighten out the manufacturing and supply chain by removing inefficiencies caused by the lack of PSG-wide coordination. The entire research and development operation was consolidated under one roof in Research Triangle Park (RTP), North Carolina. By 1999, the rest of IBM was vital and thriving again, and the stock had reached its all-time high, increasing its market capitalization more than fourfold to $169 billion. However, the Personal Systems Group continued to face a difficult competitive environment, and fierce price wars had sharply reduced its profits. Its competitors, most noticeably Dell, offered customers the ability to configure a PC to order, whereas the PSG could only offer standard predefined models. The PSG lost nearly $1 billion in 1998. In October 1999, IBM announced that up to 1,000 jobs were being cut in the PSG. The key factors for making the PSG profitable again would require getting in place a single, worldwide-integrated system at its manufacturing sites.

IBM, like many other Fortune 500 companies, had hundreds of duplicate, nonintegrated systems that had evolved in an uncoordinated manner for decades. One way to reduce costs was to reduce the number of production, logistics, and sales systems throughout the corporation. Corporate staff were asked to investigate the situation and make a recommendation. Their

(continued)

---

[13] This section was written in collaboration with Joyce Elam and Kenneth Murphy.

recommendation was that there was only one software solution big enough and broad enough to cover IBM across the board, and that was SAP[14]. IBM Corporate decided to adopt SAP as the corporate ERP solution in March 1995.

The business case was also based on PSG implementing a "group model." The concept of the group model for PSG included a common processing configuration, common architectures, education and process documentation, and overall requirements and release components. The group model embodied the following concepts (Becerra-Fernandez et al., 2005):

1. Common Processes: Business processes would be developed and configured in SAP to support common processes worldwide. Although there were legal, financial, and operating differences resulting in some sites, commonality was the cornerstone of the SAP implementation.

2. Common Development and Support: Configuration and code development would be supported by a group of programmers and analysts residing at RTP. The development groups would share one single development environment. End-user support would be located in each site to optimize responsiveness, but all fixes and enhancements would be managed centrally to maintain commonality control.

3. Common Architectures: Production would be run from one SAP production instance.

4. Common Education and Process Documentation: Training materials would be developed centrally and distributed to each manufacturing site. National languages would be accommodated.

5. Real-Time Access to Information: This would be available from all PSG production and distribution facilities, through real-time integration within SAP interfaces to PSG decision support tools and interfaces with complementary applications.

Implementing an integrated production system at the RTP site would include 300 new business processes and subprocesses and replace about twenty critical, technologically obsolete legacy systems. In addition, interfaces to many other legacy systems would need to be developed so that they could exchange data with the new ERP system, entitled Production Release 2 (PR2). Figure 3.6 shows the IT architecture map that would exist after the implementation of PR2.

The overall management structure for the PR2 project consisted of a matrix with process teams and plan teams. There were six process teams, each associated with one of the following modules in SAP: manufacturing, sales and distribution, production planning, finance and costing, procurement, and engineering change. The process teams had responsibility for designing the new business processes to be implemented in SAP. The process team leaders owned the human resources from the business side and were responsible for managing and allocating the human resources to the "plan owners." There were approximately 80 people in these teams.

Senior IT managers were the plan owners in each of these areas. Plan owners designed an overall project plan that detailed all the activities for their assigned area that had to occur during the nine-month life of the project. Plan owners were responsible for ensuring that milestones defined in their plans were met. In addition to the human resources from the process teams, these plans owners had access to the IT organization.

(*continued*)

---

[14] www.sap.com is one of the major ERP vendors.

SAP Applications Diagram – RTP

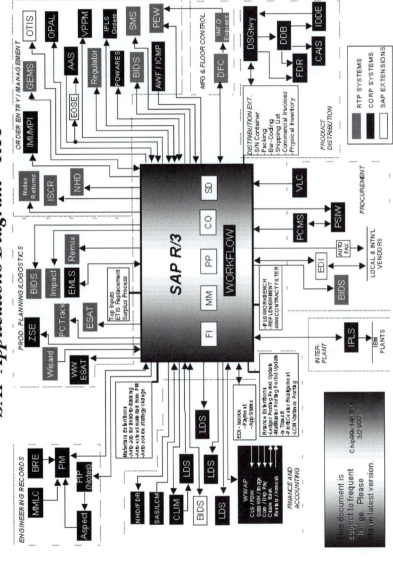

FIGURE 3.6 The IBM SAP (Source: Becerra-Fernandez et al., 2005)

As part of the process plan, IT employees configured in SAP the PSG business processes as defined by the process teams. The program plan required IT employees to develop the code to bridge SAP to the other "legacy" information systems supporting the business. In addition to building bridges to the remaining legacy systems, the IT team was responsible for extracting data from the systems being retired and placing data into SAP in support of the data migration plan. The IT team was also responsible for defining the systems architecture, which includes the hardware and software supporting the application, and the group model plan, which is the common architecture for a single system for all plants. Finally, there were three plans associated with deployment:

1. Organizational Change: Designing a plan for how jobs will change and making the changes
2. End-User Education: Designing a plan for educating the users of the system and offering training sessions
3. Deployment: Providing a liaison from the project team to the user community

An example of a high-level deployment plan is given in Figure 3.7.

Planning for PR2 deployment began in the third quarter of 1998 and continued until the go-live day. Weekly meetings were held to define responsibilities for the management of functional areas, data cleaning and migration, system testing, and user support. An extremely detailed "move to production plan" was designed that defined hour-by-hour the activities on the go-live date.

To successfully accomplish PR2 deployment, manufacturing commitments for the second quarter of 1999 had to be greatly reduced. RTP volume for the entire month of April was scheduled to be 20,000 boxes. This was equivalent to a typical week's production. The difference was off-loaded to the manufacturing plant in Guadalajara. The decision to off-load work to Guadalajara had to be made early in the planning cycle, since all components and other materials had to be delivered there. In addition, all suppliers to the RTP had to be informed of the shutdown. In some cases contracts had to be altered.

As the go-live date approached, there were still a number of serious unresolved issues. Four weeks before going live, a major problem with the implementation of the DB2 database being used by PR2 was encountered. There were also SAP software modules still being tested, and end-to-end system testing was not yet complete. Production ramp-down at RTP was completed on March 27, and at this point the team had the task of closing the books on the old legacy systems. This required working until midnight to ensure that every bit of revenue was captured. The legacy systems ran overnight batch bridges, so the team needed to allow enough time to fix any potential bridge errors.

During the shutdown period between March 27 and April 6, the focus was on data migration. The process of data conversion had begun months earlier with the data conversion managers working with the process team to define the data requirements for the SAP environment. After requirements were determined, the data conversion managers had to inform the legacy IT team of the requirements. The groups had to then agree to a data "translation" at the data level, which involved definition of field names, determination of field lengths, formatting of data, and so on. Once agreement was reached, the legacy team created programs to extract and clean the data. Once the data was moved into the test SAP system, it was tested with the assistance of a series of subroutines. This cycle of data extraction and clean-up was conducted nine times, using over 200 data conversion programs and handling more than 194,000 pieces of data.

(continued)

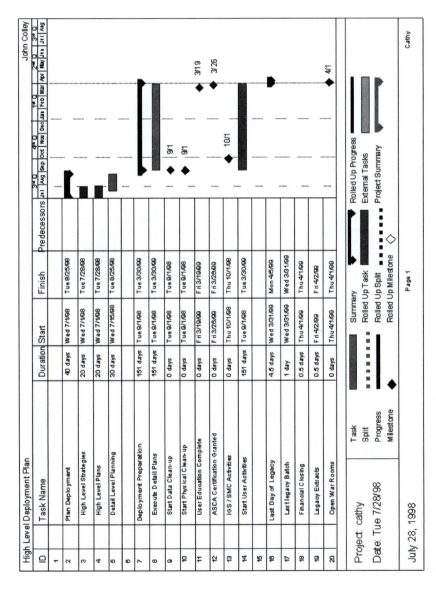

FIGURE 3.7 The SAP Implementation Project Plan

75

High Level Deployment Plan

ID	Task Name	Duration	Start	Finish	Predecessors
21	Start Production Status	0 days	Thu 4/1/99	Thu 4/1/99	
22	Start Problem Tracking	0 days	Thu 4/1/99	Thu 4/1/99	
23	SAP Conversions	2 days	Fri 4/1/99	Sat 4/2/99	
24	Verification & Validation	1 day	Sat 4/3/99	Sat 4/3/99	
25	Golden Back-up	0.5 days	Mon 4/5/99	Mon 4/5/99	
26	SAP Lock Down	0.5 days	Mon 4/5/99	Mon 4/5/99	
27	Release S&A	0.5 days	Mon 4/5/99	Mon 4/5/99	
28					
29	**SAP Go Live**	1 day	Tue 4/6/99	Tue 4/6/99	
30	System Verification	0.5 days	Tue 4/6/99	Tue 4/6/99	
31	Production Test Orders	0.5 days	Tue 4/6/99	Tue 4/6/99	
32	First Nightly Batch	1 day	Tue 4/6/99	Tue 4/6/99	
33					
34	**Post Production Support**	90 days	Tue 4/6/99	Mon 8/9/99	
35	Slow "Planned Ramp-up	0 days	Fri 4/9/99	Fri 4/9/99	
36	Exercise All "Paths"	1 day	Fri 4/9/99	Fri 4/9/99	
37	Transition "Ownership"	0 days	Mon 5/10/99	Mon 5/10/99	
38	Ramp to Production Volumes	60 days	Tue 4/6/99	Mon 6/28/99	
39	Post Implementation Review	3 days	Mon 5/24/99	Wed 5/26/99	
40	Warranty Period	90 days	Tue 4/6/99	Mon 8/9/99	

Legend:
Task, Split, Progress, Milestone, Summary, Rolled Up Task, Rolled Up Split, Rolled Up Milestone, Rolled Up Progress, External Tasks, Project Summary

Project: cathy
Date: Tue 7/28/98

Page 1

John Colley
Cathy

July 28, 1998

FIGURE 3.7 *(continued)*

The SAP deployment team instituted a "war room" for the days following ramp-up. The war room was open all the time and equipped with a direct phone line to the RTP production facility. During the first several weeks of deployment, there were three calls from the production facility per day and an executive status report at the end of the day. At the start of go-live, the team members focused all their energy on the war room and the events occurring in the RTP production facility. By May, it was clear that the system was stable. It had been a full month since PR2 had gone live at RTP. Everyone was ecstatic at the relative lack of major problems with the system rollout. It was a great relief, considering the incredible efforts and significant challenges in the months prior to the go-live date. The successful installation of PR2 in RTP allowed for the sunset several legacy systems and required 194,000 data items to be migrated from legacy systems to SAP. Only a few major problems with the system rollout had been encountered. The implementation of the ERP system proved to be a resounding success.

Due to their scope and complexity, ERP implementations have been and will continue to be a challenge. Clearly, the well-published failures indicate that not all organizations have been up to this challenge. The PSG at IBM was up to the challenge. The successful implementation demonstrates that a very large-scale ERP project can be completed successfully. Successful ERP implementations require that well-defined plans are executed in order to ensure that the project's critical success factors are addressed throughout the implementation. This case study demonstrates that the critical success factors for the implementation of ERP projects, previously described in Section 3.2, were significant to the project's success. In conclusion, the risks associated with these projects leave little room for poor project management.

Finally, this case study also confirms that ERP implementations require the unwavering commitment of upper management, who must be willing to provide the necessary resources and even intervene when required to do so. Furthermore, careful organizational and technical project planning and management must be exercised throughout the project, since the organization must be able to rely on significant project management expertise in order to be successful. In addition, project teams must be knowledgeable, diverse in business and technical expertise, and highly motivated, and they must understand the business strategy behind ERP implementations. Project managers must be cognizant of the entire landscape of IT applications and how ERP integrates with these, in addition to how the current business processes will need to change in the face of the new technology.

In this case study, IBM provides a very powerful model for how to succeed in implementing ERP solutions. Any organization beginning the process would benefit by assessing how it compares to IBM on each of the six factors. This assessment along with the practices and approaches taken by the Raleigh project team can provide very valuable guidance in successfully implementing ERP systems.

► 3.6 SUMMARY

In this chapter you learned the technologies that enable the creation of the organizational memory, or knowledge repository, the aggregate of all the corporate structured information that is used for BI. The chapter starts with a discussion of ERP systems and the critical success factors for their implementations. The chapter also describes data warehousing, the reasons why organizations implement them, the two most popular modeling methodologies used to implement them, and the challenges around deploying data warehouses. Finally, the chapter describes how to define the operating model for the enterprise and the corresponding enterprise architecture. The chapter concludes with a case study that documents the successful implementation of ERP at IBM Personal Systems Group, and how the project team successfully overcame the challenges posed by one of the largest ERP implementations to date.

► KEY TERMS

alert system
best practices database
business processes
critical success factors
content management
  system
coordination
data mart
data warehouse
dimensional modeling
diversification
document management
  system
enterprise application
  integration (EAI)

enterprise architecture
  (EA)
enterprise content
  management
enterprise resource
  planning (ERP) system
ERP implementation
entity-relational (ER)
  modeling
expertise locator system
extract/transform (or
  transfer)/load (ETL)
  software
incident report database
learning organization

lessons learned system
manufacturing resource
  planning or material
  requirements planning
  (MRP) system
middleware
operating model
replication
SMBs
unification
Web content
  management system

► REVIEW QUESTIONS

1. Describe the challenges around the deployment of ERP systems.

2. What are the six unique, critical success factors for large-scale ERP project implementations?

3. What are the two reasons why the enterprise needs to create a data warehouse?

4. Describe the two most popular data modeling techniques for data warehousing.

5. Describe the challenges around deploying a data warehouse.

6. What are the characteristics of mature data warehouses?

► APPLICATION EXERCISES

1. Review the ERP architecture of your organization or the one presented in the IBM case study in Figure 3.6. What modules are provided by the ERP system? What are the legacy systems integrated to the ERP system?

2. Review the architecture of the data warehouse of your organization or find an example in the literature. Is it a mature DW? Why or why not?

3. Describe the operating model of your organization. Given the characteristics of your organization, is that the appropriate operating model for the enterprise?

4. Go to www.teradata.com, and click on the *Enterprise Data Warehousing* option in the *Product and Services* tab. Download some of the demos on *Active Enterprise Intelligence*. Describe the components in active enterprise intelligence. What advantages do they present? Explain with some examples from the airlines, call centers, or the financial services industry.

5. Go to www.teradata.com, and click on the *Enterprise Data Warehousing* option in the *Product and Services* tab. Download some of the demos on health care solutions. Describe how health care organizations could improve quality of service while minimizing costs using data warehousing and BI.

6. Go to the Microsoft Dynamics Web page (http://www.microsoft.com/dynamics/environment. mspx) and download the Environmental Sustainability Dashboard demo. In your opinion, is this functionality something that SMBs will be interested in?

▶ REFERENCES

Bashein, B., and Markus, L. 2000. *Data Warehouses: More Than Just Mining*. Financial Executives Research Foundation.

Becerra-Fernandez, I. 2006. "Searching for Experts on the Web: A Review of Contemporary Expertise Locator Systems." *ACM Transactions on Internet Technology*, 6(4), 333–355.

Becerra-Fernandez, I., Murphy, K., and Elam, J. 2005. "Successfully Implementing ERP: The IBM Personal Systems Group Experience." *International Journal of Internet and Enterprise Management*, 3(1), 78–97.

Becerra-Fernandez, I., and Sabherwal, R. 2009. *Knowledge Management: Systems and Practices* (Armonk, N.Y.: M. E. Sharpe). Forthcoming.

Bingi, P., Sharma, M., and Godia, J. 1999. "Critical Issues Affecting an ERP Implementation." *Information Systems Management*, 16(3), 7–14.

Chenoweth, T., Schuff, D., and St. Louis, R. 2003. "A Method for Developing Dimensional Data Marts." *Communications of the ACM*, 46(12), 93–98.

Davenport, T. 1998. "Putting the Enterprise into the Enterprise System." *Harvard Business Review*, 76(4), 121–131.

Dignum, V. 2002. A Knowledge-Sharing Model for Peer Collaboration in the Non-Life Insurance Domain. In Proceedings of the 1st German Workshop on Experience Management, Berlin, Germany.

Esteves, J., and Pastor, J. 2001. "Enterprise Resource Planning Systems Research: An Annotated Bibliography." *Communications of the Association for Information Systems (CAIS)*, 7(8).

Esteves, J., and Pastor, J. 2007. "An Updated ERP Annotated Bibliography: 2001–2005."*Communications of the Association for Information Systems (CAIS)*, 19(18).

Hasselbring, W. 2000. Information System Integration: Integration. Communications of the ACM. 43, 6, 32–38.

Hayes, F. 2002. "The Story so Far." *Computerworld*. April 15.

Inmon, W., Imhoff, C., and Sousa, R. 2001. *Corporate Information Factory*, Second Edition (New York: John Wiley).

Inmon, W. 2005. *Building the Data Warehouse*, Fourth Edition (New York: John Wiley).

Jukic, N. 2006. "Modeling Strategies and Alternatives for Data Warehousing Projects." *Communications of the ACM*, 49(4), 83–88.

Kimball, R., Ross, M., Thornthwaite, W., Mundy, J., and Becker, B. 2008. *The Data Warehouse Lifecycle Toolkit*, Second Edition (New York: John Wiley).

Markus, M. L., Axline, S., Petrie, D., and Tanis, C. 2000. "Learning from Adopters' Experiences with ERP: Problems Encountered and Success Achieved." *Journal of Information Technology*, 15, 245–265.

Microsoft. 2009. Driving environmental sustainability practices with Microsoft Dynamics. Accessed from the Web at http://www.microsoft.com/dynamics/environment.mspx on April 8, 2009.

Pender, L. 2000. "Damned If You Do." *CIO Magazine*, September.

Pender, L. 2001. "Faster, Cheaper ERP." *CIO Magazine*, May.

Ponniah, P. 2001. *Data Warehousing Fundamentals* (New York: John Wiley).

Rockart, J. 1979. "Chief Executives Define Their Own Data Needs." *Harvard Business Review*, March-April, 81–93.

Ross, J. 2004. "Enterprise Architecture: Depicting a Vision of the Firm." MIT Sloan CISR Research Briefing, IV (1B), March.

Ross, J. 2005. "Forget Strategy: Focus IT on Your Operating Model." MIT Sloan CISR Research Briefing, V. (3C), December.

Ross, J., Weill, P., and Robertson, D. 2006. *Enterprise Architecture Strategy: Creating a Foundation for Business Execution*. Harvard Business School Press.

Rutherford, E. 2001. "ERP's Ends Justify Its Means." *CIO Magazine*, April.

Sen, A., and Sinha, A. 2005. "A Comparison of Data Warehousing Methodologies." *Communications of the ACM*, 48(3), 79–84.

Slater, D. 2000. "Middleware Demystified." *CIO Magazine*. May.

Songini, M. 2004. "HP Puts Part of the Blame on SAP Migration." *Computerworld*, August 18, http://www.computerworld.com/softwaretopics/erp/story/0,10801,95276,00.html?nas=EB-95276.

Sumner, M. 2000. "Risk Factors in Enterprise-wide ERP Projects." *Journal of Information Technology*, 15, 317–327.

Wailgum, T. 2007. "ERP Definition and Solutions." *CIO Magazine*. March 7.

Wailgum, T. 2008. "SAP Who? Inside One of SAP's Smallest ERP Customer Success Stories." *CIO Magazine*. September 25.

Watson, H., Ariyachandra, T., and Matyska, R. 2001. "Data Warehousing Stages of Growth." *Information Systems Management*, 18(3), 42–50.

Weber, R., Aha, D. W., and Becerra-Fernandez, I. 2001. "Intelligent Lessons Learned Systems." *International Journal of Expert Systems Research & Applications*, 20(1), 17–34.

Wheatley, M. 2000. "ERP Training Stinks." *CIO Magazine*, 13(16), 86.

Wixom, B., Watson, H., Reynolds, A., and Hoffer, J. 2008. "Continental Airlines Continues to Soar with Business Intelligence." *Information Systems Management*, 25(2), 102–112.

CHAPTER 4

TECHNOLOGIES ENABLING INFORMATION INTEGRATION

▶ 4.1 INTRODUCTION

In Chapter 3 we discussed technologies that enable the creation of organizational memories. This chapter focuses on the integration of structured information from data warehouses and ERP systems with unstructured information and information from other sources, including external public information, interorganizational information, and Web-based information.

How is information integrated? In this chapter we focus on two significant ways:

1. Synthesis of new insights from unstructured data residing in the organization's enterprise systems, such as enterprise portals and document management systems.

2. Creation of new insights via the integration of structured organizational data with external data, such as Web-based unstructured information from customer Web sites or vendor data sources.

We organize our discussion around the topics of environmental scanning, text and Web mining, and technologies such as RFID. We begin our presentation of data source integration in a BI application.

▶ 4.2 INTEGRATION OF DATA SOURCES IN A BUSINESS INTELLIGENCE APPLICATION

Creating new insights may entail different processes across different organizations. For example, some organizations may have state-of-the art enterprise systems in place and large data warehouses to capture the firm's structured data as we described in Chapter 3, while others may rely on spreadsheets and other individually developed information artifacts as their primary source of organizational memory. For this reason, the challenges that organizations face regarding knowledge discovery will be quite diverse as we look across firms. Therefore, business intelligence applications will rely on a relatively wide range of software tools as we consider differences in data sources and corporate cultures across firms. For example, some organizations will depend primarily on internal data to create new knowledge, including data from existing transaction systems, such as ERP and legacy systems. Other organizations will depend heavily on augmenting this information with external data originating from vendors, customers, publicly available data, or external "for-purchase" data. Related to the issue of external data is the topic of environmental scanning, which we discuss in detail later. The decision of whether to use external data or not is related primarily to:

1. *Business need:* For example, Hewlett Packard's BI application, which supports their computer manufacturing supply chain requires intimate knowledge of structured data from vendors that is necessary to provide the firm with important information such as availability and delivery dates for the requisite electronic components.

2. *Data availability and organizational expertise:* The lack of in-house data may be one of the reasons an organization may need to rely on external data. Similarly, lack of in-house expertise may force organizations to seek that expertise and the associated information from outside the organization.

3. *BI application sophistication:* As BI applications become increasingly complex, external or real-time data may be used to improve the breadth of intelligence and predictive ability of such implementations, by augmenting the sources of information used to create new knowledge.

4. *BI budget:* Integrating external or real-time data is typically increasingly expensive, as purchasing external data sources as well as integrating more granular and timely data command additional investments. Therefore, organizations would need to develop a business model that supports the return on investment on the purchase and integration of external data in the BI application.

For example, for Kimberly-Clark, one of Wal-Mart's top suppliers, the decision to integrate real-time data into the supply chain, also known as real-time business intelligence (RTBI), was instrumental for the organization to understand in a timely manner what was happening with a particular product in promotion. By integrating real-time data into the supply chain, Kimberly-Clark was able to support more cost-effective decision making from the supply chain perspective, in a manner that helped them increase stock levels and keep items on Wal-Mart's shelves (Wailgum, 2007a). Business Intelligence in Practice 4.1 delves into the topic of real-time BI.

Clearly the first requirement in designing an organization's architecture for knowledge creation is to have a crisp understanding of the business objectives. For example, an organization's desire to "Improve the customer response rate to a marketing campaign" would be best stated as "Currently our marketing campaign response rates are on average 1.5%. A benchmark of marketing best practices reveals that a marketing response rate of 11% is achievable, which is our new goal." The most important goal of a marketing campaign is to reach those customers who are likely to purchase the product or service offering. An effective marketing

---

Business Intelligence in Practice 4.1: Real-time Business Intelligence for Operational Risk Management

Operational risk management (ORM) relates to identifying enterprise-wide risks, controls, and performance reports in a timely manner. In this respect ORM requires external real-time data in order to understand how the enterprise is performing in relation to the organization's performance objectives. Operational risk is related to the operational performance of the enterprise as it faces daily actions, some of which may have a negative outcome. For this reason, an enterprise must have a clear understanding of how it's operating in real time, and have at any time a clear status of the business with respect to its performance objectives.

For example the BI application at Continental Airlines, described in Chapter 3, must effectively integrate external real-time data—like, for example, the FBI's "watch list" to determine whether it's safe to fly. Real-time business intelligence (RTBI) is used to ensure that the ORM is up to date and synchronized with the firm's business objectives.

By definition, RTBI "must provide the same functionality as traditional business intelligence, but operate on data that is extracted from operational data sources, with adequate speed, and provides a means to propagate actions back into business processes in an adequate time-frame" (Azvine et al., 2007). RTBI includes real-time information delivery, real-time business performance analysis, and real-time action on the business processes. Real time may not necessary require immediate or zero latency, but rather timeliness in the information-decision-action supply chain. Many current BI systems today require a certain level of manual intervention, which introduces the bottleneck between information and action. ORM requires real-time data fusion of information that is clean, timely, and relevant. For more details on the relationship between ORM and RTBI, please refer to Azvine et al., 2007.

---

strategy would entail, for example: "Target only those customers from the campaign database that are likely to be the perspective buyers," or, in other words, "Identify 35% of the customers from the campaign database that are likely to constitute 80% of the prospective buyers." By effectively identifying from the database those customers that are most likely to buy the new offering, the firm could effectively save the cost associated with trying to reach the 65% who probably would not have an interest in the new product or service, and thus achieve the maximum profit for the campaign.

Once the objectives of the BI application are clearly stated, the next step is to understand the characteristics of the data. Deep knowledge of the data sources is crucial for defining the appropriate algorithms for the application. As a rule of thumb, understanding and preparing the data consumes most of the time and resources in the implementation of the BI application, and may consume from 50% to 80% of the project resources. Data understanding includes the following steps:

1. *Data collection:* This step involves defining the data sources for the study, including as we mentioned above the use of external public data (such as vendors' components delivery dates for the HP BI application) and proprietary databases (e.g., medical doctors and their specific areas of specialty in a particular zip code). The outcome of this step includes the description of the data sources, the data owners and who maintains the data, cost (if externally purchased), storage format and structure, size (e.g., in records, rows, etc.), physical storage characteristics, security requirements, restrictions on use, and privacy requirements.

2. *Data description:* This step describes the contents of each of the BI data sources. Significant descriptors may include the number of fields (columns) and a measure of how sparse the database is (percent of records missing). Also for each data field the following items should be described: data type, definition, description, source, unit of measure, number of unique values, and range of values. In addition, other important data descriptors may include when, how, and the timeframe in which the data were collected. Finally, descriptors about which attributes are the primary and foreign keys in a relational database should also be defined.

3. *Data quality and verification:* This step defines whether any of the data should be disregarded due to irrelevance or lack of quality. In fact, according to a Gartner study (Swartz, 2007) more than 25% of critical data in Fortune 1000 companies is flawed. Gartner specifies that a number of data quality issues need to be considered: whether the organization has the data, its validity (values fall within acceptable range), consistency (same values across multiple locations), integrity (completeness), accuracy (model properties), and relevance (appropriate to business objectives). In a BI application, the GIGO (garbage-in-garbage-out) principle applies. This means that irrelevant or inconsistent data must be excluded from the analysis; otherwise it will negatively affect the results of the application results. Many data mining tools allow specifying which fields are to be ignored by the analysis model.

As part of this effort, many organizations are currently undergoing major consolidations of their data centers. For example, HP reduced the number of applications used within HP from 5,000 to 1,500 and its data centers from 85 to 6 (Foley, 2007). This project provided access to over 50,000 employees across the globe, and eventually all of HP's suppliers, distributors, and business customers.

In Chapter 5 we describe the data preparation and data mining process in detail. In Section 4.3 we present ways the acquisition of external information can be used to augment the capabilities of a firm to manage and plan for action.

▶ 4.3 ENVIRONMENTAL SCANNING

Environmental scanning is defined as "scanning for information about events and relationships in a company's outside environment, the knowledge of which would assist top management in its task of charting the company's future course of action" (Aguilar, 1967) and "the acquisition and use of information about events, trends, and relationships in an organization's external environment, the knowledge of which would assist management in planning the organization's future course of action" (Choo, 2001a, 2001b). The importance of environmental scanning is that it provides organizations with the ability to understand how changes in the external environment may impact their decision making, both at a tactical and a strategic level.

Adaptive organizations are those that have the ability to sense and interpret what may seem like noise into a meaningful course of action. In technology-intensive environments, adaptiveness takes precedence over efficiency, and organizations must translate apparent noise into meaning faster than it arrives (Haeckel, 1999). Therefore, adaptive organizations must rely on environmental scanning to effectively interpret external changes, such as changing customer needs. Changing customer needs require the organization to be able to adapt its product offerings with the required flexibility, agility, and responsiveness. Adaptive organizations come to accept changing customer needs and unpredictable change as the norm, rather than the exception. Research studies confirm that environmental scanning is a predictor of improved organizational performance; that is, firms that use advanced information systems to monitor external events show higher growth and profitability (Subramanian, Fernandes, and Harper, 1993).

Environmental scanning includes looking *for* (seeking or searching) information as well as looking *at* (viewing or using) information (Choo, 2001b). Daft and Weick (1984) proposed a model for environmental scanning based on two dimensions: environmental analyzability (EA, or perceived environmental uncertainty) and organizational intrusiveness (OI, the extent to which the organization allocates resources for information search). Based on this model, organizations may be classified into one of the four modes of environmental scanning: *undirected viewing* (EA = unanalyzable, OI = passive), *conditioned viewing* (EA = analyzable, OI = passive), *searching* (EA = analyzable, OI = active), and *enacting* (EA = unanalyzable, OI = active). See, for example, Figure 4.1.

What does this mean in terms of a firm's use of external information? An organization in the *undirected viewing* mode will tend to be "satisfied with limited, soft information and does not seek comprehensive, hard data . . . relying more on irregular contacts and casual information from external, people sources" (Choo, 2001b). A firm in the *conditioned viewing* mode "makes use of standard procedures, typically employing internal, non-people sources, with a significant amount of data coming from external reports, databases, and sources that are highly respected and widely used in the industry" (Choo, 2001b). An organization in the

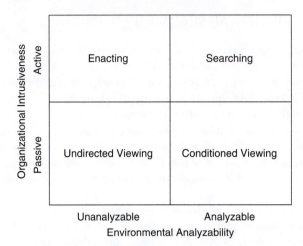

FIGURE 4.1 Organizational Classifications Based on Environmental Scanning Modes (Source: Daft and Weick, 1984; Choo, 2001b)

searching mode "systematically analyzes data to produce market forecasts, trend analysis, and intelligence reports" (Choo, 2001b). In other words, whereas information seeking and use in *conditioned viewing* is restricted to a few issues, firms in the *searching* mode view information seeking as a broad and open activity, based on their willingness to revise or update their existing knowledge. Finally, firms in the *enacting mode* "construct their own environments. They gather information by trying new behaviors and seeing what happens. They experiment, test, and stimulate, and they ignore precedent, rules, and traditional expectations" (Daft and Weick, 1984). Clearly an organization's environmental scanning mode will to a large extent define its BI strategy, with organizations in increasingly complex environments understanding the need to scan more broadly in order to reduce uncertainty. Furthermore, firms in the scanning mode need to provide available information about their customers, competitors, and the industry as a whole to their employees at large, making the case for a wider deployment of BI applications at the organizational level.

Other studies have found that the importance of environmental scanning for an organization increases with environmental uncertainty, which means that CEOs who perceive their environments as uncertain are more likely to scan the environment. In addition, the quality of the external source is the most likely predictor for organizations to engage in this activity (Auster and Choo, 1993). An organization's environment could be perceived as uncertain due to a number of reasons (Albright, 2004):

1. *Industry or market:* In this respect, an organization in a competitive environment will be under increasing pressure to understand the role

of its competitors in the market, and the relationship with its customers and suppliers, as well as be alert to emerging trends and challenges.

2. *Technology:* New technologies can have substantial impacts on business and production processes, impacting efficiencies, changes in production, infrastructure, and communication.

3. *Regulatory:* Changes in laws—such as, for example, the Sarbanes-Oxley Act of 2002 and its emphasis on documenting business processes—will have a major impact on the firm.

4. *Economic:* Fluctuations in international and national economic trends can also impact the environmental uncertainty of the firm, defining, for example, where components are sourced from in the manufacturing supply chain. For example, currency fluctuations may define whether a toy manufacturer sources its components from China or Vietnam.

5. *Social:* Market changes may also be the result of more subtle changes, such as demographic shifts in relevant customer segments.

6. *Political:* For example, the terrorist act of September 11, 2001, resulted in dramatic impacts to businesses, but in particular, it completely redefined business processes for the entire airline industry.

Text mining and *Web mining* are the most important techniques used to identify and extract external business information. Text mining refers to mining the content of unstructured data, and Web mining is defined as "web crawling with online text mining" (Zanasi, 2000). Both text mining and Web mining are described in detail in Sections 4.4 and 4.5, respectively. *Online Analyst* (Zanasi, 2000) is an example of a system for environmental scanning of competitive intelligence. This system consists of an intelligent agent that surfs the Web in an intelligent fashion: searching, reading, and analyzing documents that are retrievable online. This system is able to review many more documents than a human analyst can, even if the human analyst worked 24 hours per day. The system is able to uncover relevant information that may be unintentionally or otherwise hidden. Business Intelligence in Practice 4.2 describes other current examples in environmental scanning.

In Section 4.4 we describe how unstructured text information can be used to augment the capabilities of the BI application via text mining.

▶ 4.4 TEXT MINING

Text mining refers to mining the content of unstructured data, in the sense that this data source may not reside in a structured database but is more likely in an unstructured file. In this respect, text mining refers to discovering new insights by

---

[1] http://www.connotate.com/

Business Intelligence in Practice 4.2: Web Mining for Environmental Scanning

Cynergy was created in 1994, through the mergers of Cincinnati Gas & Electric Company (CG&E) with Public Service Indiana (PSI) Energy and Union Light, Heat & Power (ULH&P). Frequently, company employees would bookmark or copy Web sites of interest into their spreadsheets. In order to facilitate the process of environmental scanning, the firm invested in a Web mining server solution consisting of software agents that would monitor, extract, and deliver information in real time from these Web sites of interest. The company used the software agents to collect and capture real-time information about oil and gas prices, availability, weather, and other relevant developments in order to predict energy consumption, supply, and pricing (Haimila, 2003).

Other applications of environmental scanning via Web mining include using intelligent software agents to:[1]

- Harvest relevant data from disparate Web sites and monitor online consumer marketplaces in several countries at a major investment bank in order to deliver frequently updated information from source sites for pattern analysis.

- Automate the content extraction and aggregation processes at one of the oldest and largest news organization of the world. Software agents were used to collect information and metadata from newspaper feeds and Web sites, apply contextual information, and integrate this information with existing databases. Software agents were trained to pull existing information existing in numerous formats (including HTML, RSS, etc.) from numerous sites.

- Automate the information extraction related to frequent Medicaid policy changes and update corresponding business processes at a major health care organization.

In short, the technology enabled organizations to leverage the use of software agents to deliver information from specific sources. This information would later be used for trend analysis, to perform persistent searches of key products and company Web sites, and to automatically pull data that would be used to update financial models and other production spreadsheets.

---

automatically "reading" large documents (called corpora) of text written in natural language (like, for example, the English language). In terms of text mining, algorithms focus on *information retrieval* (IR), *information extraction*, and *information summarization*. In text mining, documents are indexed by the words they contain, using information retrieval (IR) (Salton, 1989) techniques. Document text mining relies on text categorization (TC) techniques to uncover new knowledge from it. TC is defined as:

"the task of assigning a Boolean value to each pair (d_j, c_i) ε D X C, where D is a domain of documents and $C = (c_1, \ldots, c_{|C|})$ is a set of predefined categories." (Sebastiani, 2002)

If a value of T is assigned to (d_j, c_j) it means that d_j is filed under c_i, whereas a value of F would mean a decision not to file d_j is filed under c_j. Text categorization relies on IR indexing techniques, which are used in the construction of document classifiers (Sebastiani, 2002). IR indexing techniques consist of calculating a function—such as, for example, multivariate regression, nearest neighbor classifiers, probabilistic Bayesian models, decision trees, neural networks, symbolic rule learning, and support vector machines (Dumais and Chen, 2000). In information retrieval, the content of documents is indexed by the words they contain (Salton, 1989). IR indexing techniques consist of calculating the functions **term frequency (TF)** and **term frequency inverse document frequency (TFIDF)**. The function TFIDF consists of the product of a term frequency and its inverse document frequency, which depends on the frequency of occurrence of a specific keyword term in the text and the number of documents it appears in. The *term frequency* (TF) refers to how frequently a term occurs in the text, which represents the importance of the term. The *inverse document frequency* (IDF) increases the significance of terms that appear in fewer documents, while downplaying terms that occur in many documents. TFIDF then identifies those terms that are frequently used in one document but infrequently used across the corpora or collection of documents. The net effect is that terms like *astrophysics*, which may occur frequently in a scientist's white paper but infrequently across the whole corpora of white papers in that organization, would result in a good indexing term.

Text mining techniques can be classified in four main layers (Chen, 2001):

1. ***Natural language processing (NLP)* or linguistic analysis** is used to identify key concept descriptors (the *who, what, when,* or *where*), which are embedded in the textual documents. In linguistic analysis the unit of analysis is the word. These functions can be combined with other linguistic techniques such as *stemming, morphological analysis, Boolean, proximity, range,* and *fuzzy search*. For example, a stemming algorithm is used to remove the suffix of a word. *Stoplists* are used to eliminate words that are not good concept descriptions, such as prepositions (e.g., *and, but,* etc.). Linguistic techniques can be combined with statistical techniques—for example, to represent grammatically correct sentences. Also, **semantic analysis** is used to represent meaning in stories and sentences.

2. ***Statistical and co-occurrence analysis*** is used like the TFIDF function mentioned above. For example, **link analysis** is used to create conceptual

associations and automatic thesauri for keyword concepts. Also, similarity functions are used to compute co-occurrence probabilities between concept pairs.

3. ***Statistical and neural networks clustering and categorization***, like the ones that will be discussed in Chapter 5, are used to group similar documents together, as well as communities into domain categories. Neural network techniques—such as, for example, Kohonen neural networks—work well for large-scale clustering text mining tasks, and the results can be graphically visualized and intuitive.

4. ***Visualization and human computer interfaces (HCI)*** can reveal conceptual associations, which can be represented in various dimensions, such as one-, two-, and three-dimensional views. Furthermore, interaction techniques, such as drill-down or zooming, can be incorporated to infer new knowledge.

Figure 4.2 depicts the text mining process. Business Intelligence in Practice 4.3 describes the text mining efforts at Travelocity.

Section 4.5 describes how one special type of text mining can be used to improve our understanding of our customers' needs and wants: Web mining.

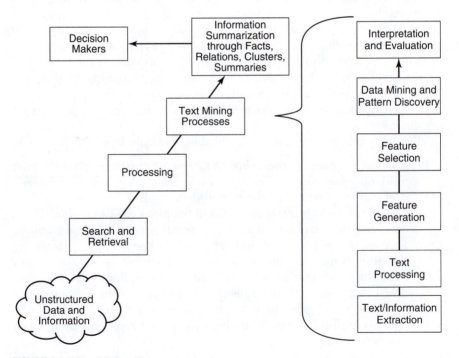

FIGURE 4.2 Text Mining Process
(Source: Adapted from Sullivan, 2001, and Auvil and Searsmith, 2003)

Business Intelligence in Practice 4.3:
Text Analytics Will Take You Places

American Airlines was the first to offer customer access to its electronic reservation system through its historic SABRE system. In 1996 Travelocity. com (a subsidiary of SABRE Holdings, itself a subsidiary of American Airlines) was launched, becoming the first Web site that allowed customers to access SABRE's reservation system. The idea was that customers would be able to find fare and schedule information, as well as reserve, book, and purchase tickets without the help of a travel agent. Currently, the site also offers consumers the ability to book hotel rooms, rental cars, cruises, vacations, and last-minute travel packages.

Travelocity.com, like many Web-based companies, has an abundance of unstructured textual data, contained in over 600,000 customer e-mails, call center documents, and other sources of data. Recognizing the impossibility of manually exploring each of these documents, the company turned to text mining in order to take advantage of this resource and identify potential customer service issues. The focus of the initiative was to pull out information related to facts, opinions, requests, trends, and trouble spots from the corpora of unstructured data. The firm plans to integrate these findings with structured data in their data warehouse to identify trends. For example, if customers typically comment on an issue with a given frequency, and this frequency is observed as going up or down, it will be important to review what may be actually causing these trends (Havenstein, 2007).

More recently the company has turned to **text analytics**, which is viewed as the "voice of customer technology" designed to discover the customer *sentiments* from the communications instead of a *nugget* of information. For example, Travelocity receives around 30,000 customer satisfaction survey responses, 50,000 e-mails, and 400,000 calls from customers each month (CIO Staff, 2008). Given the proliferation of blogs and chats as mechanisms for customers to express themselves, text analytics are the technology of choice to analyze the content of social networking sites.

How would you describe this job? It's finding a digital needle in a virtual haystack.

▶ 4.5 WEB MINING

Web-based companies operate in hypercompetitive environments that create the need to better understand their customer's preferences. This need, coupled with the abundance of Web-based data, sets the stage for organizations to try to discover new knowledge from the logs maintained by their organization's

Web servers. Uncovering the customers' path through the data may in fact allow firms to personalize their Web pages, anticipate new sales, and increase the average purchase per customer visit, thus improving overall profitability. Perhaps e-business could be credited with providing the impetus for knowledge discovery of competitive trends via mining of Web-based data. The business need for mining the contents of Web data is clear:

> *"Companies venturing in e-commerce have a dream. By analyzing the tracks people make through their web site, they'll be able to optimize its design to maximize sales. Information about customers and their purchasing habits will let companies initiate e-mail campaigns and other activities that result in sales. Good models of customers' preferences, needs, desires, and behaviors will let companies simulate the personal relationship that businesses and their clientele had in the good old days."* (Edelstein, 2001)

Web mining is defined as "web crawling with online text mining" (Zanasi, 2000). In contrast with mining of internal information sources, which tend to be numeric data sources (described in Chapter 5), much of the data that exist on the Web is text data. In fact, it is estimated that 80% of the world's online content is based on text (Chen, 2001). This can lead to difficulties when mining the Web. There are several differences between traditional data mining and Web mining. One significant difference is that Web mining requires linguistic analysis abilities. Web mining requires techniques from both information retrieval and artificial intelligence domains. Web pages are indexed by the words they contain, using information retrieval (IR) techniques (Salton, 1989). Web content mining relies on text categorization (TC) techniques to uncover new knowledge from it. Therefore, Web content mining techniques are rather different from the DM techniques described in Chapter 5.

There are three types of uses for Web mining (Kosala and Blockeel, 2002; Jackson, 2002). These are:

1. *Web structure mining:* Mining the Web structure consists on examining how documents on the Web are structured, seeking to discover the model underlying the Web link structures. In Web structure mining, *intra-page structure* mining is used to evaluate the arrangement of the various HTML or XML tags within a Web page. On the other hand, *inter-page* structure refers to hyperlinks connecting one Web page to another. Web structure mining can be used to categorize Web pages and to uncover the relationship between Web sites and their similarities (Jackson, 2002).

2. *Web usage mining:* Also known as *clickstream analysis*, it consists of identifying the user navigation patterns through the Web pages in a domain. Web usage mining is used to uncover Web surfers' behaviors, by examining their interactions with the Web site, including their mouse clicks, queries, and transactions. Web usage mining includes three main

tasks: *preprocessing, pattern discovery,* and *pattern analysis* (Jackson, 2002):

a. *Preprocessing* consists of converting data about the Web page's use, content, and structure, preparing datasets for pattern discovery that may originate from different data sources. This step is the most challenging in Web usage mining, since it involves data collection from multiple servers (including *proxy servers*), cleansing extraneous information, and using data collected by *cookies* for identification purposes.

b. *Pattern analysis* is a step that takes advantage of visualization and online analytical processing (OLAP) techniques, like the ones discussed in Chapter 6, to aid understanding of the data, notice unusual values, and identify possible relationships between the variables.

c. *Pattern discovery* is a step involving the use of DM techniques, similar to those discussed in Chapter 5, except that certain variations may be considered. For example, in a market basket analysis study of items purchased in an online store, the click-order for the items added to the shopping cart may be interesting, and is not typically studied in typical market basket analysis of customer purchases in the corresponding brick-and-mortar setting.

3. *Web content mining* is used to discover what a Web page is about and how to uncover new knowledge from it. Web content data include analysis of the semistructured and unstructured content used to create the Web page, which includes the text, images, audio, video, hyperlinks, and *metadata*. Web content mining is based on text mining and IR

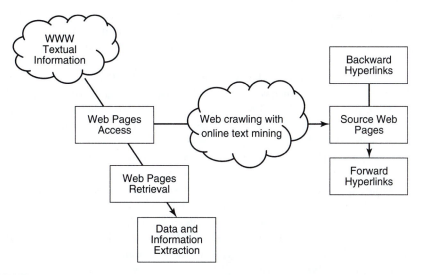

FIGURE 4.3 The Web Mining Process

techniques like the ones described in the prior section. These techniques consist of the organization of large amounts of textual data for the most efficient retrieval. Information retrieval techniques have become increasingly important, as the amount of semistructured as well as unstructured textual data present in organizations has increased dramatically. IR techniques provide a method to efficiently access these large amounts of information.

Figure 4.3 depicts the Web mining process. Business Intelligence in Practice 4.4 describes how Web mining can be used to search for images on the Internet.

BI in Practice 4.4: Mining the Web for Images

Given all the effort to mine the textual content of the Web, what can we do about mining the images on the Web? Current research aims to overcome some of limitations intrinsic to the problem of indexing images, which is that images are not usually annotated using semantic descriptors. Early developments in image retrieval systems were based on using keyword-based image retrieval techniques, which seek to match keywords from the user query to those keywords used to annotate the images. Undoubtedly, annotating images is impractical and tedious, and by all means subjective.

The method *content-based image retrieval (CBIR)* aims to find images via the specific features of the queried image, such as color histogram, shape, and so on. This method allows the automatic extraction of features from the images, and avoids the subjectivity associated with keyword-annotation-based methods. CBIR may show some performance limitations—for example, it may often find irrelevant images with similar features as those of the queried image.

A third method proposed by Chen et al. (2001) effectively combines both visual and semantic feature vectors from the images and the textual content of the Web pages where the images are found. This approach extracts text information from the Web pages that contain the images in order to semantically describe the images. The extracted text description is then combined with image features to form a robust combination of both visual and semantic descriptors.

Other approaches combine user-provided relevance feedback in order to improve the image retrieval results (Li, Chen, and Zhang, 2002). In other words, images may be appropriately tagged by users to further improve indexing results. Integrating user-provided relevance feedback has been shown to help improve the image retrieval performance when used in a database of 100,000 images.

Web mining can be useful in the development of expertise locator systems (ELS) as described in Section 4.8. Mining Web data can bring about extraordinary rewards, including developing a personalized relationship with online customers, improving the profitability of online stores through improved processes, and growing online revenues. Section 4.6 describes in detail how customer relationship management can in fact deliver this promise.

▶ 4.6 APPLICATION OF WEB MINING IN CUSTOMER RELATIONSHIP MANAGEMENT

Customer relationship management (CRM) consists of mechanisms and technologies used to manage the interactions between a company and its customers. The first adopters of CRM solutions were database marketers seeking to automate the process of interacting with their customers. Applications in CRM can be characterized as *operational* or *analytical*. **Operational CRM** includes the support of call centers and sales force automation. Most global companies have implemented such systems. Through operational CRM, firms are able to establish a single view and point of contact for each customer. In contrast, firms using **analytical CRM** employ data mining techniques to create new insights about their customers in order to better understand and serve their clients.

Early adopters of CRM include firms in competitive markets such as financial services, retailing, and telecommunications, who initially invested in analytical CRM applications for one or more of the following purposes (Schwenk, 2002):

a. Integrate the customer viewpoint across all *touchpoints*, since many CRM solutions combine infrastructure components such as *enterprise application integration* (EAI) technology and data warehouses, as well as OLAP and data mining. The goal of CRM is to construct an integrated view of the customer, to understand the customer touchpoints and therefore create new insights about the client that will enable organizations to better recognize and service the client's needs.

b. Respond to customer demands in "Internet time," because online environments have changed the dynamics of decision making, requiring organizations to react to increasingly complex customer requests at faster speeds. Furthermore, the study and analysis of online data can be used to improve and personalize products and services. Finally, analysis of Web data can provide important insight into customer behaviors and preferences, which can be used to improve online content and design.

c. Gain more value from BI investments, since knowledge discovery can be used to conduct market segmentation studies that determine which customers could be targeted for certain services and products, in order to *narrowcast* (that is, send targeted e-mails) customers.

As an example of a successful CRM application, consider the case of Mexican grocery retailer Soriana[2], which uses market basket analysis CRM functionality in order to determine the success of its marketing campaign and the price elasticity of its products (Lamont, 2002). Also, the Brazilian company Redecard[3] uses CRM to analyze MasterCard, Diners Club, and other credit and debit card transactions together with its customer data to determine, using market segmentation analysis, which customers to target for certain products (Lamont, 2002).

The first step in the design of the CRM process is to identify the customer market segments that may yield the highest profits. This step involves sorting through large datasets in order to discover the data "gold nuggets," which are the mining promise. CRM software in a sense automates some of the efforts in the DM process used to find predictors of purchasing behaviors. Furthermore, CRM applications may also integrate the results of the DM study into predefined campaign management software. Campaign management software is used to effectively manage the planning, execution, assessment, and refinement of the myriad marketing campaigns at an organization. Campaign management software may also be instrumental in monitoring a company's communications with its customers, including direct mail, telemarketing, customer service, point of sale, and online interactions.

In many CRM applications, data mining prediction models are used to calculate a *customer score*, which is a numeric value assigned to each customer database record that specifies the probability that the customer in question will behave in a specific manner. For example, *customer churn* is a measure of customer attrition, and is defined as the number of customers who discontinue a service during a specified time period divided by the average total number of customers over that same period. Data mining prediction models can be used to estimate customer churn, meaning that a high *churn score* assigned to a specific customer record represents a high probability that the customer will indeed discontinue the service. The set of churn scores could then be used to target those customers in that segment for specific marketing campaigns designed to retain those customers.

Consider a DM study at a large national bank, which revealed that many of its customers only take advantage of the checking account services it provides. Typically, customers at this institution deposit their payroll check, only to move the funds once they become available, to investment accounts and other service providers outside the bank. The integrated capabilities of DM and CRM can automatically trigger a target marketing promotion for customers with sizable deposits, designed to encourage them to make their investments through the bank's offerings, keeping their money at the bank. DM and CRM can be integrated to sharpen the focus of prospects, therefore increasing marketing response and effectiveness. More details about the relationship between DM and CRM are described by Berson, Smith, and Thearling (2000). Business Intelligence in Practice 4.5 describes how to mine the Deep Web.

[2] http://www.soriana.com

[3] http://www.redecard.com.br

Business Intelligence in Practice 4.5: Mining the Deep Web

Have you ever heard about the Deep Web? It refers to repositories that are not always indexed by automated search engines like Google or Yahoo. We refer to the Shallow Web (also the Surface Web or the Static Web) as the content that most robotic search engines or Web crawlers index, in traversing the Internet by means of following URL links. It is speculated that the Deep Web may be from 5 to 500 times as large as the Shallow Web, meaning that most search engines only index about 20% of the Web (Ratzan, 2006). The Deep Web is not indexed by most search engines because it consists of sites that are proprietary (command a fee), require registration (login and password), are blocked by local Web masters or by a search engine, are dynamic (created on demand), have a special format (like spreadsheets), or are host searchable databases.

The next frontier in Web mining will be to discover new knowledge from the massive coffers of unstructured information now held under the auspices of social network sites like Facebook, LinkedIn, and MySpace. Companies are anxious to draw insights from the members of those communities, about topics ranging from brand recognition and reputation to the influence a particular user may exert on members of the community. As such, social network sites are ripe for mining analytics focused on customer needs, site content, market competition, brand recognition and reputation, product and customer loyalty, and an "influence metric" for each member of the social community (Kanaracus, 2008). How likely are my friends to buy a specific fragrance, pair of jeans, and designer glasses once I share with them that I had to have them? If my influence metric is significant, then we could predict that my social network site "friends" would likely follow with similar purchases. And how is this influence expected to carry on to other realms—like, for example, political orientation?

So what does the future hold? One thing is for sure, new technologies for mining the Web will continue to support the old adage that *the truth is out there*.

▶ 4.7 RADIO FREQUENCY IDENTIFICATION

What do the following scenarios have in common?

It used to take seven workers to unload materials at Boeing's Auburn (Washington) plant where the aircraft maker builds parts for its planes . . . Now the only worker needed to move the parts is the supplier's truck driver who delivers the goods. Boeing has no employees of its own working the door." (Kharif, 2005)

Like most health care facilities, Washington Hospital Center (WHC) in the nation's capital used to struggle with asset management: finding the right pieces of equipment when employees needed them. But two and a half years ago, WHC, one of the 25 largest hospitals in the country, sought to address that knowledge management problem . . . in order to track them online." (Raths, 2008)

"One of the most vexing problems for magazine publishers is trying to figure out just how many people read printed copies of magazines, rather than letting them languish in stacks of unread mail. Other questions have been raging since the dawn of the printing press, such as: how long and often do readers spend reading the pages? Do readers skip around among the articles? Do they read from front to back or from back to front? And does anybody look at the advertisements? Historically, these have been mostly unanswerable questions, left to estimates and guesswork. But a marketing research company . . . announced . . . it is testing . . . technology to measure magazine readership in public waiting rooms." (Wailgum, 2007b)

All of these examples are based on the integration of one innovative technology: radio frequency identification (RFID). RFID emerged from the domain of radio and radar applications, and was originally described by Harry Stockman as a technology for "point-to-point communication, with the carrier power generated at the receiving end and the transmitter replaced by a modulated reflector, represents a transmission system which possesses new and different characteristics. Radio, light, or sound waves (essentially microwaves, infrared, and ultrasonic waves) may be used for the transmission under approximate conditions of specular reflection" (1948, p.1196). RFID has seen many different implementations, as described in the examples above, where the technology has been used to capture information that can be recovered later via radio waves.

Commercial activities employing RFID didn't commence until the 1960s, but the first important implementations would not be seen for another twenty years, as innovations related to transportation interests such as toll collection were launched (Landt, 2001). RFID combines radio broadcast and radar technology, and essentially combine two parts:

1. An antenna that receives and transmits the signal.

2. The RFID tag, an integrated circuit that modulates and demodulates a radio frequency signal, and processes and stores information. RFID tags can be passive, active, or semipassive.

Passive tags have no battery and the power is supplied by the reader, requiring a one hundred times stronger power level to power up the circuitry than for active or semiactive tags. When the passive tag encounters radio waves from the reader, the coiled antenna within the tag forms a magnetic field that draws power to the tag, energizing the circuits in the tag. The tag then sends the data stored in the tag's memory. Active tags have a battery or power supply, and semipassive tags have a power supply that powers the tag. The battery can serve as a partial or complete power source for the active tag's circuitry and antenna; some active tags may even be equipped with replaceable batteries, while others may be sealed (IBM, 2007).

RFID tags and services in health care are expected to grow into a $2.1 billion industry by 2016, in applications ranging from asset management, as in the example described above, to improving the flow of patients and throughput of their surgical rooms (Raths, 2008). Today, a great majority of RFID applications involve improving the management of the supply chain and inventory tracking. RFID tags are for the most part used to monitor the location of the goods, which is later communicated to back-end systems using network software. In this regard, Wal-Mart has led the implementation of RFID, insisting that tags be included in all of their shipments. For example, Sam's Club, a Wal-Mart division, recently announced that firms supplying them with goods would need to meet their RFID tagging requirements or else agree to pay a service fee (Bachelor, 2008). Clearly, a mandate of this sort is likely to pressure manufacturers to include RFID tags in all their products, and it is estimated that around 40% of all U.S. manufacturers will deploy RFID by 2010 (Kharif, 2005). One of Wal-Mart's top suppliers, Kimberly-Clark, was an early adopter of RFID, starting early on the evolution of the capabilities of their supply chain to a demand-driven supply network (Wailgum, 2007a). This vision requires the establishment of a highly integrated suite of supply chain systems that provide end-to-end visibility and as close to real-time information as possible.

RFID technology is expected to continue to create sizable profit returns in health care, manufacturing, and retail. RFID is expected to have an increasingly important role in increasing the intelligence of supply chains, health care applications, and intelligent devices. Some privacy advocacy groups warn us, though, that this exciting new technology that continues to deliver such profitable improvements could also pose grave dangers if it was ever implanted in humans, as it could be misused by authoritarian governments that seek to limit the freedom of individuals (Monahan and Wall, 2007). To what extent an intelligent magazine found at the doctor's office, which broadcasts how long the unaware reader spends gazing at a particular advertisement, is considered an intrusion on the reader's freedom is yet to be determined. Business Intelligence in Practice 4.6 presents the ways RFID technology can also pose concerns to privacy pundits.

Business Intelligence in Practice 4.6: RFID to Track Conference Attendees

Supply chain optimization, intelligent transportation systems, asset management—it all makes perfect sense, but how about tracking conference attendees? IBM used RFID technology embedded in name tags to "follow" conference attendees at its Information On Demand 2007 global conference (Thibodeau, 2007). The purpose of the RFID tag was to track attendance into conference sessions in order to extract product and training interest. The use of tags is also expected to help with conference management and to identify the most popular sessions.

(continued)

> However, although many of these experiments are well-intentioned, some privacy groups objections are translating into new legislations aimed at restricting their use (Hamblen, 2007). For example, some privacy advocacy groups are urging consumers to microwave new underwear to disable RFID tracks so that they may not be tracked. By far, the loudest cry of objections is centered around the implantation of RFID tags on individuals without their consent. Other pieces of legislation focus on restricting government from tracking individuals or integrating RFID data with personal information.
>
> What does all this translate to? There's no chance of sneaking out of the conference to sightsee and do a little site exploration if Big Blue is watching!

In Section 4.8 we review a case study of how Web content mining was used to improve the capabilities of expertise locator systems at NASA.

CASE STUDY 4-8

AN APPLICATION OF WEB CONTENT MINING TO EXPERTISE LOCATOR SYSTEMS

Business visionaries predict that the organization of the future will most likely structurally resemble the modern-day movie industry, a contrast to the traditional vertically structured firms. One of the challenges that this organization of the future will face is how to identify the experts required in order to accomplish its goals—for example, when a firm organizes the creation of a blockbuster movie, only to later disband once the project has been accomplished. Would this challenge be any different if the new project entails the design of a next generation space shuttle or the latest high-performance driving machine? Intrinsic to this scenario is the utilization of expertise locator systems (ELS) to assemble the project team. Consider the following scenario:

You are part of a project working to build a new cryogenic handling storage facility. You encounter a problem: a valve fails upon testing. There is a design problem. What to do? You may go back and rework the problem, through the same process with the same company and NASA engineers, or you may go to Expert Seeker and form the Rapid Answer Collaborative Knowledge Expert Team (RACKET). Expert Seeker finds:

1. *A collection of scientists from the University of Arizona Center for Cryogenics Studies*
2. *A valve manufacturing expert from a plant in Detroit*
3. *A cryogenic expert that worked on problems during shuttle launches and has transferred to Marshall Space Flight Center*
4. *A collection of technical white papers and lessons learned that NASA has published from similar projects*

The team takes two days and collaborates by video teleconference and the Internet to pinpoint the design problem and find the solution to fix it. (Chris Carlson, NASA engineer; Becerra-Fernandez, 2006)

(continued)

Typically, most ELS tend to rely on self-assessment to collect experts' competencies, which offers many limitations. Early examples of such systems are HP's CONNEX, NSA's KSMS, and Microsoft's SPuD (Becerra-Fernandez, 2006). Web content mining has shown great promise in the development of ELS that are used to locate experts based on information sources that may already exist within the organization (e.g., in corporate memories and intranets) as well as outside (e.g., on the Internet). For example, an ELS could be designed to identify experts based on their published documents, which would essentially require an automatic technique to identify the experts' names, as well as a way to associate experts' names with their corresponding skill keywords, mined from those published documents. Some examples of these types of ELS are cited by Yimam-Seid and Kobsa (2003), including:

1. Bellcore's Expert/Expert Locator (Streeter and Lockbaum, 1988), which uses latent semantic indexing to build an expertise index using the collection of technical documents produced by experts.

2. Contact Finder (Krulwich and Burkey, 1995), which monitors discussion groups to locate experts based on the postings' content.

3. MITRE's Expert Finder (Mattox, Maybury, and Morey, 1999), which locates experts by identifying the relationship between experts and published documents in the organization's intranet.

Another example of an expertise-locator KM system is the NASA Expert Seeker Web Miner[4], which included the design of a name-finding algorithm to discover from within the organization's Web pages the names of the NASA experts who authored these pages. Traditional IR techniques[5] were used to discover skill keywords from the content of these pages. Then the skill keywords were matched with the identified expert names.

Typically, IR techniques use as input a set of inverted files, which is a sequence of words that reference the group of documents in which the words appear. These words are chosen according to a selection algorithm that determines which words in the document are good index terms. In a traditional IR system, the user enters a query, and the system retrieves all documents that match that keyword entry. Expert Seeker Web Miner was based on an IR technique that went one step further. When users queried the system for an expert in a particular field, the system ran a document search based on the user query. Since the user was looking for experts in a specific subject area, the system returned names of those experts whose names appeared in the matching documents (excluding Web masters and curators). The experts' names were ranked according to the number of matching Web pages in which each individual name appeared, so those experts who published more documents on the topic requested by the user would appear at the top of the list.

The process used for assigning keywords to experts in Expert Seeker was carried out in four stages:

1. First, all the relevant content data from published documents, in this case Web pages published by each expert describing their current research, were transferred to a separate server area for further processing. For this study, the unstructured data included all the Web pages on the NASA-Goddard Space Flight Center domain.

(continued)

---

[4] This version of Expert Seeker was developed to support the needs of Goddard Space Flight Center.

[5] See, for example, *Selection by Discriminant Value* in (Frakes and Baeza-Yates, 1992), about an algorithm for selecting index terms.

2. The goal of the second stage was to identify all instances of expert names by programmatically examining the content of each Web file. The name data were compared to the X.500 personnel directory databases. All the names in the employee database were organized into a map-like data structure beforehand that was used in the Web content mining process. This map consisted of all employee names referenced by their last name key. In addition, each full name was stored in every possible form that it could appear. An individual document was first searched for all last name keys. Subsequently, the document was searched a second time using all values of the matching keys.

3. The third stage of the indexing process involved identifying keywords within the HTML content. This was done using a combination of word stemming and frequency calculation. First the text was broken up into individual words, through string pattern matching. Any sequence of alphabetical characters was recognized as a word, while punctuation, numbers, and white space characters were ignored. The resulting list of words was processed to determine whether a word was included in a *stoplist*. The resulting list of words was then processed with a *stemming* algorithm. This was done to group together words that may be spelled differently but have the same semantic meaning. In this manner, a person who entered "astronomical" as a query term would most likely also be interested in documents that match the term "astronomy."

4. Once the stemming process was completed, the algorithm calculated the frequency of each term. TFIDF was used during the keyword selection process in the determination of good index terms. However, other indexing algorithms could have been used instead with comparable results.

In summary, in this context expertise was determined based on the assumption that if an expert's name recurrently appears in many Web documents along with a document keyword, then that expert must have significant knowledge of the domain defined by the keyword. The keywords mined from the Web content served the purpose of associating experts with the skill set defined by the keyword. Figure 4.4 shows the architecture for Expert Seeker, and the data sources are described in Table 4.1. For more details about Expert Seeker, refer to the works by Becerra-Fernandez (2000, 2001, 2006).

Theoretically, a large document count for a search query should produce more accurate results. Table 4.2 illustrates preliminary results for Web mining accuracy and precision for a set of skill keyword query terms. Precision was determined by testing whether a keyword entered as a query term correctly described the expertise for the corresponding employee. The precision values for the keywords in Table 4.2 are represented by the percentage of correct matches within the top 15 results for the keyword. Precision is also measured by reviewing which experts the system identified for each keyword. A test for precision was performed with the GSFC CIO, who had intimate knowledge of the Center's competencies, and was able to determine whether those experts identified by Expert Seeker were indeed experts in their fields. Recall was not calculated, because it would be hard to determine whether the names appearing in the NASA Web documents completely reflected all the employees of that organization. The results showed a high precision for scientific or research related skill terms, and less precision for the more managerial or administrative related skill terms. This may be due to the highly scientific and research-oriented nature of the document body. These results showed that the system can retrieve experts from the document body with a substantially high degree of precision, in particular for scientific and research-related keywords.

(*continued*)

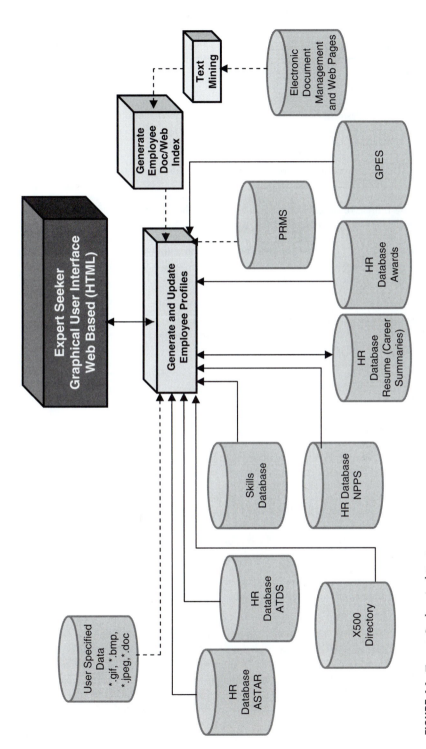

FIGURE 4.4 Expert Seeker Architecture

103

Table 4.1 Description of the Data Sources for Expert Seeker

User Specified Data: This information is optionally user-supplied. For example, experts can opt to provide career summaries that will be used by Expert Seeker to augment the expertise search. A database table to hold this information was created and linked to the system, initially populated from the NPPS human resources database. Other user-supplied data could include pictures, publications, patents, hobbies, civic activities, etc.

ASTAR: This human resources database view provides the experts' in-house training courses.

ATDS: This human resources database view provides the experts' workshops and academic classes employees are planning to take.

X.500: This database view provides the experts' general employee data such as first name, last name, work address, phone, organization, fax, and email. X.500's unique identifier is also used to cross-reference employees in different databases.

Skills Database: This database view provides a set of skills and subskills that are used by Expert Seeker to index the expertise search. The KSC Core Competency team defined this set of skills and subskills as a refinement to a previous Center-wide skills assessment.

NPPS Database: This human resources database view provides the experts' formal education, including professional degrees and the corresponding academic institutions. NPPS is also the source for the employee's department, used by the directorate search mode. The contents of this database were also used to initially populate the career summary section table.

KPro: This database view will be populated with project participation information through a new project management system under development at NASA/KSC.

GPES: The Goal Performance Evaluation System (GPES) is a system developed at KSC. This database view serves as the data source for profile information such as employees' achievements. GPES will replace the Skills Database since GPES will also be populated with KSC's strategic competencies and levels of expertise.

Data Mining: Expert Seeker expertise search is augmented through the use of data-mining algorithms, which build an expert's profile based on information published by employees on their WebPages. Similarly, a document repository could be mined for expertise using these algorithms.

SAGE: The Searchable Answer Generating Environment (SAGE) is an expertise-locator system developed and hosted at the Florida International University Knowledge Management Laboratory to identify experts within Florida's universities. Expert Seeker users can define the search scope to be within KSC or to expand it to universities in Florida. The latter means that Expert Seeker would launch an expert search to SAGE, and the results of this search would be integrated into one output at the Expert Seeker GUI.

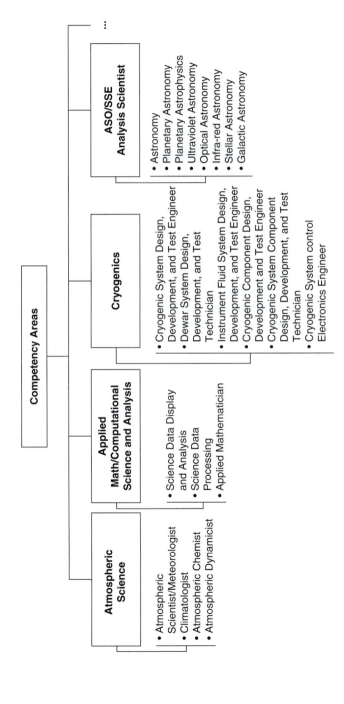

FIGURE 4.5 Competence Taxonomy for NASA Goddard Space Flight Center

Table 4.2 Precision Results for Sample Skill
Keyword Query

Keyword	Precision (Top 15 results)
Astrophysics	87%
Astronomy	92%
Comet	92%
Climate	92%
Ocean	73%
Atmosphere	87%
Management	64%
Human resources	53%

Finally, Web mining can also aid in the development of **knowledge taxonomies**, or *ontologies*. Taxonomy is the study of the general principles of scientific classification. Ontology is an explicit formal specification of how to represent the objects, concepts, and other entities that are assumed to exist in some area of interest and the relationships that hold among them. In the case of ELS, the taxonomy is used to identify the critical knowledge areas used to describe and catalog people's knowledge or competency areas. The development of adequate knowledge taxonomies and ontologies could be an expensive, time-consuming, and complex process, typically requiring the collaboration of a cross-functional group tasked with defining the organization's most significant knowledge areas. In addition, the process of developing knowledge taxonomies could be complex because these decisions could play on organizational politics, since lack of representation in the knowledge taxonomy could be considered threatening to organizational subunits. Figure 4.5 depicts an excerpt from the competence taxonomy developed for NASA Goddard Space Flight Center. The complete taxonomy includes 57 competency areas, many of them with up to 12 additional subareas specified.

▶ 4.9 SUMMARY

In this chapter you learned about the technologies that enable the creation of organizational memories, via the integration of structured information from enterprise systems with unstructured information and information from other sources including real-time data. The chapter describes environmental scanning and the role that external public information, inter-organizational information, Web-based information, as well as customer relationship management tools play on organizational memories. The chapter also presents the topics of text mining and Web mining, and describes the implementation of NASA's Expert Seeker Web Miner, an expertise locator system that employed Web content mining to identify experts based on the content of the Web sites published by NASA's scientists on Goddard Space Flight Center's intranet portal. Finally, we described RFID and the increasingly important role this technology is playing in increasing the intelligence of supply chains, health care applications, and intelligent devices.

▶ KEY TERMS

analytical CRM
data collection
data description
data preparation
data quality and
    verification

expertise locator system
    (ELS)
information retrieval (IR)
knowledge taxonomy
linguistic analysis
link analysis
operational CRM

semantic analysis
target-sell
term frequency inverse
    document frequency
    (TFIDF)
text analytics

▶ REVIEW QUESTIONS

1. Describe the steps involved in the data understanding process.

2. Why is understanding of the business problem essential to knowledge discovery?

3. Describe the importance of environmental scanning.

4. Describe text mining. What is TFIDF?

5. Describe the three types of Web DM techniques. Which one is used in the NASA Expert Seeker case study?

▶ APPLICATION EXERCISES

1. The University of Sheffield, Natural Language Processing Group, publishes a site for the dissemination of the General Architecture for Text Engineering (GATE) (gate.ac.uk), which is an open source infrastructure for developing and deploying software components that process human language. Describe how GATE could be used to automatically identify the names of people in a corporate intranet and transform them into hyperlinks to be used in a general mailer via e-mail.

2. Rapid-I distributes the open source software RapidMiner (http://rapid-i.com/content/blogcategory/38/69/), formerly YALE (Yet Another Learning Environment), an environment for machine learning and data mining experiments. View their interactive tour in the company Web site, and then describe how you would use this environment in your organization.

3. Download the open source software RapidMiner environment (http://rapid-i.com/content/blogcategory/38/69/) and view the tutorial published by the company. Then describe how you would implement an expertise locator system like Expert Seeker at your organization using RapidMiner.

4. Design the ELS architecture for your organization, including defining existing information sources that will be used by the application.

▶ REFERENCES

Aguilar, F. 1967. *Scanning the Business Environment* (New York: Macmillan).
Albright, K. 2004. "Environmental Scanning: Radar for Success." *The Information Management Journal*, May/June, 38–45.

Auster, E., and Choo, C. 1993. "Environmental Scanning by CEOs in Two Canadian Industries." *Journal of the American Society for Information Science*, 44(4), 194–203.

Auvil, L., and Searsmith, D. 2003. Using Text Mining for Spam Filtering Supercomputing. Automated Learning Group, National Center for Supercomputing Applications, University of Illinois.

Azvine, B., Cui, Z., Majeed, B., and Spott, M. 2007. "Operational Risk Management with Real-Time Business Intelligence." *BT Technology Journal*, 25(1), 154–167.

Bachelor, B. 2008. "Sam's Club Tells Suppliers to Tag or Pay." *RFID Journal*, January 11.

Becerra-Fernandez, I. 2000. "The Role of Artificial Intelligence Technologies in the Implementation of People-Finder Knowledge Management Systems." *Knowledge Based Systems*, 13(5), 315–320.

Becerra-Fernandez, I. 2001. "Locating Expertise at NASA–Developing a Tool to Leverage Human Capital." *Knowledge Management Review*, 4(4), 34–37.

Becerra-Fernandez, I. 2006. "Searching for Experts on the Web: A Review of Contemporary Expertise Locator Systems." *ACM Transactions on Internet Technology*, 6(4), 333–355.

Berson, A., Smith, S., and Thearling, K. 2000. *Building Data Mining Applications for CRM* (New York: McGraw Hill).

Chen, H. 2001. *Knowledge Management Systems: A Text Mining Perspective* (Tucson: University of Arizona).

Chen, Z., Wenyin, L., Zhang, F., Li, M., and Zhang, H. 2001. "Web Mining for Web Image Retrieval." *Journal of the American Society for Information Science and Technology*, 52 (10), 831–839.

Choo, C. 2001a. *Information Management for the Intelligent Organization: The Art of Scanning the Environment*, Third Edition (Medford, N.J.: Information Today).

Choo, C. 2001b. "Environmental Scanning as Information Seeding and Organizational Learning." *Information Research*, 7(1). Available at: http://InformationR.net/ir/7-1/paper112.html.

CIO Staff. 2008. "Panning for Gold in Customer Chats." *CIO*, September 5.

Daft, R., and Weick, K. 1984. "Toward a Model of Organizations as Interpretation Systems." *Academy of Management Review*, 9(2), 284–295.

Dumais, S., and Chen, H. 2000. Hierarchical Classification of Web Content. In Proceedings of the 23rd ACM International Conference on Research and Development in Information Retrieval (SIGIR'00), Athens, Greece.

Edelstein, H. 2001. "Pan for Gold in the Clickstream." *Information Week*, March 12.

Frakes, W., and Baeza-Yates, R. 1992. *Information Retrieval: DataStructures and Algorithms* (Upper Saddle River, N.J.: Prentice Hall).

Foley, J. 2007. "Inside HP's Data Warehouse Gamble." *Information Week*, January 1/8.

Gilbert, A. 2002. Smart Carts on a Roll at Safeway. CNET News, October 28. Accessed through the Web at http://news.cnet.com/2100-1017-963526.html on August 24, 2008.

Gray, P., and Watson, H. 1998. *Decision Support in the Data Warehouse* (Upper Saddle River, N.J.: Prentice Hall).

Haeckel, S. 1999. *Adaptive Enterprise* (Boston: Harvard Business School Press).

Haimila, S. 2003. "Web Mining Synergy." *KM World*, May 1.

Hamblen, M. 2007. "Privacy a Hot Topic as RFID Tagging Grows in Use." *Computerworld*, September 20.

Havenstein, H. 2007. "Travelocity.com Dives into Text Analytics to Boost Customer Service." *Computerworld*, November 14.

IBM. 2004. IBM and Safeway Create Enjoyable Grocery Shopping Experience, IBM White Papers, March 2. Accessed at http://www-1.ibm.com/industries/wireless/doc/content/bin/Safeway_1.pdf on August 24, 2008.

IBM. 2007. "Keeping Tabs on RFID–It's Way More than Barcodes and It's Changing the Way the World Works, *Ideas from IBM*, June 12. Accessed at http://www.ibm.com/ibm/ideas-fromibm/us/rfid/061207/images/RFID_061207.pdf on August 24, 2008.

Jackson, J. 2002. "Data Mining: A Conceptual Overview." *Communications of the Association for Information Systems*, 8, 267–296.

Jenkin, T. A. 2008a. How IT Supports Knowledge Discovery and Learning Processes on the Web. In the Proceedings of the Hawaii International Conference on System Sciences (HICSS), Waikoloa.

Jenkin, T. A. 2008b. Using Information Technology to Support the Discovery of Novel Knowledge in Organizations. Thesis (PhD, Management), Queen's University.

Jenkin, T. A., Chan, Y. E., and Skillicorn, D. B. 2007. Novel-Knowledge Discovery–Challenges and Design Theory. In the Proceedings of the Annual Conference of the Administrative Sciences Association of Canada, Ottawa.

Kanarakus, C. 2008. "Service Aims to Mine Social Networks for Consumer Insight." *CIO Magazine*, March 26.

Kharif, O. 2005. "RFID's Second Wave." *Business Week*, August 9.

Kosala, R., and Blockeel, H. 2000. "Web Mining Research: A Survey." *ACM SIGKDD Explorations*, 2(1), 1–15.

Kovalerchuck, B., Triantaphyllou, E., Ruiz, J., Torvik, V., and Vityaev, E. 2000. "The Reliability Issue of Computer-Aided Breast Cancer Diagnosis." *Journal of Computers and Biomedical Research*, 33(4), 296–313.

Krulwich, B., and Burkey, C. 1995. Contact Finder: Extracting Indications of Expertise and Answering Questions with Referrals. In Working Notes of the 1995 Fall Symposium on Intelligent Knowledge Navigation and Retrieval, Cambridge, Mass. Technical Report FS-95-03, AAAI Press, 85–91.

Lamont, J. 2002. "CRM Around the World." *KM World*, 11(9), October.

Landt, J. 2001. Shrouds of Time: The History of RFID. Association for Automatic Identification and Data Capture Technologies (AIM) Publications. Retrieved from http://www.aimglobal.orgon 2008-08-16.

Lawrence, R., Almasi, G., Kotlyar, V., Viveros, M., and Duri, S. 2001. "Personalization of Supermarket Product Recommendations." *Data Mining and Knowledge Discovery*, 5, 11–32.

Li, M., Chen, Z., and Zhang, H. 2002. "Statistical Correlation Analysis in Image Retrieval." *Pattern Recognition*, 35(12), 2687–2693.

Marsdent, P. 1990. "Network Data and Measurement." *Annual Review of Sociology*, 16, 435–463.

Mattox, D., Maybury, M., and Morey, D. 1999. Enterprise Expert and Knowledge Discovery. In Proceedings of the 8th International Conference on Human–Computer Interaction (HCI International '99), Munich, Germany, August, 303–307.

Monahan, T., and Wall, T. 2007. "Somatic Surveillance: Corporeal Control through Information Networks." *Surveillance & Society*, 4(3), 154–173.

Raths, D. 2008. "Hospitals Play Tag—RFID Finds a Niche in Healthcare." *KM World*, July 11.

Ratzan, L. 2006. "Mining the Deep Web: Search Strategies that Work. *Computerworld*, December 11.

Salton, G. 1989. *Automatic Text Processing* (Boston: Addison-Wesley Longman).

Schwenk, H. 2002. "Real-Time CRM Analytics: The Future of BI?" *KM World*, 11(2), February.

Sebastiani, F. 2002. "Machine Learning in Automated Text Categorization." *ACM Computing Surveys*, 34(1), 1–47.

Stockman, H. 1948. "Communication by Means of Reflected Power." *Proceedings of the Institute of Radio Engineers*, 36(10), 1196–1204.

Streeter, L.A. and Lochbaum, K. (1988). An expert/expert-locating system based on automatic representative of semantic structure. In proceedings of the 4th IEEE conference on Artificial Intelligence Applications. IEEE. San Diego, CA 345–349.

Subramanian, R., Fernandes, N., and Harper, E. 1993. "Environmental Scanning in U.S. Companies: Their Nature and Their Relationship to Performance." *Management International Review*, 33(3), 271–286.

Sullivan, D. 2001. *Document Warehousing and Text Mining: Techniques for Improving Business Operations, Marketing, and Sales* (New York: John Wiley).

Swartz, N. 2007. "Gartner Warns Firms of 'Dirty Data'." *The Information Management Journal*, May/June, 6.

Thibodeau, P. 2007. "IBM Uses RFID to Track Conference Attendees." *Computerworld*, October 16.

Vats, N., and Skillicorn, D. B. 2004a. The ATHENS System for Novel Information Discovery. Department of Computing and Information Science, Queen's University, Technical Report 2004-489.

Vats, N., and Skillicorn, D. B. 2004b. Information Discovery within Organizations Using the Athens System. Proceedings of the 2004 Conference of the Centre for Advanced Studies on Collaborative Research, Markham, Ontario, pp. 282–292.

Wailgum, T. 2007a. "Kimberly-Clark's Secrets to RFID Success." *CIO*, July 30.

Wailgum, T. 2007b. "RFID Chips in Your Magazines." *CIO*, December 12.

Yimam-Seid, D., and Kobsa, A. 2003. "Expert Finding Systems for Organizations: Problem and Domain Analysis and the DEMOIR Approach." *Journal of Organizational Computing and Electronic Commerce* 13(1), 1–24.

Zanasi, A. 2000. Webmining through the Online Analyst. Proceedings of the First Data Mining Conference. Cambridge University, Cambridge, UK.

CHAPTER 5

TECHNOLOGIES ENABLING INSIGHTS AND DECISIONS

▶ 5.1 INTRODUCTION

In Chapter 4 we discussed technologies that enable information integration. In this chapter we discuss technologies that enable insights and support decision making. The process of creating new insights from information is known as **business analytics**. Organizations relying on business analytics make extensive use of data, statistical and quantitative analysis, explanatory and predictive modeling, and fact-based decision making (Davenport and Harris, 2007). Relevant technologies for business analytics, including different data mining technologies that have their origin in statistics and artificial intelligence, are discussed and illustrated in this chapter.

How are new insights discovered from existing information? We focus on two significant ways:

1. Discovery by using existing information about how decisions are made in order to build systems that make similar decisions

2. Discovery by finding useful patterns in observations, typically embodied in explicit data

We organize our discussion around the topics of business analytics, the CRISP-DM process, and statistical as well as intelligent data mining technologies. We begin with our presentation of how business analytics can be used to create new insights.

▶ 5.2 TECHNOLOGIES TO CREATE INSIGHTS: USING DATA MINING TO CREATE NEW EXPLICIT KNOWLEDGE

As we described in Section 1, the essence of business analytics is to embed analytical decisions into business processes on an ongoing, repeatable basis instead of treating analytics as an ad hoc activity (Davenport and Harris, 2007). Thus, firms that want to follow a business analytics strategy will need to embed analytics in their most important business processes.

Perhaps the reference to data mining evokes the process of extracting the "gold" knowledge buried in enterprise databases, with the expectation that this gold will give a firm a significant competitive advantage. The gold mined from the databases refers to patterns buried between the data variables, which represent new insights about the previously unknown relationships among these variables. These families of techniques are also collectively known as **knowledge discovery in databases (KDD)**, or more commonly, **data mining (DM)**. The beginnings of KDD as a discipline can be traced to the early 1990s when the first workshop on KDD was held (Piatetsky-Shapiro and Frawley, 1991), although the natural and social science fields have been using these techniques for many years prior as the basis for scientific investigation. KDD has been defined as the process of applying statistical or intelligent algorithms to uncover and interpret patterns from data generated by these algorithms (Fayyad et al., 1996). Many practitioners use the terms KDD and DM interchangeably, although for others KDD is viewed as involving the whole business intelligence process, whereas DM may refer more specifically to the actual application of DM techniques.

Business analytics is considered to be a component of business intelligence by other authors, as well as in this book. For example, one author views analytics in relation to business intelligence as follows: "The use of analytics in business is not new. Operations research methodology (which is a large component of analytics) started to be applied to business 60 years ago, right after World War II . . . Business intelligence now gives us standard and ad hoc reports, query, and drill-down capabilities . . . Analytics adds advanced statistical analysis, forecasting, predictive modeling, and optimization" (Gray, 2007, p. 203). While recognizing analytics as a component of BI, authors have argued about the difference between business analytics and data mining. Some authors view the two as distinct, arguing that business "analytics comes with hypothesis testing . . . data mining is more the act of discovery that lacks a hypothesis" (Adelman, Moss, and Kelly, 2005). Others view business analytics and data mining as synonymous. For example, according to Kohavi and colleagues (2002, p. 45), "data mining and analytics are used interchangeably here to denote the general process of exploration and analysis of data to discover and identify new and meaningful patterns in data. This definition is similar . . . [to] knowledge discovery." So although there is some difference in opinion regarding the differences among the three terms—business analytics, data mining, and knowledge discovery—they have also been viewed as interchangeable (Kohavi, Rothleder, and Simoudis, 2002), and we follow the latter strategy. These technologies are used to create new insights from uncovered relationships and patterns from existing data and information, and can provide organizations with a competitive advantage.

DM applications have made noteworthy contributions to scientific discovery—for example, in breast cancer diagnosis (Kovalerchuk et al., 2000). Recall that in Chapter 1 we described some of the factors driving BI, namely:

1. **Exploding data volumes** ready for analysis, marked by the convergence of improved and inexpensive data storage capabilities, regulatory

requirements, and the abundance of customer data resulting from the explosion of e-commerce applications.

2. **Increasing decision complexity** resulting from increased competition across industries and countries, globally distributed organizations, and the increasing requirement to incorporate both structured and unstructured information in decision making.

3. **Need for quick reflexes** as decision makers increasingly need to respond efficiently and effectively to environmental changes, with greater accountability for their actions.

4. **Technological progress**, as powerful computing power has become increasingly accessible and less expensive, thereby supporting increasingly complex computational requirements.

In addition, the growth of DM in the commercial arena has been fueled by the increased availability of robust, flexible, and integrated analytic capabilities. For example, as described in Section 4.6, many CRM software applications include integrated DM prediction models used to calculate a customer *score*, which is a numeric value assigned to each customer database record that indicates the probability that the customer in question will behave in a specific manner.

In the early days of BI, DM applications were implemented to improve the process of bank credit applications, and it was estimated that as many as 95% of the banks were already using DM by 1996 (Smith and Gupta, 2000). An early application of BI describes a project in which a financial institution sought to identify the characteristics of borrowers who defaulted in their loans and thus to better identify those customers who were likely to default on their loans. This application used 1,000 observations and 20 factors to mine a set of rules from the data, creating a model that accurately predicted loan defaults with a 66% success rate (Witten, 2000). Too bad bank officers decided not to pay attention to their BI models before the subprime mortgage crisis![1]

The literature abounds with examples of how retailers, both brick-and-mortar as well as *e-tailers* (a portmanteau or compound of the words "electronic" and "retailer"), have successfully implemented DM to improve their marketing and operating processes. Safeway is one prominent example of a brick-and-mortar retailer. IBM[2] designed a DM application for this British grocer to allow its customers to set up and transmit their shopping lists ahead of time for pickup at the store. Since this convenient application implied that customers would forego the urge for impulsive buying, Safeway decided to turn

---

[1] During the years of 2006–2007 leading up to the subprime mortgage crisis, many U.S. mortgages were issued to borrowers that had a lesser ability to repay the loans based on a set of factors, so that when house prices began to decline in those same years, mortgage delinquencies soared, resulting in a decline in capital available at financial institutions in the United States and around the world.

[2] www.ibm.com

to DM to personalize recommendations for their shoppers, by creating a list of grocery items that matched a customer's profile (IBM, 2004). Recommendations would be generated based on a customer's prior purchasing patterns, as well as by matching to what other clients with similar profiles may have purchased in the past. In Business Intelligence in Practice 5.1, we describe a successful DM implementation for electronic commerce.

Business Intelligence in Practice 5.1: Data Mining Applications for e-Commerce

One successful e-tailer implementation is the case of eBags,[3] a Web-based storefront of handbags, suitcases, wallets, and other similar products. What distinguished the eBags DM implementation was how the firm was able to identify which Web pages were in fact garnering the greatest number of purchases. Using this information, eBags explored how Web content could lead to more effective Web sales, and how it could be used to personalize the customers' experience using their demographics and buying preferences. Among other demographic data, eBags would use the customer's zip code to feature specific items. As an example, online customers from affluent neighborhoods would be offered designer items, while discounted offers would be featured to shoppers from less wealthy ones (Stevens, 2001).

Another prominent e-tailer is Proflowers,[4] an online resource that describes itself as "connecting consumers with fresh-from-the-field flowers." The most important challenge in the flower industry is to deliver the goods to the consumer as soon as possible from the time the flowers are picked, in order to maximize the period that consumers will enjoy the product. Proflowers was able to use DM to improve the management of its Web-storefront traffic, by modifying its Web site throughout the day to optimize inventory, via highlighting slower selling products and downplaying better selling ones (Stevens, 2001).

Success stories abound in the practitioner literature that quantify the value of applying DM techniques to create new business insights. Probably, the most popular DM applications are in the marketing arena. Each time a customer purchases a product or service, a record of the transaction is stored in the enterprise system. In many cases, these transactions include buyer demographics. Tying the customer's profile with the transaction can lead to better information about which purchasers are likely to later buy this product, as well as which other products this customer is likely to purchase, therefore expanding

[3] http://www.ebags.com/
[4] http://www.proflowers.com

product cross-sales. We saw some examples of such applications in Chapter
Here is a summary of other successful DM applications:[5]

1. *Banking:* Trading and financial forecasting applications, like those used for
   determining derivative securities pricing, futures price forecasting, and
   stock performance, provide a fertile ground for the application of DM
   techniques. DM techniques have been successfully implemented to develop scoring systems used to identify credit risk and fraud. Other potential
   applications include modeling the relationship between corporate strategy,
   financial health, and corporate performance. A Capital One analytics
   initiative resulted in a 20% growth in earnings per share per year through
   the creation of new credit card products with different interest rates,
   incentives, direct mail packaging, and other variations for the purpose of
   attracting new customers (Davenport, 2006).

2. *Target Marketing:* Intelligent DM techniques like artificial neural networks can be utilized for target marketing, including market segmentation.
   With this approach, marketing departments can classify customers according to specific demographic characteristics, such as gender and age group,
   as well as their consumer behavior. These techniques can also optimize
   direct marketing campaigns by categorizing customers who are increasingly likely to respond to new product offerings based on prior purchasing
   patterns. For example, Harrah's clustering application enabled it to better
   segment its customers and increase the profitability of its rewards program
   (Lee et al., 2003).

3. *Insurance:* Clustering DM techniques have been used for categorizing
   groups of customers to predict claim frequencies and determine premium
   pricing. In addition, these techniques have also proven successful in
   uncovering instances of claim fraud and have been used to improve
   customer retention. For example, Progressive Insurance uses analytics
   to design new products that target customers who may exhibit certain risk
   characteristics (e.g., motorcycle riders) that may be offset by other positive
   factors (high credit scores and no accidents) (Davenport, 2006).

4. *Telecommunications:* Predictive DM techniques, such as artificial neural
   networks, for example, have been used mostly to attempt to reduce churn
   (described in Chapter 4), which is a measure of customer attrition.
   Customer churn is defined as the number of customers who discontinue
   a service during a specified time period divided by the average total
   number of customers over that same period. DM can also be used to
   predict the conditions that may cause a customer to return to or restart the
   service. In addition, association techniques like market basket analysis have

---

[5] For an extensive review of articles on data mining techniques and applications to specific business
problems see (Bishop 1994; Widrow, Rumelhart, and Lehr, 1994; Wong, Bodnovich, and Selvi, 1997;
Smith and Gupta, 2000).

identify which telecommunication products customers are
[purchas]e together. Finally, Verizon uses business analytics to better
[identify] factors leading to superior performance (Davenport, 2006).

[Oper]*ations Management:* Predictive DM techniques, like artificial neural
networks, have been used for planning and scheduling, project management, and quality control. For example, Huber + Suhner, a global leader in
the development of systems for radio frequency, wireless, and fiber optic
applications, used analytics to improve its operations. Huber + Suhner was
able to integrate its customer, product, project, and sales data together into
reports that combined data such as earnings, costs of sales, budgets, and so
on (Holbrook, 2004).

6. *Retail Sales Forecasting:* DM methods have also been successfully applied
to sales forecasting, taking into consideration multiple market variables,
including customer profiling based on purchasing habits. For example,
association techniques like market basket analysis can help understand
customer clusters based on purchasing patterns and which products are
likely to be purchased together. Marriott International achieved a unique
competitive advantage by using analytics to establish the optimal price for
its guest rooms (Davenport, 2006).

7. *Systems Diagnosis:* DM can be used to uncover diagnostic rules from a
database of documented faults. This type of analysis is useful to predict
device failures and thus develop a schedule for preventive maintenance
that can avoid costly outages. Furthermore, mining existing faults can lead
to design and manufacturing improvements. For example, diagnostic rules
were mined from 600 documented faults in rotating machinery (such as
motors and generators) and then compared to the same rules elicited from
a diagnostic expert, and it was found that the mined rules provided slightly
better performance than the ones elicited from the expert (Witten, 2000).

Today, applications of business analytics and data mining abound in fields as
diverse as cutting costs in servicing ATMs to better predicting hurricanes. One of
the most interesting recent analytics applications is in crime-fighting, an implementation that earned the police department at Richmond, Virginia, the Gartner
2007 BI Award for Excellence (Harvey, 2007). This implementation, described in
Chapter 1, required the integration of crime report data with other relevant
information sources such as weather, traffic, sports events, and paydays for large
employers. Cluster results revealed, for example, that robberies increased on
paydays near check-cashing stores. Armed with these outcomes, police were able
to take preventive measures that resulted in a decrease in crime rates by 21% by
2006, and by an additional 19% by 2007 (Harvey, 2007). In the years to come, other
related projects at Richmond will explore how other factors such as city design,
road networks, and shopping mall hours may also affect the incidence and gravity
of urban crime (Harvey, 2007).

Other interesting applications of DM techniques include facilitating the classification of a country's investing risk based on a variety of factors (Becerra-Fernandez, Zanakis, and Walczak, 2002), and identifying the factors associated with a country's competitiveness (Zanakis and Becerra-Fernandez, 2005), described in more detail in Section 5.7.

▶ 5.3 THE BUSINESS ANALYTICS PROCESS

Business analytics can mean different things for different organizations. Some organizations have a mature and well-planned enterprise architecture and large data warehouses as described in Chapter 3, while others may have small databases. The problems faced by the users of DM systems may also be quite different. Therefore, the developers of DM technologies face a difficult process when attempting to build tools that are applicable across the entire spectrum of needs and corporate cultures. Early efforts to apply analytics to business operations faced the need to learn, primarily via trial and error, how to develop an effective approach to the process of KDD. In fact, as early DM adopters witnessed an exploding interest in the application of techniques, it became apparent there was a need to develop a standard process model for KDD. This standard should be well reasoned, nonproprietary, and freely available to all BI practitioners. In 1999, a consortium of vendors and early adopters of DM applications for business operations—consisting of Daimler-Chrysler (then Daimler-Benz AG, Germany), NCR Systems Engineering Copenhagen (Denmark), SPSS/Integral Solutions Ltd. (England), and OHRA Verzegeringen en Bank Groep B.V. (The Netherlands)— developed a set of specifications called the **cross-industry standard process for data mining (CRISP-DM)**[6] (Chapman et al., 2000; Two Crows, 1999; Brachman and Anand, 1996). CRISP-DM is an industry-neutral and tool-neutral process for data mining that provides a hierarchical process model for defining the basic tasks of the BI process.

Figure 5.1 summarizes the steps in the DM process, also known as the CRISP-DM process methodology, which we will describe in more detail in Chapter 8. In Chapter 4, we discussed in detail the first two steps of this process and how insights may be uncovered from unstructured data. In this chapter, we examine the application of the DM process to structured data.

Once the objectives of the study have been clearly established via measurable business goals and the process of data understanding has been completed, the next task involves the **data preparation**. The steps for the data preparation task are:

a. *Selection:* This step involves defining the predictor variables and the sample dataset. The process of selecting the predictor variables is critical, because DM algorithms will not perform well if inconsequential variables (fields or database columns) are considered as potential predictors. This is

---

[6] www.crisp-dm.org

Business Understanding	Data Understanding	Data Preparation	Modeling	Evaluation	Deployment
Determine Business Objectives *Background / Business Objectives / Business Success Criteria*	**Initial Data Collection** *Initial Data Collection Report*	**Data Set** *Data Set Description*	**Generate Test Design** *Test Design*	**Evaluate Results** *Approved Models / Assessment of Data Mining Results w.r.t. Business Success Criteria*	**Plan Deployment** *Deployment Plan*
Situation Assessment *Inventory of Resources / Requirements / Assumptions / Constraints / Risk and Contingencies / Terminology / Costs and Benefits*	**Data Description** *Data Description Report*	**Selection** *Rationale for Inclusion/ Exclusion*	**Build Model** *Parameter Settings / Models*	**Review Process** *Review of Process*	**Produce Final Report** *Final Report / Final Presentation*
Determine Data Mining Goal *Data Mining Goals / Data Mining Success Criteria*	**Data Quality Verification** *Data Quality Report*	**Cleaning** *Data Cleaning Report*	**Model Evaluation** *Model Description / Assessment*	**Determine Next Steps** *List of Possible Actions / Decision*	**Plan Monitoring and Maintenance** *Maintenance Plan*
Produce Project Plan *Project Plan*	**Exploratory Analysis** *Exploratory Analysis Report*	**Construction** *Derived Variables / Generated Records / Transformation*			**Review Project** *Experience Documentation*
		Integration *Merging / Aggregation*			
		Formatting *Rearranging Attributes / Reordering Records / Within-Value / Reformatting*			

FIGURE 5.1 CRISP-DM Data Mining Process Methodology (Source: SPSS, 2009)

what is known as the garbage-in-garbage-out (GIGO) principle, which means that if insignificant variables are fed into the DM model, the outcome will be meaningless. Basically this is the reason why DM requires an understanding of the domain and an awareness of which are the potential variables that could influence the outcome. As a rule of thumb, the number of predictors (columns) must be smaller than the number of observations (rows) in the dataset. In fact, the number of observations should be at least 10 to 25 times the number of predictors. An increase in the number of predictors results in a proportional increase in the computational requirement to build the model. Often times the complete dataset to be fed through the model may be extremely large, so a sample of the dataset can be selected to represent the complete dataset. When selecting a representative sample for the complete dataset, it's appropriate to pay attention to the constraints imposed by sampling theory.

b. *Construction and transformation of variables:* Often, many of the variables involved in the DM model will need to be transformed or constructed from the existing raw data. For example, ratios and combination of various fields may need to be calculated. Furthermore, certain algorithms like *Market Basket Analysis*, for example, may require data to be transformed to categorical format (integer) from its original continuous format. Finally, the specific model may require transformations that group raw data values in ranges such as *low*, *medium*, and *high*.

c. *Data integration:* The dataset required by the DM model may reside on multiple disjoint databases, which will need to be consolidated for the model to use. Data consolidation may also require redefinition of some of the data fields to allow for consistency. Different databases may, for example, relate to the same data entry slightly differently. As an example, one database record may use the full customer name (e.g., Florida International University), whereas the corresponding record in another database field may use an abbreviation (FIU). These incompatibilities must be reconciled prior to data integration.

d. *Formatting:* This step involves the reformatting and reordering of the data fields, as required by the DM model.

The next task in the DM process comprises the **model building and validation**. The task frequently involves repeatedly trying several options until the best quality model emerges. Therefore, developing an accurate model is an iterative process. Furthermore, different algorithms could be tried with the same data set and the results then compared to see which model yields the best accuracy results. For example, both neural network and rule induction algorithms could be applied to the same dataset to develop a predictive model. The results from each algorithm could be compared for accuracy in their respective predictive quality. Sections 5.4 and 5.5 delve into the topic of model building in detail.

Following model development, the models must be *validated*. Prior to the model construction, a subset of the data is set aside for validation purposes. This means that the validation data set is not used to develop or train the model but to calculate the accuracy of the predictive qualities of the model. The most popular validation technique in **n-fold cross validation**—specifically, **ten-fold validation**. Ten-fold validation divides the total validation dataset into ten approximately equal-sized datasets, using each of the ten validation sets a single time, to evaluate the model comparing the accuracy with that resulting from using the remaining nine training sets. For each of the ten models (the last model includes using the whole dataset), the accuracy is determined, and the overall model accuracy is determined as the average of each of the accuracies of the model validation samples.

The next task in the DM process comprises the **model evaluation and interpretation**. Once the model is developed, the validation dataset is fed through the model. Since the output for the validation dataset is known—for example, the customers with a "bad risk" loan rating in a given dataset—the model outcomes or predicted results can be compared with the actual outcomes in the validation dataset. This comparison represents the accuracy of the model. If the model accuracy is around 50%, then the model will not be acceptable, because essentially that is the same accuracy as for a random occurrence. What constitutes an acceptable model reliability depends on the context in which the model will be used and how risk averse the organization is toward incorrect outcomes. Section 5.6 discusses the issues around model evaluation in more detail.

Finally, the last task in the DM process is **deployment**. This task implements the "live" DM model within an organization to aid the decision-making process. A valid model must make sense, and a pilot implementation is always required prior to live deployment. Once the model has been effectively deployed, it's important to continue to monitor how well the model predicts the outcomes and the benefits that the model brings to the organization. For example, a clustering model may be deployed to identify fraudulent Medicare claims. When the model identifies potential instances of fraud and these instances are validated as indeed fraudulent, the savings to the organization from the deployment of the model should be captured. These early successes will then act as "flag-bearers" for the DM efforts, and will in effect create enthusiasm about continued implementation of other DM applications within the organization.

CRISP-DM is only one of the institutions that have ongoing efforts toward streamlining the DM process. Other similar efforts include:

1. *Customer Profile Exchange (CPEX):*[7] Offers a vendor-neutral, XML-based open standard for facilitating the privacy-enabled interchange of customer information across disparate enterprise applications and systems.

---

[7] http://www.cpexchange.org

2. *Data Mining Group (DMG):*[8] Is an independent, vendor-led group, which develops DM standards, such as the predictive model markup language (PMML).

The goals that CRISP-DM, CPEX, and DMG standards pursue are to facilitate the planning, documentation, and communication in business analytics initiatives and to serve as a common reference framework for the DM industry. In fact, these standards help people, rather than software systems, communicate about analytics initiatives. Many of these standards were the outcome of practical experience from the implementation of DM projects.

We describe the steps in the process of developing the DM model in the next two sections.

▶ 5.4 THE DATA MINING MODEL: DESCRIBING WHAT HAPPENED

Recall from Chapter 4 that the first step in the DM process is to understand the goals of the application, followed by understanding the characteristics of the data. As we discussed before, it's estimated that this step may consume from 50% to 80% of the project resources, and it includes the **data collection** (defining the data sources for the study), **data description** (describing the contents of each of the DM data sources), and **data quality and verification** (which defines whether any data should be ignored due to lack of quality or relevance to the study).

No matter what the goals of the study are, the DM techniques used for the study could originate from the fields of statistics (like, for example, ANOVA) or computer science (an example is artificial neural networks). The first step in order to define which DM technique to use for the application is to identify the goals of the study, which can be either to **describe** what happened or to **predict** what will happen. In this section we focus on explaining how DM techniques can be used to describe what happened.

Once the purpose of the study has been defined, the next step is to understand the characteristics of the input and outcome data that will be used. Input or predictor variables and output or outcome variables could be either continuous or discrete (also known as categorical). In general, continuous data is numerical data that could conceivably be measured in smaller units—for example, time, weight, age, or money. Notice that even though most people in the United States can't think of a unit of measurement for money smaller than the penny, a fraction of a cent is conceivable. On the other hand, discrete data can't conceivably be measured in smaller units. For example, the number of married men in a room is a discrete number, because no man could be partly married.

To describe what happened means to segment or cluster data based on certain input characteristics, with no specific outcome to predict in mind.

---

[8] http://www.dmg.org

Descriptive techniques are used to look for patterns in prior activities or actions that affect these actions or activities. If the goal of the study is just to cluster or find associations that may exist among the data, then a specific outcome will not need to be associated with each set of predictor variables. In this sense, a data set that describes the customer base could be clustered in order to identify customer segments, but the model would not be used to predict a specific outcome, but rather would be used to understand how these observations may group together based on certain affinities among them. For example, in looking for criminal activity in financial transactions such as money laundering, one would look for unusual behaviors among the bank customers. Typically, criminal activity would be an "outlier" among well-defined customer clusters. Techniques to accomplish this segmentation include affinity (or association) and clustering techniques. Descriptive techniques can be of two types:

1. *Affinity or association:* These techniques serve to find which items are closely associated in the database, including market basket analysis (MBA) and link analysis. For example, a goal of the DM study could be "to identify the products that customers are likely to purchase together," which could help a supermarket interested in developing marketing campaigns targeting items that historically are purchased together. The results from MBA reflect rules that describe associations between products that people purchase together. One example would be "If wine is purchased, then cheese and crackers are also purchased 80% of the time."

2. *Clustering:* These techniques are used to uncover the natural groupings of data that may not be as obvious through casual inspection. The goal here is to create clusters of input records based on a set of characteristics that recognizes them as similar. For example, a business goal could be "to identify the Medicare billing records that look unusual," by creating clusters that classify billing records based on characteristics such as patient age, criticality of their diagnosis, and so on.

Table 5.1 summarizes some of the different descriptive techniques, including both association and clustering methods and their applicability pertaining to the characteristics of the input variables. Note that for all these techniques, the output variable is not defined. Market basket or association analysis can include the use of two techniques: Apriori, or generalized rule induction (GRI), is an association rule algorithm that requires the input fields to be discrete. Apriori is generally faster to train than GRI. Apriori allows only the specification of logical (or dichotomies) for the input variables, such as (True, False) or (1, 0) to indicate the presence (or absence) of the item in the market basket. Generalized rule induction is an association rule algorithm, which is capable of producing rules that describe associations between attributes to a symbolic target and is capable of using continuous or logical data as its input. Other clustering techniques include genetic algorithms and fuzzy logic.

Table 5.1 Summary of Applicability of Clustering and Association Techniques

Goal	Input Variables (Predictor)	Output Variables (Outcome)	Statistical Technique	Examples
Find large groups of cases in large data files that are similar on a small set of input characteristics	Continuous or discrete	No outcome variable	K-means cluster analysis	• Customer segments for marketing • Groups of similar insurance claims
Create large cluster memberships			Kohonen neural networks	• Cluster customers into segments based on demographics and buying patterns
Create small set associations and look for patterns between many categories	Logical	No outcome variable	Market basket or association analysis with apriori	• Identify which products are likely to be purchased together • Identify which courses students are likely to take together
Create small set associations and look for patterns between many categories	Logical or numeric	No outcome variable	Market basket or association analysis with GRI	• Identify which courses students are likely to take together
Create linkages between sets of items to display complex relationships	Continuous or discrete	No outcome variable	Link analysis	• Identify a relationship between a network of physicians and their prescriptions

Business Intelligence in Practice 5.2 describes how one organization used technology to cluster its customers in one hundred customer segments that would drive their loyalty program and provide them a significant competitive advantage.

Business Intelligence in Practice 5.2: Harrah's Customer Clusters Lead to Higher Firm Profitability

Harrah's Entertainment,[9] the world's largest provider of branded casino entertainment, began its operations in Reno, Nevada, some seventy years ago. Harrah's vision, communicated in its Web site, is "focused on building loyalty and value with its customers through a unique combination of great service, excellent products, unsurpassed distribution, operational excellence, and technology leadership."

Harrah's vision of using technology to improve customer satisfaction dates to the 1980s, when the company leadership embarked in the implementation of a customer loyalty program that provided customers the opportunity to earn points as they spent more across the different properties owned by the company. Motivated by the economic slowdown caused by the dot-com bust of the late 1990s, a new strategy to increase sales through an innovative rewards program was necessary to improve the firm's customer service and marketing. The new rewards would require a new technology infrastructure, which included an enterprise-wide data warehouse that integrated customer data from all of its properties. The data warehouse would effectively interconnect and consolidate client data from all the organizational transactional systems, slot machines, hotel management information systems, and reservation systems. Customer data would include such details as customer stay, demographic data, preference data, every play in the slot machines, games played at the game tables, and customer betting patterns.

In addition, Harrah's invested in an award-winning CRM system used to analyze customer information for new patterns and insights. Harrah's developed systems to cluster its customers into approximately one hundred different market segments, and created individualized marketing programs based on the specific segments. Market segments would project to a specific business value to Harrah's, which was used to develop appropriate marketing and advertising for each segment, translating into competitive advantage for the firm.

The new segmentation capability provided company employees with the necessary decision-making tools to improve the firm's marketing profitability. Harrah's distinguished itself from its competitors by investing in the technology necessary to substantially improve its loyalty rewards program, resulting in measurable improvements in customer satisfaction and winning numerous practitioner awards. (Compiled from Lee et al., 2003)

---

[9] www.harrahs.com

In Section 5.5 we describe how DM techniques can be used to predict what will happen.

▶ 5.5 THE DATA MINING MODEL: PREDICTING WHAT WILL HAPPEN

In Section 5.4 we described the first step in a DM study, which is to identify whether the goal of the study is to describe what happened or to predict what will happen. In this section we focus on explaining how DM techniques can be used to predict what will happen.

To predict what will happen means to develop a model that uses historical data to predict an outcome based on a set of input characteristics. Predictive techniques require the use of past history with the intent to predict future behavior. DM techniques in this category serve to classify the outcome variable—for example, *customers*—into predefined categories. For example, if it was discovered that there is a clear relationship between certain employment aspects of past loan holders and their subsequent loan defaults, a new loan applicant matching that criteria could be labeled as a "bad risk." Then, based on a set of attributes, we can predict that a particular new loan applicant is not likely to repay the loan, and therefore, denied the loan application. If the goal of the study is to develop a predictive model, the study requires having historical data, which includes inputs or predictor variables associated with given outputs or outcomes. For example, in order to develop a model to predict credit risk, it will be necessary to have collected a data set of prior customer data, including variables that could be used to predict credit risk, such as credit score, credit card debt, and years of education, as well as a credit risk outcome variable for that particular customer. As a rule of thumb, this data set should include at least 10 observations (or customers or rows of data) for each predictor (or inputs or columns of data). DM techniques used to predict what will happen are classified into three categories: *statistical* methods, *connectionist* methods, and *rule induction* methods.

5.5.1 Statistical Data Mining Methods

The objective of **statistical DM techniques** is to find how two or more variables are related to each other—in other words, the *correlations* between the variables. One common way to find this relationship is to try to identify a mathematical equation that can describe the relationship between the input variables and the outcome, also known as *curve fitting*. There are a number of curve fitting methods. One of these methods is the *least squares method*, which seeks to fit a straight curve among the outcomes by minimizing the sum of the squares of the deviation of the outcome versus the predicted values. Another method is nonlinear correlation, which is appropriate when the outcome function can't be described by a straight line but can be described by a polynomial or exponential function. Finally, *multivariate correlation* techniques are appropriate when the relationship between variables in the correlation is linear, but the problem space is multi-dimensional. Table 5.2 summarizes the different statistical techniques and their

Table 5.2 Summary of Applicability of Statistical Techniques

Goal	Input Variables (Predictors)	Output Variables (Outcomes)	Statistical Technique	Examples
Find linear combination of predictors that best separate the population	Continuous	Discrete	Discriminant analysis	• Predict instances of fraud • Predict whether customers will remain or leave (churners or not) • Predict which customers will respond to a new product or offer • Predict outcomes of various medical procedures
Predict the probability of outcome being in a particular category	Continuous	Discrete	Logistic and multinomial regression	• Predict insurance policy renewal • Predict fraud • Predict which product a customer will buy • Predict that a product is likely to fail
Output is a linear combination of input variables	Continuous	Continuous	Linear regression	• Predict expected revenue in dollars from a new customer • Predict sales revenue for a store • Predict waiting time on hold for callers to an 800 number • Predict length of stay in a hospital based on patient characteristics and medical condition
For experiments and repeated measures of the same sample	Most inputs must be discrete	Continuous	Analysis of variance (ANOVA)	• Predict which environmental factors are likely to cause cancer
Predict future events whose history has been collected at regular intervals	Continuous	Continuous	Time series analysis	• Predict future sales data from past sales records

applicability pertaining to the characteristics of the input and output variables. Inferential statistical techniques are differentiated from descriptive statistics. Inferential techniques are used to generalize from data and thus develop models that generalize from the observations, whereas descriptive statistics are used to characterize data that have already been collected and directly measured.

Both connectionist and rule induction methods (nonstatistical) are differentiated from statistical techniques in that the latter require a hypothesis to be specified beforehand. In addition, statistical techniques often are subject to stringent assumptions, such as normality of the sample data, uncorrelated error, or homogeneity of variance. However, statistical techniques provide for a more rigorous test of hypotheses.

5.5.2 Connectionist Methods: Neural Networks

Connectionist methods use artificial **neural networks** (ANN) techniques. ANN refers to a computer-based representation of what is theorized to be the human brain's physiological structure. ANN can be used as a predictive technique (backward propagation network) or as a clustering technique (Kohonen network). ANN originated with the seminar work by McCulloch and Pitts (1943), and later Minsky (1954) would write his doctoral dissertation on modeling the human brain via neural computation.

One of the most important features of ANN is that they can "learn." The most popular neural network algorithm is the multilayered feed-forward neural network with the back-propagation learning rule (Bishop, 1994; Fu, 1994; Hornick, Stinchcombe, and White, 1989; Smith and Gupta, 2000; Walczak, 2001; Wong et al., 1997), which is known to exhibit superior performance to other neural network paradigms (Walczak, 1998). The training process involves first assigning a random initial value between zero and one for the network weights, and then presenting the network with a set of inputs and associated outputs. The ANN output is compared with the actual value for the output, and an error (the difference between actual and predicted output) is computed. This error propagates back from the output nodes adjusting the weights associated with the appropriate neuron. This process continues iteratively, as several examples are being presented in sequence to the network. The process stops when the training process converges (i.e., the error values stabilize below an acceptable threshold). Alternatively, in some cases the process may also stop if it is determined that it will not converge (i.e., the error is not yet within an acceptable threshold and it is not improving with additional iterations). Back-propagation calculates the difference between calculated results of using the network weights and the outputs of the training set, and feeds back the error network by adjusting the weights in a recursive fashion in order to minimize the error. Network training is accomplished by seeking the set of values for the weights that minimizes an error function, such as the sum-of-squares errors. Figure 5.2 represents a simple two-layer ANN consisting of five input variables, one hidden layer, and two outcome variables. In this figure, each of the circles represents a neuron. For example, this neural network was being used to predict credit rating outcome (Low Risk or High

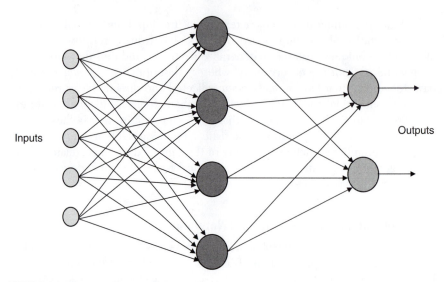

FIGURE 5.2 Two-Layer Neural Network

Risk) given five customer input characteristics: years of education, credit rating, credit card debt, owns house, and owns pet; and the weights correspond to the strength of the connection between each of the neurons. If the connection strength is close to 0, it means that the input variable doesn't impact the outcome. For instance, in this example the weight of the neuron for "owns pet" is likely to have a much smaller value (possibly close to zero) than the weight associated with "credit rating" (which is likely to be close to 1). Another characteristic of ANN is that the model can continue to learn, as the network can be retrained with new observations.

Table 5.3 summarizes the connectionist methods and their applicability pertaining to the characteristics of the input and output variables. *Memory-based*

Table 5.3 Summary of Applicability of Noninferential Predictive Techniques

Goal	Input (Predictor) Variables	Output (Outcome) Variables	Data Mining Technique	Examples
Predict outcome based on values of nearest neighbors	Continuous, discrete, and text	Continuous or discrete	Memory-based reasoning (MBR)	• Predict medical outcomes
Predict outcome in complex nonlinear environments	Continuous or discrete	Continuous or discrete	Neural networks	• Predict expected revenue • Predict credit risk

reasoning is a DM technique that looks for the nearest neighbors of known data samples, and combines their values to assign classification or prediction values for new data samples. MBR uses a distance function to find the nearest element to a new data sample, and a combination function to combine the values at the nearest neighbors to make a prediction. For more information on MBR refer to the work by Berry and Linoff (1997).

5.5.3 Symbolic Data Mining Methods: Rule Induction

Decision tree and rule induction methods, also known as *symbolic* techniques, are used to infer the "rules" that classify or partition the dataset. BI inductive algorithms are used to classify the dataset as a function of its characteristics, by developing a branching scheme that will predict the outcome based on the values of several attributes (Breiman et al., 1984; Fayyad et al., 1996). **Rule induction** methods provide automated techniques that are used for discovering how to generate classification schemes that resemble a decision tree (Breiman et al., 1984; Apte and Hong, 1996; Apte and Weiss, 1997). Once the tree has been created, it is simple to transform the conditional attribute branches into the programming code conditional statements (IF-THEN-ELSE). Different decision tree and rule induction methods are applicable depending on the characteristics of the data.

The classification and regression tree (CART) algorithm, which has become one of the most popular methods to build a **decision search tree**, was first described by Breiman et al. (1984). Other classification methods include chi-squared automatic interaction detector (CHAID) and C5.0 (a more recent version of ID3, C4.0, and C4.5). C5.0 and CART are similar classification methods, the most important differences being how C5.0 treats discrete variables. CART always performs a binary split of a continuous variable at each node, whereas C5.0 assumes one branch for each value taken on by the discrete variable (Berry and Linoff, 1997). CHAID can also be used to build decision trees, but its use is restricted to discrete variables (Hartigan, 1975).

The classification process begins at the top of the tree, also known as the root node. An attribute is selected to divide the sample at the root node. Then the test at the root node tests all samples, which pass to the left if True, or to the right if False. At each of the resulting nodes (called the parent nodes), further tests serve to continue classifying the data (creating children nodes). The algorithm is applied recursively to each child node until either all examples at a node are in one class, or all the examples of that node have the same values for all attributes. Every leaf of the tree represents a branching (classification) rule. Rule-based solutions translate the tree by forming a conjunct of every test that occurs on a path between the root node and the leaf node of the tree (Apte and Weiss, 1997). The algorithm makes its best split first, at the root node, each following split having smaller and less representative population, and the decision tree will continue growing as long as new splits improve the ability of the tree to separate the records (Berry and Linoff, 1997).

Traditional statistical prediction methods attempt to fit a model to data. Decision trees, on the other hand, partition the data based on the relationships between inputs and the output variable. The resulting decision tree indicates the inputs or predictors having a strong impact on the output, since the stronger the impact, the closer it will be to the root node (meaning higher in the tree structure hierarchy), and to subgroups that have concentrations of cases with specified characteristics (Breiman et al., 1984). In other words, variables at the root node represent the strongest classifiers, followed by the next strongest classifiers at each of the leaf nodes.

Figure 5.3 depicts the outcome decision tree for a targeting marketing initiative for a new product developed by a financial services firm. The resulting decision tree identifies Age in Years as the most significant predictor for customers that are likely to purchase the new product, with those over 44.14 years being 67% more likely to purchase the new product. Therefore the target marketing initiative would seek to prospect all the customers in the database older than 44.14 years. Upon analysis of the data for those customers younger than 44.14, the distribution among those likely to purchase the product or not was close to random (50%),

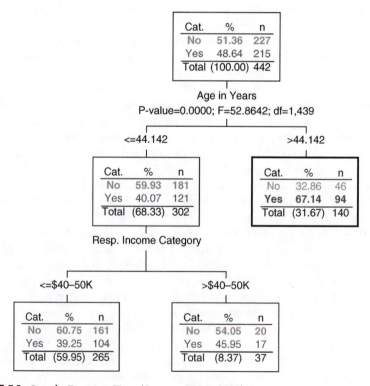

FIGURE 5.3 Simple Decision Tree (Source: SPSS, 2009)

Table 5.4 Summary of Applicability of Decision Tree Techniques

Goal	Input (Predictor) Variables	Output (Outcome) Variables	Decision Tree Technique	Examples
Predict by splitting data into more than two subgroups (branches)	Continuous, discrete, or ordinal	Discrete	Chi-square automatic interaction detection (CHAID)	• Predict which demographic combinations of predictors yield the highest probability of a sale • Predict which factors are causing product defects in manufacturing
Predict by splitting data into more than two subgroups (branches)	Continuous	Discrete	C5.0	• Predict which loan customers are considered a "good" risk • Predict which factors are associated with a country's investment risk
Predict by splitting data into binary subgroups (branches)	Continuous	Continuous	Classification and regression trees (CART)	• Predict which factors are associated with a country's competitiveness • Discover which variables are predictors of increased customer profitability
Predict by splitting data into binary subgroups (branches)	Continuous	Discrete	Quick, unbiased, efficient, statistical tree (QUEST)	• Predict who needs additional care after heart surgery

therefore that node was further exploited using the Income variable. The next level of the tree depicts that among the younger clients, those with income lower than $40,000–50,000 are not likely to buy the product, so the marketing campaign would purposely exclude those clients. The decision points of the trees can be translated intuitively into software conditional statements, such as:

IF < client.age > GT THAN < 40.14 > THEN send_marketing_campaign

and many DM packages provide the code along with the representation of the decision tree.

One of the advantages offered by rule induction algorithms is that the results may be directly inspected to understand the variables that can be effectively used to classify the data. Table 5.4 summarizes the various rule induction methods.

Typically, several different methods could be applied to any problem with similar results. Business Intelligence in Practice 5.3 describes how data mining, specifically artificial neural networks, can be used to predict power consumption at an electric utility and thus improve power system energy consumption.

Business Intelligence in Practice 5.3: Using Data Mining to Improve Energy Consumption in Power Systems

The power load forecast depends primarily on the weather. In cold regions, the highest heating load is in the winter, while air conditioners account for the biggest load in warm areas during the summer. Therefore, the power load forecast relies on an accurate weather forecast, for the next 24, 48, and 72 hours, and provides the necessary information to plan for the adequate power generation capacity. Electric utilities need to be extremely careful about these plans, because power stations have considerable startup costs and cannot be turned on and off within minutes if the power load is greater than expected. For example, nuclear power plants, which are the most efficient generators, take several days or weeks to place online; coal- or oil-fired stations, which are the next most efficient, may take about a day to fire up. Other types of generators with lower startup costs are typically more inefficient and costlier to operate. Electric utilities must carefully plan how to effectively place their units online to meet their load, and typically run complex algorithms on a real-time basis in order to identify the best power plant generation mix.

The function of load forecasting is sometimes delegated to an entire group of planners. To a large extent, temperature is the most significant predictive factor in forecasting the power load. However, other factors such as the day of the week, wind speed, and humidity may also affect the outcome. Research into how to improve the load forecasting has explored the use of neural networks to predict the energy consumption for a specified area and period of time. Using a database containing actual historical data that includes

(continued)

features such as ambient temperature, wind speed, humidity, and day of the week (among others), and the actual corresponding power that was consumed per hour, a network can be trained that can be used later to predict the load that will be consumed on a per hour basis for 24, 48, and 72 hours. The Electric Power Research Institute[10] is offering neural network-based tools to perform this specific function.

In Section 5.8 we describe one study that explored how statistical, neural networks, and rule induction techniques were used to develop predictive models to predict the competitiveness of nations. In Section 5.9 we discuss how to evaluate the results of the DM model.

▶ 5.6 THE DATA MINING MODEL: UNDERSTANDING WHAT HAPPENED

The BI process is an iterative process. Once the model has been developed the results must be evaluated. The potential for errors and their consequences must be carefully considered when performing a DM exercise. An intelligent computer system can make two types of errors when trying to solve a problem. To simplify the argument, let's assume that the possible solutions can only be "yes" or "no". One instance of this could be in a medical diagnosis of a serious disease, such as cancer. The two possible errors are: (1) an indication of "no" when the true answer is "yes", and (2) an indication of "yes" when the true answer is "no". The former is called the user's risk, and the latter is called the developer's risk. Depending on the application of the system, one type of error may be tolerable while the other may not be. For example, in the case of a system used to predict the presence of cancer in a patient, a false positive medical diagnosis ("yes" when the answer is truly "no") or vice versa can be very costly in terms of the seriousness of the error. On the other hand, a system designed to select a type of wine for a meal may tolerate such an error quite acceptably. Figure 5.4 illustrates the iterative nature of the CRISP-DM process.

Once the results of the DM study have been obtained, it's extremely important to carefully evaluate the cost of errors when the performance of the model is examined. For example, Table 5.5 presents the results of a study to predict the diagnosis of patients with heart disease based on a set of input variables. In the table, the columns represent predicted values for the diagnostic and the rows represent actual values for diagnostic of patients undergoing a heart disease examination. Actual values are coded in the cells, with percentages coded in parenthesis along the actual values. In this table, the predictions made along the shaded quadrant (*Actual No disease/Predicted No disease*) represent patients that

---

[10] http://www.epri.com/

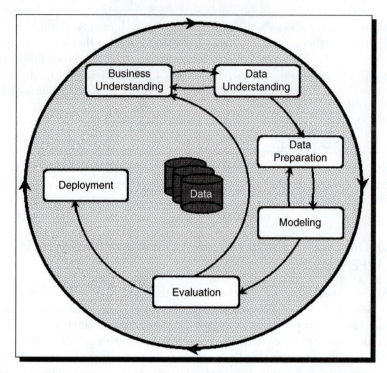

FIGURE 5.4 The Iterative Nature of the KDD Process (Source: SPSS, 2009)

were correctly predicted as being healthy. That means that 118 patients (or 72% of a total of 164 patients) were diagnosed with *No disease* and they were indeed healthy. Looking at the shaded quadrant (*Actual Presence of disease/Predicted Presence of disease*), 96 patients (or 69.1% of a total of 139 patients) were diagnosed with *Presence of disease* and they were indeed sick. For the patients in these two quadrants, the classification algorithm correctly predicted their heart disease diagnosis. However, the patients whose diagnosis falls off this diagonal (the quadrants that are not shaded) were incorrectly classified. In this example, 46 patients (or 28% of a total of 164 patients) were diagnosed with the disease when in fact they were healthy. Furthermore, 43 patients (or 30.9% of a total of 139 patients) were incorrectly diagnosed with no disease when in fact they were sick.

Table 5.5 Classification Table Results (SPSS, 2009)

Heart Disease Diagnostic	Predicted No Disease	Predicted Presence of Disease
Actual No Disease	118 (72%)	46 (28%)
Actual Presence of Disease	43 (30.9%)	96 (69.1%)

In summary, 70.6% of the patients were correctly classified with the prediction algorithm in this example. Note that in this example, the cost of incorrectly giving a patient sound bill of health when in fact the patient is sick is considered much higher than incorrectly predicting the patient to be sick when in fact the person is healthy. The former may cause the patient to die without the proper care, whereas the latter will give the patient a jolt, but further tests are likely to be reassuring.

Based on the goals of the study (predictive or association) and the characteristics of the data, the appropriate DM technique can be selected among many possible alternatives, and in fact, often more than one technique could be used for a given study and would most likely yield similar results. The next section describes a study that used three different BI techniques to predict the competitiveness of nations.

CASE STUDY 5-7

CAN KNOWLEDGE DISCOVERY UNCOVER THE FACTORS THAT HELP PREDICT THE COMPETITIVENESS OF NATIONS?

A nation's competitiveness is defined by the U.S. President's Commission on Industrial Competitiveness (1985) as "the degree to which a nation can, under free and fair market conditions, produce goods and services that meet the test of international markets while simultaneously expanding the real incomes of its citizens," thus improving their quality of life. Although many authors view competitiveness and productivity as synonyms (Porter, 1990), these two terms are related but different, in that "productivity refers to the internal capability of an organization, while competitiveness refers to the relative position of an organization against its competitors" (Cho and Moon, 1998). Country risk—namely, the evaluation of the creditworthiness and the economic performance of a country—is regularly assessed in two magazines: *Euromoney* and *Institutional Investor*. Country risk may be viewed as a component rather than a substitute for competitiveness (as is innovation); both country risk and innovation are input variables in our study. In particular, because of recent pressures introduced by globalization, it is important to have a model for the analysis of a country's competitive position in the international market and the factors associated with a high outcome, and not simply an internal measure of a country's productivity. Competitiveness can be viewed as a nation's relative competitive positioning in the global market among other nations of similar economic development (Cho and Moon, 1998).

The factors for the competitiveness measure are based on the economic theories of exchange, supply and demand, unit total cost (or unit labor costs), and market behavior, and may be used to define competitiveness in one of the following ways (Artto, 1987):

1. Cost competitiveness: the most common measure, based on unit labor costs
2. Price competitiveness: measured relative to export prices
3. Non-price competitiveness: based on cost and price competitiveness measures

(continued)

Since 1982, the Institute for Management Development (IMD),[11] jointly with the World Economic Forum, produces the most extensive comparisons of nations' competitiveness via the annual publication of the World Competitiveness Yearbook (WCY). It develops a competitiveness score ranking a select group of country members of the Organization for Economic Co-operation and Development (OECD)[12] and newly industrialized countries based on 288 (for 1999) socioeconomic and political indicators, of which 42 were background information not used in the rankings. Surveys of 4,160 executives provided 1/3 of the 1999 data, while 2/3 of the data were taken from international and individual country statistics. The WCY provides a competitiveness score for each country by synthesizing all collected information into eight major factors: (1) Domestic Economy, (2) Internationalization, (3) Government, (4) Finance, (5) Infrastructure, (6) Management, (7) Science and Technology, and (8) People. The undisclosed methodology of the WCY is hard to guess, as Oral and Chabchoub (1996) found after detailed mathematical programming modeling by (sub)factor levels, suggesting the need for other statistical or mathematical programming techniques. The research described here focuses on the use of DM techniques to identify important factors associated with determining a country's competitiveness and the development of knowledge-based models to predict a country's competitiveness score (Zanakis and Becerra-Fernandez, 2004).

The 1999 WCY competitiveness score was used in this study as the dependant variable. The 1999 WCY was used to match the year available (late 1990s) for the data collected in the study for countries included in the 1999 WCY. Guided by the content of the eight factors in the WCY, the study used data collected from a variety of databases (World Bank, UN, World Factbook, IMD, etc.) data on 47 promising variables for 43 countries included in the 1999 WCY.

Table 5.6 presents a summary of the influential results in describing country competitiveness using each of the four methods of stepwise regression (SWR), weighted nonlinear programming (WNLP), neural networks (NN), and classification and regression trees (CART). The results of the study confirmed the findings presented in the WCY related to the profound impact that the technological revolution (computers, telecommunications, and the Internet) has had on the competitiveness of nations. These findings are not surprising, since the availability of effective telecommunication and Internet systems is considered a key asset in a nation's competitiveness. Nations seeking to improve their competitiveness will also need to consider making investments in IT-related education, since those skills will be necessary to operate the new technology infrastructure. Equally important, the study confirmed that the list of most significant predictors for country competitiveness didn't vary all that much across methods, although in this case the resulting models for SWR and NN displayed higher reliabilities. Interestingly enough, the results of the study matched pretty closely the results of the WCY report. For more information about this study, refer to the work by Zanakis and Becerra-Fernandez (2004).

---

[11] http://www02.imd.ch/

[12] Organisation for Economic Co-operation and Development, http://www.oecd.org/home/

Table 5.6 Predictors for Country Competitiveness According to Different Data Mining Algorithms

Summary of influential input variables

Abbreviation	Input variable	SWR	WNLP	NN	CART
COMP	Computers per 1,000 people	**X**	**X**	**X**	X
LB_STRUT	Labor force structure in population aged 15–64 (millions)	**X**	X	X	X
RISK	Composite international country risk rating (1–100 best)	**X**	**X**	**X**	
UAV	Uncertainty avoidance index	X	**X**	X	
BAL_TRAD or BAL_RANK	Balance of trade imports/exports or rank		**X**	X	**X**
PPP	Purchasing power parity GDP	X	X	X	
PROD	Overall productivity (US$ per person employed)	X	X	X	**X**
RD_EXP	Research and development expenditure (US$ millions)	X	X	X	
URBAN	Urban population percentage		X	X	X
IMPORT	Import of goods and services (% of GDP)	X	X	X	
MAS	Masculinity index	X	X	X	
DOM_SAV	Gross domestic savings (% of GDP)	X	X	X	
CO	Carbon dioxide damage (% of GDP)	X	X		
DOM_INV	Gross domestic investment (% of GDP)	X	X		
PRI_CON	Private consumption (% of GDP)		X		X
LAB_COST	Labor costs		X	X	
PHONE	Telephone lines per 1,000 people	X		X	
WAT_RUR	Access to water (% of rural population)	X	X		
INTELL	Intellectual property (patent applications filed)	X		X	
NAT_DEBT	Domestic debt (% of GDP)				X
LAB_PER	Labor force (% of population)				X
LETERACY	Adult literacy rates (% of population)		X		
INT_RAT	Real short term interest rates				X
BNK_RAT					X

(continued)

Table 5.6 (*continued*)

Summary of influential input variables

Abbreviation	Input variable	SWR	WNLP	NN	CART
	Ratio of bank liquid reserves to bank assets				
CAP_EXP	Capital expenditure (% of total expenditure)				X
SEW_URB	Access to sewage (% of urban population)			X	
EMRD	Employed engineers and scientists in R&D (% of employed in technology)	X			
SEW_RUR	Access to sewage (% of rural population)		X		
EXPORT	Export of goods and services (% of GDP)	X			

Note: Bold X indicates important variable in best model for each method.

▶ 5.8 EFFECTIVE IMPLEMENTATION OF BUSINESS ANALYTICS

Perhaps the late entry of DM into the realm of business, as compared to its use for scientific discovery, relates to business' prior inability to achieve a consolidated enterprise view of its underpinning data structures, which only came about recently through the proliferation of enterprise systems. Furthermore, many of these DM techniques require substantial computational power and access to memory to perform complex mathematical calculations such as matrix inversions, which until recently may not have been available at the desktop. Clearly, the advent of more powerful computers at our desktops and lower memory costs, as well as the proliferation of enterprise systems, data warehouses, and data marts, have enabled business to overcome these early barriers. In fact, according to the **Storage Law** (Fayyad and Uthurusamy, 2002) the capacity of digital data storage worldwide has doubled every nine months for the last decade, at twice the rate predicted by **Moore's Law** for the growth of computing power. However, many critics point out that this growing capacity has resulted in a phenomenon called "**data tombs**" (Fayyad and Uthurusamy, 2002), or **data stores** where data are deposited to "merely rest in peace," just in case one day the business may be able to analyze them. In many cases there is a strong possibility that these data will never be analyzed, and the promise to discover new business intelligence that could be used to improve services, profits, or products, will not be achieved.

Furthermore, even though many of the DM techniques have been used for over ten years for scientific applications, these same technologies have entered the business arena only in the past few years, often bundled with other software offerings such as CRM, sales force automation tools, and enterprise systems. Even in those cases, adequately implementing the DM models frequently requires in-depth knowledge of the algorithmic requirements, in addition to how to use the software itself and a deep understanding of the business context and the problem that needs to be resolved. Perhaps due to these reasons, the deployment of analytics in organizations is still considered an art that requires a number of actors to partake in the activity, including the project leader, the DM client, the DM analyst, the DM engineer, and the IT analyst (Jackson, 2002). The project leader has the overall responsibility for the management of the study. The DM client understands the business problem, but in general doesn't have the adequate technical skills to carry out the study. The DM analyst translates the business needs into technical requirements for the DM model. The DM engineer develops the DM model together with the DM client and analyst. The IT analyst provides access to hardware, software, and data needed to carry out the project. In some large projects, a number of DM analysts and engineers may be involved. Clearly, managing the number of actors involved in the study is indeed a challenging task that must be carefully coordinated by the project leader.

There are eight common mistakes that organizations seeking the deployment of DM technologies must avoid (Glaser and Stone, 2008; Griffin, 2006; King, 2007):

1. *User expectations are too high:* Avoid being overly impressed by a vendor's claims and slick outcome charts with high visual appeal. Installing the software is a far cry from delivering any form of operational intelligence. One way to get around this mistake is to work with vendors to use actual company data to produce all the functionality demos. This will give users a better idea of what can actually be accomplished with the application.

2. *Putting the right tools in the wrong hands:* DM tools bring about maximum business value when they are placed in the hands of front-line managers. DM models could also improve the productivity of executives, but managers are usually the ones who stand to gain the most in terms of improved decision-making ability and driving profitability throughout the organization. One example of this principle is Virgin Entertainment, which created a DM application for its store managers to calculate buyer conversion rates every 15 minutes and compare it across each of its 13 megastores, resulting in an overall 20% sales increase (King, 2007).

3. *Dishing up data that users need to figure out how to use:* Once the DM analysis points out certain outcomes, who will take charge? Often DM reports will point out performance problems, but offer no help in how to improve performance. If the analysis points out errors leading to claim denials or operating room turnover, who is accountable for fixing the problem? The organization needs to be ready to appoint someone responsible to ensure that mechanisms are in place to address those findings (Glaser and Stone, 2008).

4. *Training users only at the beginning of the project:* As DM users become increasingly versed in the capabilities of the technology, they will need to expand their knowledge. Furthermore, often new software versions will include more complex capabilities that could enhance the DM models in use throughout the organization.

5. *Going for a quick win rather than planning for the long haul:* Organizations are often so focused on the BI application that they don't take the care to develop a solid enterprise architecture. Properly defining the underpinning, high-quality data is the only viable path to reliable BI outcomes. If your organization resembles a land of 10,000 databases, take the time to carefully design and implement the enterprise architecture (Ross, Weil, and Robertson, 2006).

6. *The organization goes for the big bang:* This pitfall refers to the organization seeking to resolve all the master data issues in a single initiative. Perhaps one alternative is to begin with a pilot—say, with the customer data element—then gradually expand throughout the organization. A grandiose, big bang project is likely to exhaust its proponents before the project gains are accomplished. As with any other type of project, it's best to start with more manageable projects that bring quicker returns on investments.

7. *Data roles and governance are not adequately addressed:* One byproduct of engaging in a DM project is that it will bring to light issues around data quality. Data stewards as well as appropriate governance structures will need to be established to guarantee that the necessary operational changes do indeed take place.

8. *The organization fails to demonstrate value:* If the business value from implementing the DM model is not clear, the idea of adopting BI will quickly loose its luster in the organization. Just like in any other software project, return on investment must be frequently shown to ensure sustained executive commitment.

In Section 5.9 we describe how to integrate analytics into decision support.

▶ 5.9 REAL-TIME DECISION SUPPORT: INTEGRATING RESULTS WITH ACTION

Once the results from the analytics study are acceptable, it's necessary to put the results into action in order to drive business value. **Real-time decision support** refers to putting analytics into action. Many organizations may have had statistics around for years, but if they don't put them into action they will not achieve their strategic goals. For example, baseball, like most other sports, is full of statistics that describe the players' prowess, such as batting averages, strikeout/walk ratios, and many other stats that fascinate fans of all ages. However, in spite of the proliferation of descriptive statistics in baseball, these analytics were in many instances not used to win games, and coaches often relied on gut feeling to make the most critical decisions in the game. In *Moneyball* (Lewis, 2004), the author writes about how one team, the Oakland A's, was able to win in spite of owning a roster of lesser paid players due to their innovative use of analytics. The book describes how the team's general manager was able to overcome severe economic limitations by recruiting a team of players who nobody wanted, but who together were able to earn him the American League record for wins by putting to use an analyst methodology.

A necessary condition for real-time decision support is the integration of the analytics into other existing systems. Thus real-time decision support requires that the analytics process be both "interactive" as well as "invisible." Advocates of making analytics invisible argue that it is primarily concerned with making it easy, convenient, and practical to explore very large databases without years of training as data analysts (Fayyad and Uthurusamy, 2002). In fact, according to this view, this goal requires that the following challenges be addressed:

1. *Scaling analysis to large databases:* Current decision support techniques require that data sets be loaded into the computer's memory to be manipulated. This requirement offers a significant barrier when very large databases and data warehouses must be scanned to identify patterns.

2. *Scaling to high-dimensional data and models:* Typical statistical analysis studies require humans to formulate a model and then use techniques to validate the model via understanding how well the data fit the model. However, it may be increasingly difficult for humans to formulate models a priori based on a very large number of variables, which increasingly add dimension to the problem. Models that seek to understand customer behavior in retail or Web-based transactions may fall in this category. Current solutions require humans to formulate a lower dimensional abstraction of the model, which may be easier for them to understand.

3. *Automating the search:* DM studies typically require the researcher to enumerate the hypothesis under study a priori. In the future, analytics algorithms may be able to perform this work automatically.

4. *Finding patterns and models understandable and interesting to users:* In the past, DM projects focused on measures of accuracy (how well the model predicts the data) and utility (the benefit derived from the pattern, typically money saved). New benefit measures like understandability of the model and novelty of the results must also be developed. In addition, DM techniques are expected to incorporate the generation of meaningful reports resulting from the study.

Some of these current challenges are being resolved today through the increasing availability of vertically integrated decision-support solutions. For example, in CRM software, analytics operations are streamlined through the use of standardized models, which may include the most widely used data sources. For instance, a standardized model for financial services would most likely include customer demographics, channel, credit, and card usage, as well as information related to the promotion and actual response. In order to streamline the analytics process, the metadata[13] type for each table must be predefined (nominal, ordinal, interval, or continuous) while subsequent operations are based on this information including the pre-specification of algorithms that are appropriate to solve specific business problems (Parsa, 2000). For example, based on the results presented earlier in Table 5.5, a vertically integrated application to predict which loan customers are considered a good risk will automatically implement the C5.0 algorithm if the input variables are continuous and the outcome is discrete.

An additional limitation in the deployment of analytics today is the fact that the successful implementation of analytics at any organization may require the integration of disparate systems, since there are few plug-and-play solutions. All of these requirements translate into dollars, making many DM solutions sometimes quite expensive. As we said before, making the business case based on realistic estimations of ROI is essential for the success of the knowledge discovery initiative. Finally, effective application of the analytics to decision-support applications requires the solution to be seamlessly integrated into existing environments. This requirement makes the case for vendors, researchers, and practitioners to adopt standards like the CRISP-DM standard presented in Section 5.2.

Referring back to the Harrah's example, the firm developed a real-time decision-support model that included the customer data collection, analysis via their clustering algorithms, specialized marketing interventions via their loyalty program, and new customer response data collection to close the loop back to data. In the words of Harrah's then CIO (Boushy, 2003):

> "It's the idea of the active enterprise. We want to make our interactions with customers whether they take place on the phone, on our website, or at a slot machine more dynamic and proactive. We're taking what we've done with our data warehouse, operational systems, and our CRM environment and integrating them in an active environment, so when someone checks in to a hotel, we know exactly what needs to take place on the property to provide them with a seamless experience."

Only when analytics drive decisions does the organization realize competitive returns.

► 5.10 SUMMARY

In this chapter you learned about the DM process, the goals for the implementation of DM techniques in organizations, design considerations, and specific types of DM techniques. Business Intelligence in Practice features that describe the implementation of DM techniques were presented, each based on different methodologies, including the use of

---

[13] Metadata refers to data about data, and it is used to describe data, in particular unstructured data such as video, audio, documents, images, or e-mail files.

decision trees or rule induction as a knowledge-modeling tool. The second of these features illustrates the use of neural network DM application to predict load consumption. A case that describes how the three types of predictive techniques were used in the unusual context of predicting country competitiveness was also presented. We explained issues about deployment of the analytics capability—in particular, real-time decision support. Finally, we discussed practical insights into the pitfalls that should be avoided to ensure the successful deployment of DM.

▶ KEY TERMS

back-propagation
  algorithm
business analytics
business understanding
clustering techniques
CRISP-DM
customer profile
  exchange (CPEX)
data collection
data description
data mining (DM)
data preparation
data quality and
  verification

data stores
data tombs
data warehouse
decision tree
knowledge discovery in
  databases (KDD)
market basket analysis
Moore's Law
neural networks
operational CRM
paired leaf analysis
personal profile
potential predictors

predictive DM
  techniques
real-time decision
  support
rule induction algorithms
sample set
statistical DM techniques
Storage Law
target-sell
ten-fold (n-fold) cross
  validation
tree construction

▶ REVIEW QUESTIONS

1. Describe the six steps in the CRISP-DM process.

2. Why is understanding the business problem essential to knowledge discovery?

3. Describe the three types of DM techniques.

4. Describe some of the barriers to the use of data mining.

5. Describe the eight pitfalls that should be avoided when implementing DM applications.

▶ APPLICATION EXERCISES

Identify which DM techniques you would select to solve the following exercises. Explain your answer. Include a description of the input and output variables that would be relevant in each case. Note that more than one technique may apply for each of these problems.

1. Predict fraudulent credit card usage based on purchase patterns.

2. Predict instances of fraud related to Medicare claims.

3. Predict which customers are likely to leave their current long-distance provider.

4. Predict whether a person will renew his or her insurance policy.

5. Predict who will respond to a direct mail offer.

6. Predict that a generator is likely to fail.

7. Predict which specialized voice services a person is likely to purchase from the local telecommunications provider.

8. Identify factors resulting in product defects in a manufacturing environment.

9. Predict the expected revenue from a customer, based on a set of customer characteristics.

10. Predict the cost of hospitalization for different medical procedures.

11. Create customer segments in a marketing campaign.

12. Segment among university graduates those that are likely to renew their alumni membership.

13. Go to www.spss.com/clementine/ and download the Clementine tutorial and demonstration to review the data mining tool.

14. Go www.sas.com/ and compare the features of their Enterprise Miner tool with those of Clementine. Do they support the same data mining techniques?

15. Go to www.cognos.com and view a demo of how this tool is used for analytics. Compare the Cognos user interface and functionality with that of Clementine.

16. Go to the Wikipedia page on data mining and review any other two current data mining software vendors. How much overlap do you find among the functionality each of the packages offer?

▶ REFERENCES

Adelman, S., Moss, L., and Kelly, C. 2005. "What Is the Difference between Analytics and Data Mining?" *Information Management Online*, February 4. Last accessed from http://www.information-management.com/news/1019393-1.html on March 9, 2009.

Apte, C., and Hong, S. 1996. "Predicting Equity Returns from Securities Data." In Fayyad, U., Piatetsky-Shapiro, G., Smythand, P., and Uthurusamy, R. (Eds.) *Advances in Knowledge Discovery and Data Mining* (Menlo Park, Calif.: AAAI Press and Cambridge, Mass.: MIT Press), 542–560.

Apte, C., and Weiss, S. 1997. "Data Mining with Decision Trees and Decision Rules." *Future Generation Computer Systems*, 13, 197–210.

Artto, E. W. 1987. "Relative Total Costs–An Approach to Competitiveness Measurement of Industries." *Management International Review*, 27, 47–58.

Becerra-Fernandez, I., Zanakis, S., and Walczak, S. 2002. "Knowledge Discovery Techniques for Predicting Country Investment Risk." *Computers & Industrial Engineering*, 43(4), 787–800.

Becerra-Fernandez, I., Gonzalez, A., and Sabherwal, R. 2004. *Knowledge Management: Challenges, Solutions, and Technologies* (Upper Saddle River, N.J.: Prentice Hall).

Berry, M. and Linoff, G. 1997. *Data Mining Techniques for Marketing, Sales and Customer Support* (New York: John Wiley).

Berson, A., Smith, S., and Thearling, K. 2000. *Building Data Mining Applications for CRM* (New York: McGraw Hill).

Bishop, C. 1994. "Neural Networks and Their Applications." *Review of Scientific Instruments*, 65(6), 1803–1832.

Brachman, R. and Anand, T. 1996. *The Process of Knowledge Discovery in Databases: A Human-Central Approach. In Advances in Knowledge Discovery and Data Mining.* AAAI Press, Menlo Park, CA/MIT Press, Cambridge, MA, pp. 37–57.

Breiman, L., Friedman, J., Olshen, R., and Stone, C. 1984. *Classification and Regression Trees* (Boca Raton, Fla.: Chapman & Hall).

Boushy, J. 2003. "Head it Up at Harrah's." *CIO Magazine*, February 1. Accessed at http://www.cio.com/article/31695/Stanley_and_Boushy_Head_Up_IT_at_Harrah_s on March 9, 2009.

Chapman, P., Clinton, J., Kerber, R., Khabaza, T., Reinartz, T., Shearer, C., and Wirth, R. 2000. *CRISP-DM 1.0 Step-by-Step Data Mining Guide*. Technical report. SPSS.

Chen, H. 2001. *Knowledge Management Systems: A Text Mining Perspective*. (Tucson: The University of Arizona).

Cho, D. S., and Moon, H. C. 1998. "A Nation's International Competitiveness in Different Stages of Economic Development." *Advances in Competitiveness Research*, 1(6), 5–19.

Davenport, T. 2006. "Competing on Analytics." *Harvard Business Review*, January, 2–10.

Davenport, T., and Harris. 2007. *Competing on Analytics: The New Science of Winning*. (Cambridge, Mass.: Harvard Business School Press).

Edelstein, H. 2001. "Pan for Gold in the Clickstream." *Information Week*, March 12.

Fayyad, U., Piatetsky-Shapiro, G., Smyth, P., and Uthurusamy, R. 1996. "From Data Mining to Knowledge Discovery: An Overview." In Fayyad, U., Piatetsky-Shapiro, G., Smythand, P., and Uthurusamy, R. (Eds.) *Advances in Knowledge Discovery and Data Mining* (Menlo Park, Calif.: AAAI Press and Cambridge, Mass.: MIT Press), 1–33.

Fayyad, U., and Uthurusamy, R. 2002. "Evolving Data Mining into Solutions for Insights." *Communications of the ACM*, 45(8), 28–21.

Frakes, W., and Baeza-Yates, R. 1992. *Information Retrieval: DataStructures and Algorithms*. (Upper Saddle River, N.J.: Prentice Hall).

Fu, L. 1994. *Neural Networks in Computer Intelligence* (New York: McGraw-Hill).

Gilbert, A. 2002. "Smart Carts on a Roll at Safeway." CNET News, October 28. Accessed at http://news.cnet.com/2100-1017-963526.html on August 24, 2008.

Gonzalez, A. J., Daroszweski, S., and Hamilton, H. J. 1999. "Determining the Incremental Worth of Members of an Aggregate Set through Difference-Based Induction." *International Journal of Intelligent Systems*, 14(3).

Gordon, M. D., and Lindsay, R. K. 1986. "Toward Discovery Support Systems: A Replication, Re-examination, and Extension of Swanson's Work on Literature-Based Discovery of a Connection between Raynaud's and Fish Oil." *Journal of the American Society for Information Science* 47(2), 116–128.

Gray, P. 2007. "Bookisms: Strategy & Alignment, Analytics & Risk Reduction: Looking to the Future." *Information Systems Management*, 24(2), 201–207.

Gray, P., and Watson, H.J. 1998. *Decision Support in the Data Warehouse* (Upper Saddle River, N.J.: Prentice Hall).

Harvey, I. 2007. "Fighting Crime with Databases." *CBC News*, August 6.

Hartigan, J. A. 1975. *Clustering Algorithms* (New York: John Wiley).

Holbrook, K. 2004. "Adding Value with Analytics." *Strategic Finance*, 86(5), 40–43.

Hornik, K., Stinchcombe, M., and White, H. 1989. "Multilayer Feedforward Networks Are Universal Approximators." *Neural Networks*, 2(5), 359–366.

IBM. 2004. IBM and Safeway Create Enjoyable Grocery Shopping Experience. IBM White Papers, March 2. Accessed at http://www-1.ibm.com/industries/wireless/doc/content/bin/Safeway_1.pdf on August 24, 2008.

Jackson, J. 2002. "Data Mining: A Conceptual Overview." *Communications of the Association for Information Systems* 8, 267–296.

Jenkin, T. A. 2008a. "How IT Supports Knowledge Discovery and Learning Processes on the Web." In The Proceedings of the Hawaii International Conference on System Sciences (HICSS), Waikoloa.

Jenkin, T. A. 2008b. Using Information Technology to Support the Discovery of Novel Knowledge in Organizations. Thesis (PhD, Management), Queen's University.

Jenkin, T. A., Chan, Y. E., and Skillicorn, D. B. 2007. "Novel-Knowledge Discovery–Challenges and Design Theory." In The Proceedings of the Annual Conference of the Administrative Sciences Association of Canada, Ottawa.

Kohavi, R., Rothleder, N., and Simoudis, E. 2002. "Emerging Trends in Business Analytics." *Communications of the ACM*, 45(8), 45–45.

Kovalerchuck, B., Triantaphyllou, E., Ruiz, J., Torvik, V., and Vityaev, E. 2000. "The Reliability Issue of Computer-Aided Breast Cancer Diagnosis." *Journal of Computers and Biomedical Research*, 33(4), 296–313.

Lamont, J. 2002. "CRM around the World." *KM World*, 11(9), October.

Lawrence, R., Almasi, G., Kotlyar, V., Viveros, M., and Duri, S. 2001. "Personalization of Supermarket Product Recommendations." *Data Mining and Knowledge Discovery*, 5, 11–32.

Lee, H., Whang, W., Ahsan, K., Gordon, E., Faragalla, A., Jain, A., Moshin, A., and Shi, G. 2003. Harrah's Entertainment Inc.: Real-Time CRM in a Service Supply Chain. Stanford University case GS50.

Lewis, M. 2003. *Moneyball: The Art of Winning an Unfair Game* (New York: W. W. Norton).

Minsky, M. L. 1954. "Theory of Neural-Analog Reinforcement Systems and Its Application to the Brain-Model Problem." Doctoral dissertation, Princeton University.

McCulloch, W. S., and Pitts, W. 1943. "A Logical Calculus of the Ideas Immanent in Nervous Activity." *Bulletin of Mathematical Biophysics*, 5, 115–133.

Nonaka, I., and Takeuchi, H. 1995. *The Knowledge Creating Company* (New York: Oxford University Press).

Oral, M., and Chabchoub, H. 1996. "On the Methodology of the World Competitiveness Report." *European Journal of Operational Research*, 90(3), 514–535.

Parsa, I. 2000. "Data Mining: Middleware or Middleman." Panel on KDD Process Standards (Position Statement), Proceedings from the Sixth ACM SIGKDD International Conference on Knowledge Discovery and Data Mining, August.

Piatetsky-Shapiro, G., and Frawley, W. J.(Eds.). 1991. *Knowledge Discovery in Databases* (Menlo Park, Calif.: AAAI Press/MIT Press).

Porter, M. E. 1990. *The Competitive Advantage of Nations* (New York: The Free Press, Macmillan).

Ross, J., Weil, P., and Robertson, D. 2006. *Enterprise Architecture as Strategy Creating a Foundation for Business Execution* (Cambridge, Mass.: Harvard Business School Press).

Salton, G. 1989. *Automatic Text Processing* (New York: Addison-Wesley).

Swanson, D. R. 1986. "Fish Oil, Raynaud's Syndrome, and Undiscovered Public Knowledge." *Perspectives in Biology and Medicine*, 30(1), 7–18.

Swanson, D. R. 1990. "Medical Literature as a Potential Source of New Knowledge." *Bulletin of the Medical Library Association*, 78(1), 29–37.

Schwenk, H. 2002. "Real-Time CRM Analytics: The Future of BI?" *KM World*, 11(2), February.

Smith, K. A., and Gupta, J. N. D. 2000. "Neural Networks in Business: Techniques and Applications for the Operations Researcher." *Computers and Operations Research*, 27, 1023–1044.

SPSS. 2009. *IBM SPSS Modeler*. SPSS was acquired by IBM in October 2009. (Chicago: SPSS).

Stevens, L. 2001. "IT Sharpens Data Mining's Focus." *Internet Week*, August 6.

Two Crows. 1999. *Introduction to Data Mining and Knowledge Discovery* (Potomac, MD.: Two Crows Consulting).

U.S. President's Commission on Industrial Competitiveness. 1985. *Global Competition: The New Reality* (Washington, D. C.: U.S. Government Printing Office).

Vats, N., and Skillicorn, D. B. 2004a. *The ATHENS System for Novel Information Discovery*. Department of Computing and Information Science, Queen's University, Technical Report 2004-489.

Vats, N., and Skillicorn, D. B. 2004b. Information Discovery within Organizations Using the Athens System. Proceedings of the 2004 Conference of the Centre for Advanced Studies on Collaborative Research, Markham, Ontario, pp. 282–292.

Walczak, S. 2001. "An Empirical Analysis of Data Requirements for Financial Forecasting with Neural Networks." *Journal of Management Information Systems*, 17(4), 203–222.

Walczak, S. 1998. "Neural Network Models for a Resource Allocation Problem." *IEEE Transactions on Systems, Man and Cybernetics*, 28 B(2), 276–284.

Widrow, B., Rumelhart, D. E., and Lehr, M. A. 1994. "Neural Networks: Applications in Industry, Business and Science." *Communications of the ACM*, 37(3), 93–105.

Witten, I. 2000. Adaptive Text Mining: Inferring Structure from Sequences. Proceedings of the 34th Conference on Information Sciences and Systems. Princeton University, NJ. March 15–17.

Wong, B. K., Bodnovich, T. A., and Selvi, Y. 1997. "Neural Network Applications in Business: A Review and Analysis of the Literature (1988–1995)."Decision Support Systems 19, 301–320.

Zanakis, S., and Becerra-Fernandez, I. 2005. "Competitiveness of Nations: A Knowledge Discovery Examination." *European Journal of Operations Research*, 166(1), 185–211.

CHAPTER 6

TECHNOLOGIES ENABLING PRESENTATION

▶ 6.1 INTRODUCTION

In Chapter 5 we described the technologies that help us to create new insights from information and help us use insights to make better decisions. Specifically, we discussed data mining and business analytics and how they enable real-time decision support. The results of insight creation capability, whether they are intended to facilitate real-time decision making or learning, need to be provided to users in such a fashion that they can be best utilized. In this chapter we describe those technologies supporting the presentation capability of BI (based on the format, content, and role of the user) that will make BI more valuable to users.

Here we focus on how we disseminate the discovered insights to make BI more valuable to concerned users. The importance of the presentation capability of BI is that organizational members need technologies to support decision making that may have short-term impacts known as tactical decisions or longer term impacts known as strategic decisions. In the past, the organization's MIS department was responsible for creating reports that queried the different business applications in order to obtain the necessary information that would support managers with their tactical and strategic decisions. As could be expected, it would often take a long time to code the algorithms that would produce the necessary reports, so there was a considerable time lag between the time the managers identified the information needed to support their decisions and the time it would take to obtain this information. The beauty of BI and the technologies that enable the presentation of the resulting information, which we describe in this chapter, is that they provide the tools for decision makers to improve their decisions and present these results on the fly.

We start with a discussion of technologies that support tactical decision making, including *online analytical processing (OLAP)* in Section 6.2 and *visual analytics* in Section 6.3. In addition, *performance dashboards*, discussed in Section 6.4, provide presentation capabilities to multiple indicators, originating from myriad internal and external sources of information, in a rich, colorful, and visual way. Similarly, *scorecards*—in particular, *balanced scorecards* discussed in Section 6.5—provide the needed support to strategic decision making by providing presentation capability to outcomes compared to a specific target. All of these technologies serve important roles within the organization—in particular, they provide those insights required to support adequate corporate *IT governance*, discussed in Section 6.7, and corporate *performance management*, presented in Section 6.8.

We start with a discussion of online analytical processing.

▶ 6.2 ONLINE ANALYTICAL PROCESSING

Transactional databases like those in the ERP systems described in Section 3.2 are accessed by **online transaction processing (OLTP)** applications, in particular to attend to user requests—for example, to input information into the transaction system. Similarly, **online analytical processing (OLAP)** refers to technology that enables the user to interact and present the data in the data warehouse as described in Section 3.3, usually integrating graphical tools. OLAP is used essentially to query the DW, and the response to these complex queries is precalculated by the software in order to respond to these requests rapidly (Wrembel and Koncilia 2007). The term OLAP was coined by Edgar Codd (1970), who described in this seminal paper most of the ideas that would come to define an entire industry—the field of relational database management.

OLAP supports the presentation of data in a multidimensional format called a **cube**, which essentially enables the DW data to be viewed across a set of **dimensions**, which serve to categorize the numeric facts in the DW known as the **measures**. For example, a spreadsheet is a two-dimensional array that may be used to collect customer purchases (rows), which may include a combination of product lines (columns). Measures are the numbers the users will be analyzing—for example, the total number of customer purchases or the amount of money customers spent. Dimensions are used to summarize the data and how users are likely to want to view these data—for example, by region, customer market segment, product line, or time (month, quarter, year). Dimensions are organized as hierarchies (like day, month, quarter, year, etc.), which are useful for drilling down or rolling up when analyzing the data.

One of the features of OLAP is that it allows organizing the data into *cubes*. For example, we could organize the customer yearly purchases across the past five years, forming a data cube, where the variable year is the third dimension for the data cube. Then the measures in the data cube can be manipulated to summarize or aggregate the values across any of these three dimensions (customer purchases, quarter, year), much like you manipulate the cells (tiny cubes, called cubies, or cubelets) that make up each of the faces in a Rubik's cube. OLAP offers the ability to have more than three dimensions; therefore the word hypercube is often used to describe this specific functionality.

When an analyst manipulates the data cube in various ways, he or she is known to **pivot** a table in the cube. A pivot table is a data summarization tool—for

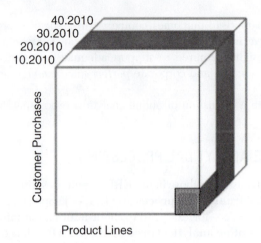

40.2010
30.2010
20.2010
10.2010

Customer Purchases

Product Lines

FIGURE 6.1 OLAP Cube, with Data Slice and Dice

example, in a spreadsheet—that allows an analyst to see the data from different angles. An analyst may want to pivot or view the data in various ways. For example, customer purchase data may be viewed by region, with revenues down the page and products across the page for a specific quarter. Alternatively, the table may be pivoted or reoriented, to display revenue down the page and periods across for a specific product. In addition, OLAP cubes enable *slicing* and *dicing* the data, which is basically allowing users to view the data from any of the dimensions represented in the cube, either by presenting only a slice of data—say, for a particular year—or a dice of the data—for example, only a particular customer segment. Figure 6.1 shows an OLAP cube for the customer purchase data described above, a slice of data for the third quarter of 2010, and dice of the data representing a customer segment for the first two quarters of 2010.

While the aforementioned example oversimplifies the use of OLAP, the sheer volume of electronic commerce clickstream data requires that many of these techniques be automated in order to find patterns in the data. For example, a business analyst may need to create new knowledge from millions of clickstream records generated by customer traffic to a Web site each day, aggregated to customer records with hundreds of attributes (Kohavi, Rothleder, and Simoudis, 2002). Without a presentation infrastructure like OLAP, business analysts would need to rely on data analysts to perform the data mining and extract the information from the results so that it can in fact aid decision making. The relevance of OLAP is that it allows business analysts to manipulate the analytic results across the different dimensions, so that the results of the analysis can quickly be reflected into business actions. In this way, analytics is able to make an impact in all areas of business, including sales, marketing, supply chain, and finance, as we described in Chapter 5.

Ideally, business users should be able to analyze and present the newly discovered knowledge. In the past, a gap could be observed between the analytics and the business. This gap was characterized by challenges that included the fact that most analytic tools are designed for quantitative analysts and not for the broader base of business users, who need the output translated into the language and visualizations appropriate for their business needs (Kohavi et al., 2002). We discuss how visualization can support BI in Section 6.3.

▶ 6.3 VISUAL ANALYTICS

Visual analytics (which is related to the terms data visualization, information visualization, scientific visualization, and knowledge visualization) refers to the use of computer graphics to create a visual representation of large collections of information. Visual analytics has been defined as "the science of analytical reasoning facilitated by visual interfaces . . . to synthesize information and derive insights from massive, dynamic, ambiguous, and often conflicting data; detect the expected and discover the unexpected, provide timely, defensible, and understandable assessments; and communicate assessments effectively for action" (Thomas and Cook, 2005, p. 4). In general, the purpose of visualization is to use visual tools and techniques to combine information, in particular large amounts of information, in a way that will enable knowledge discovery.

Why is visualization important? It is important because seeing patterns among the raw data may require years of training and expertise, something that computer graphics can certainly expedite. Consider as an example Dr. Jones, a hurricane researcher whose research involves the development of hurricane models. Thirty years ago, when the field of computer graphics was in its infancy, Dr. Jones would run his models in Fortran language, which produced a three-inch-thick printout of rows and columns that described the predicted hurricane trajectory in the form of u (horizontal) and v (vertical) wind components. To Dr. Jones, an expert meteorologist, the rows and columns depicted the hurricane trajectory, which he could certainly "see" in the data, but to his student assistant (one of the authors) the rows and columns seemed like an endless and boring list of very small numbers! Clearly, visual analytics would have helped the student assistant see the same hurricane trajectory that is communicated to TV viewers today as they prepare for the next approaching hurricane—this is the power of visualization. Visualization helps users see patterns in the data that otherwise would seem like a meaningless collection of text or numbers.

Although the area of visual analytics has seen a huge impetus in terms of its capabilities in the last thirty years, additional research is still needed to overcome some of the technical challenges the field is currently facing. Business Intelligence in Practice 6.1 describes how advancement in visual analytics is critical to the safety of our nation and the world.

Business Intelligence in Practice 6.1: The Need for Visual Analytics in Emergency Response

The need to accelerate the visual analytics research agenda is no more obvious than in the effort to counter future terrorist attacks in the United States and around the globe, which defines the charter of the National Visualization and Analytics Center[1], located at the Pacific Northwest National Lab and supporting the U.S. Dept. of Homeland Security. This research agenda presents recommendations to advance the state of the art in the major visual analytics research areas (Thomas and Cook, 2005, p. 4), which are as follows:

1. *The science of analytical reasoning* provides the reasoning framework required to build both strategic and tactical visual analytics technologies for threat analysis, prevention, and response. The goal is to develop tools that maximize our ability to perceive, understand, and reason about complex and dynamic data and situations. In short, these tools are intended to facilitate the quality of the analysts' decision making while minimizing their investment of time, including effective ways to support large-scale collaboration and teamwork.

2. *Visual representation and interaction technologies* provide the mechanism for allowing users to see and understand large volumes of information at once, facilitating the process of analytical reasoning. The issue at hand here is for interaction theory to consider the time constraints imposed by urgent analytical tasks. Also, this recommendation is concerned with the design and creation of reusable components and tools that address all types of data in order for first responders to take better actions.

3. *Data representations and transformations* relates to the fact that the quality of visualization is most directly affected by the quality of the data representation that underlies it. Data transformation refers to converting data into more meaningful forms. For example, as we described in Section 3.2, using a cube to represent data in the DW is a transformation. Also, text data from Web-based transactions may need to be transformed into numeric data before they are properly analyzed. Finally, adding metadata to videos or pictures may improve the cognitive value the enterprise can gain from unstructured data types. This recommendation is concerned with augmenting the analytical value of information by highlighting what's interesting within the data.

4. *Production, presentation, and dissemination* involve reducing the time it takes to create material that summarizes the analytical results

(continued)

[1] www.pnl.gov/agenda.stm

(production), in a way that helps the audience understand the results (presentation) to be disseminated with their audience (dissemination). The information may need to be described according to the context of the audience who will use it, whether first-responders or the public at large.

Finally, the resulting approaches, algorithms, and tools that are the outcome of these research activities must be developed on a common evaluation infrastructure platform, which addresses issues around privacy and security and is based on an interoperable architecture. Only then can visual analytics help us safeguard our nation.

In addition, visual analytics can help with the day-to-day planning and operations of field sales representatives, as illustrated in Business Intelligence in Practice 6.2.

Business Intelligence in Practice 6.2: Improving Sales Performance via Visual Business Intelligence

Field sales representatives' organizational structures—for example, for those working in pharmaceutical and health care businesses—often must be reorganized in order to respond to business resource constraints (Morrison, 2006). Sales structures are often organized into territories, which may be defined by the rep's home location, established networks, and so on. Visual information mapping tools are helpful in building these sales structures.

Using color coding to map the sales territories offers several advantages: it allows managers to see whether the territories cover the same geographic size and whether there are split territories, meaning that representatives must travel through another rep's territory to reach their own clients. Furthermore, it can improve overall restructuring changes by allowing supervisors to visualize how a territory may be alternatively managed if its rep leaves the organization.

Visual information mapping tools may also allow combining and integrating different values associated with operational parameters to create "balanced" territories. In addition, visual maps may also provide an excellent medium to communicate new sales structures to the field representatives. Other applications in the pharmaceutical industry may include cluster analysis for clinical trials, development of targeted marketing campaigns, and illustration of the presence of disease trends, thus improving business performance through visual analysis.

In Section 6.4, we describe performance dashboards.

► 6.4 PERFORMANCE DASHBOARDS

As we described in Chapter 2, the concept of the performance dashboard is not new, since it's based on the earlier use of executive information systems and the results of significant research on human-computer interfaces, especially on the relative benefits of using tables and graphs to display information. Digital dashboards display BI insights in various ways (tables, charts, graphs, maps, colors, and speedometers), in a customizable interface and a navigable layout, so that users can interactively obtain pertinent information about the current situation. **Performance dashboards** are designed to be similar to car dashboards, providing multiple indicators, originating from many internal and external sources of information, in a rich, colorful, and visual way. A performance dashboard serves as an " 'organization magnifying glass'—something that focuses the work of employees so everyone is going in the same direction . . . [it] helps them clearly and concisely communicate key strategies and goals to all employees on a personal basis every day . . . . It should measure performance, reward positive contributions and align efforts so that workers in every group and level of the organization are marching together toward the same destination" (Eckerson, 2005). In a later section we explore how dashboards and scorecards can help an organization effectively manage its IT governance process and the overall organization's performance.

Performance dashboards are not the exclusive purview of managers and executives, as increasingly front-line employees may utilize operational dashboards, like those utilized by call center personnel. So while an executive may be interested in viewing financial, customer, and operational metrics aggregated for a month or quarter, a call center agent may see metrics that relate to the individual customer calling in, including their sales and product lines per hour (Howson, 2008). Figure 6.2 depicts the use of a performance dashboard across the different functional business areas of forecasting, inventory, production, and sales, and also how these metrics can be used to influence different types of advertising campaigns.

In order for a performance dashboard to accomplish its goal of helping improve organizational performance, it must meet three basic characteristics, known as the "Three Threes" (Eckerson, 2006):

1. *Three applications*: It seamlessly integrates a monitoring application, an analysis application, and a management application.

2. *Three layers*: It integrates a monitoring layer, an analysis layer, and a detailed information layer, allowing users to drill down to the root cause of a problem with increasingly detailed views as users dig into a specific problem.

3. *Three types*: It can support operational, tactical, or strategic decision making, as we will see later.

The difference between performance dashboards and scorecards is that a dashboard presents multiple numbers in various ways, whereas a scorecard

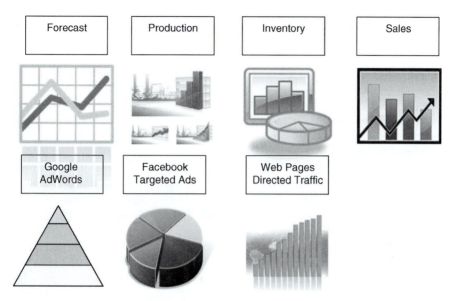

FIGURE 6.2 Performance Dashboard

compares a given outcome metric with a target, highlighting perhaps in red when a specific metric falls below the target while showing perhaps in green all the metrics that meet their targets. Real-time dashboards are further illustrated in the case study described in Section 6.8. In Section 6.5 we describe scorecards and one specific type of strategic scorecard known as the balanced scorecard.

▶ 6.5 BALANCED SCORECARDS

As we described in Section 6.4, a scorecard is also a graphical display similar to a dashboard but different in nature. Whereas dashboards graphically display various sources of information, scorecards monitor and show performance by focusing on certain outcome metrics and comparing them to a target, threshold, or forecast (Howson, 2007). Furthermore, as we described before, scorecards are typically used to monitor tactical and strategic goals, whereas dashboards may be more appropriate for operational and tactical metrics. One of the most commonly used managerial approaches for scorecards is the **balanced scorecard**, which focuses on four organizational perspectives: financial, customer, internal business process, and learning and growth.

The balanced scorecard is an overall approach for organizational assessment developed by Kaplan and Norton (1996), which provides a more comprehensive view of the firm's competitiveness that goes beyond the traditional financial measurements. The goal of the balanced scorecard is to include in the firm's assessment additional measures that are required for future growth and will eventually translate to financial gains. In this way, the balanced scorecard captures measures that may translate to both short-term and long-term success of the organization.

The original purpose of the balanced scorecard was to provide a framework for organizations to quantify the intangible assets of an organization. Typically, firms would be focused on measuring performance based on financial metrics, which are the utmost definition of a firm's success. In addition, many organizations would also measure customer satisfaction, retention, and growth, which have been correlated to financial success. Both financial and customer metrics are lagging indicators in the sense that they measure past performance. The balanced scorecard also includes two leading indicators: internal processes and intangible assets. Internal processes refer to the internal operations of the organization, in the sense of the efficiency and effectiveness of their business processes. Finally, intangible assets are considered to be the "source of sustainable value creation . . . describe how the people, technology, and organization climate combine to support the strategy. Improvements in learning and growth measures are lead indicators for internal processes, customer, and financial performance" (Kaplan and Norton, 2004, p. 10). Figure 6.3 depicts the balanced scorecard indicators grouped according to the four organizational perspectives of financial, customer, internal business process, and learning and growth, and it illustrates the interactions among the four metric structures.

As an illustration of one organization's balanced scorecard, Table 6.1 depicts the balanced scorecard for the College of Business Administration (CBA) at Florida International University (FIU).[2] The balanced scorecard identifies both the vision and mission statements of the college, as well as the key metrics that will be used to assess past performance, in terms of meeting both financial objectives as well as student learning objectives at both the undergraduate and graduate levels. The scorecard also measures value creation for the organization in terms of intangible assets, such as how the faculty supports the organization's strategy through their contributions to research and participation on boards. Finally, improvements in learning and growth are measured, for example, through metrics on the professional development of both faculty and staff.

Organizations can use the balanced scorecard as a means to link their long-term strategic objectives with their short-term actions through four management processes (Kaplan and Norton, 1996):

1. *Translating the vision*: The balanced scorecard can help business leaders build consensus around the firm's vision and business strategy to express an integrated set of objectives and measures.

2. *Communicating and linking*: The balanced scorecard lets business leaders communicate their business strategy across all levels of the organization,

[2] The authors wish to acknowledge Dean Joyce Elam of Florida International University College of Business Administration for contributing the balanced scorecard to this section.

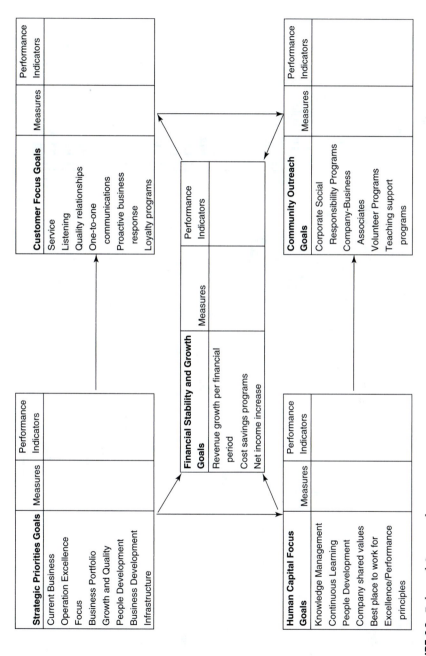

FIGURE 6.3 Balanced Scorecard

Table 6.1 FIU College of Business Administration Balanced Scorecard 2008–2009

Vision Statement

Our vision is to be internationally-recognized for providing a high-quality, technology-enabled educational experience rooted in our Miami location and focused on the unique requirements of doing business in a global and interconnected market.

Core Values

Excellence We pursue excellence in all we do and nurture this pursuit in others.

Ethics We are committed to doing the right thing in both our words and deeds.

Professionalism We hold ourselves to the highest standards of expertise and of professional conduct.

Innovation We embrace change, uncommon thinking, creativity, and the entrepreneurial spirit.

Collegiality In working together, we respect each other and welcome diverse viewpoints.

Mission Statement

Our mission is to create enduring educational value for our students, for our alumni, and for the business, professional, and academic communities we serve:

- **For our students** whom we prepare to succeed in a rapidly changing, technology-driven global business environment;

Goals and Objectives

Strategic Priorities

1. **Maintenance of Accreditation**

2. **Focus** – Build excellence and international recognition through investments in programs and faculty in the areas of international business, entrepreneurship, and professional services – accounting, finance, real estate, and insurance.

3. **Program Portfolio** – Continually evaluate portfolios of programs to ensure excellence in teaching and learning and market need.

4. **Growth and Quality** – Increase quality of undergraduate students while maintaining current enrollment, grow graduate enrollment by 50% over next five years while increasing quality of admitted students.

5. **Faculty** – Recruit, develop and support an outstanding faculty.

6. **Funding** – Acquire needed funds to support the college's mission.

7. **Space** – Complete construction of Phase II of the Business School Complex.

Strategic Initiatives 2008–2009

1. **Maintenance of Accreditation** Implement review recommendations.

2. **Undergraduate Programs** Continue implementation of *Assurance of Learning System* and enhanced undergraduate career services.

3. **Graduate Programs** Complete scheduled program reviews and implement recommended changes.

Key Metrics

Undergraduate Programs

L1. Assurance of Learning Outcomes
L2. Use and Manage Technology Outcome
L3. Quality of Students
L4. Student Recognitions
L5. Head Count – # of Graduates
L6. FTE enrollment – % of Enrollment Targets Met
L7. Placement – Satisfaction and Outcomes
L8. Satisfaction with Advising
L9. Quality of Instruction
L10. Expectations Met
L11. Rankings

Graduate Programs

L12. Assurance of Learning
L13. Quality of Students
L14. FTE enrollment – % Enrollment Target Met
L15. Placement – Satisfaction and Outcomes
L16. Expectations Met
L17. Rankings

R1. Publications in Premier Journals
R2. Citations in Social Service Index
R3. Editorial Board Membership
R4. Recognition and Awards

- **For our alumni** to whom we provide opportunities for continuing professional development and a legacy that appreciates as our excellence grows;
- **For the business and professional communities** to whom we offer knowledgeable graduates, educational programs, research, and collaborative projects;
- **For the academic community** to whom we bring new knowledge by creating an environment that nurtures high-quality research and the development of future scholars.

1. **Faculty** Recruit replacements for faculty members who resign or retire and recruit new incremental faculty members.
2. **External Relations** Expand membership on our advisory boards and our community involvement.
3. **External Visibility** Maintain rankings.
4. **Internal Processes** Maintain technology for new School of Business Complex.
5. **Revenue Generation** Secure private funding for faculty support, student support, and the building; grow executive and professional education program; and plan for new value-added programs.

Core Competencies and Definition of Metrics

(L)earning, Instruction, and Student Services Provide educational programs and learning experiences that prepare individuals to make sustained contributions to organizations and society in a global environment and are recognized for excellence. Deliver outstanding student services.

(R)esearch and Scholarship Identify and address important business and economic issues through discovery, application, and dissemination of knowledge.

(S)ervice and Outreach Offer expertise to government agencies, business and professional organizations, and others, to promote economic development and to provide value-added educational and professional programs.

(E)xternal Relations and Development Enhance opportunities for mutually beneficial collaboration between the College and its constituents and grow private investments in the College.

(P)eople Attract, develop, and retain highly qualified faculty and staff.

(I)nternal Operations Cultivate an efficient and effective operation that enables faculty and staff to achieve the mission of the College.

S1. Revenues from EPE Programs
S2. Participation on Boards

E1. Corporate Community Participating in Advisory Boards
E2. Membership in Business Alumni Chapter
E3. New Private and Corporate Donations

P1. Adequacy and Quality of Faculty
P2. Professional Development Support of Faculty and Staff

I1. Technology Availability and Quality
I2. User Satisfaction and Use of Technology Resources

aligning both individual and departmental objectives to the overall firm's strategy.

3. Business planning: The balanced scorecard enables the coordination of diverse initiatives across the firm using a common set of long-term strategic objectives.

4. Feedback and learning: The scorecard allows the organization to identify where it may be falling short according to the short-term results from the perspective of the financial, customer, internal processes, and learning; then the organization can proceed to create learning opportunities strategically targeted to meet those deficiencies.

For intangible assets (which consist of human capital, information capital, and organizational capital) to create value, they must be aligned with the organization's strategy. Furthermore, these intangible assets must be integrated with the organization's functions and not be structured in a silo or specialization. This means that only organizations that align and integrate their intangible assets investments, which include BI initiatives with their business strategy, are able to create value from their intangible assets. Few organizations are successful in the alignment and integration of their intangible assets. In one research study, only about one-third of the firms interviewed were able to report strong alignment of both the human resources and information technology priorities with the enterprise strategy (Kaplan and Norton, 2004).

Although the balanced scorecard is an effective way for an organization to articulate its tactical and strategic goals, it is often not sufficient to achieve alignment of the IT function with the overall organizational objectives. IT alignment can only be accomplished through effective IT governance. Balanced scorecards and IT governance are interrelated subjects, as it's often through the balanced scorecard that the organization can observe how effective its IT governance is. Because of the importance of the topic of IT governance and its significance for the organization to achieve its objectives, we discuss this subject in Section 6.6.

▶ 6.6 IT GOVERNANCE

IT governance refers to "specifying the decision rights and accountability framework to encourage desirable behavior in the use of IT (Weill and Ross, 2004). The goal of IT governance is to determine who makes the key IT decisions in the organization and how. Just as the CFO does not sign every payment authorization at the firm, senior management cannot be accountable for all the IT-related decisions that are made in the organization. It is important to set up a mechanism for IT governance that will encourage desirable behaviors in using IT. A well-designed IT governance ensures that these decisions are consistent with the strategy of the organization.

Research has shown that top-performing firms generate up to 40% higher return on IT investment than their competition (Weill and Broadbent, 1998). Research has also shown that top-performing firms designed governance structures linked to performance measures on which they excelled. These performance measures were seen to "harmonize" business objectives and provide a governance approach, mechanisms, and performance goals and metrics for the organization (Weill and Ross, 2004). This leads to the conclusion that the "effective IT governance is the single most important predictor of value an organization generates from IT" (Weill and Ross, 2004, p. 4).

How exactly does an organization design effective IT governance? Effective IT governance must address three questions: what decisions to make, who should make the decisions, and how to make and monitor the decisions. In answering the first question, five interrelated IT decisions must be addressed (Weill and Ross, 2004):

1. *IT Principles:* These are a related set of high-level statements about how IT is used in business. In order to define their IT principles, organizations are urged to draft a short list of business principles that define their business strategy (e.g., leverage economies of scale, standardize processes and technologies where appropriate), which lead to a set of IT principles (e. g., benchmarked lowest total cost of ownership, architectural integrity). IT principles serve both as an education tool about IT strategy and as a guide to investment decisions.

2. *IT Architecture:* This refers to the "organizing logic for data, applications and infrastructure, captured in a set of policies, relationships, and technical choices to achieve desired business and technical standardization and integration" (Weill and Ross, 2004, p. 30). As we described in Section 3.3, the enterprise architecture depends on the level of standardization and integration for data, applications, and infrastructure that is appropriate for the organization.

3. *IT Infrastructure:* This refers to the foundation of the planned technical and human IT capability that is available to the business as shared services. Investing in the right infrastructure will ensure the business is agile enough to support future digitized business processes. IT infrastructure includes the technology components (computers, database software, operating systems), the human infrastructure (knowledge, skills, standards), shared services that don't change over time, and shared and standard applications that change less regularly (accounting, budgeting, HR).

4. *Business Applications Needs:* These include the fast-changing business applications, such as insurance claim processing, loan applications, or a customer complaints support system. Business applications typically have to respond to two conflicting goals: creativity (finding new ways to deliver customer value) and discipline (ensuring that applications leverage the existing enterprise architecture).

5. *IT Investment and Prioritization:* These involve how the organization decides how much to spend on IT, what to spend it on, and ensuring that the enterprise's investments are aligned with its strategic priorities. Business leaders must be provided with incentives to sacrifice their respective unit needs for the benefit of the enterprise.

In terms of allocating decision rights, the more business-oriented IT decisions (principles, business application needs, and investment) will typically involve a governance model that involves more "federal" structures, such as committees, cross-functional teams, and such, while technical decisions rest more within the purview of technical decision makers with input from the rest of the business units. There are numerous mechanisms for implementing IT governance, which include various decision-making structures that span executive committees, process teams with IT members, and capital approval committees. In addition, alignment processes serve as management techniques for securing the enterprise-wide involvement in the effective management and use of IT. Finally, an important aspect of governance is the communications mechanisms that are used to share within the organization the outcomes of key IT governance decisions. In Business Intelligence in Practice 6.3, we explore how some organizations are demonstrating IT value through their implementation of the balanced scorecard.

Business Intelligence in Practice 6.3: Achieving IT Value through Balanced Scorecards

Implementing the use of balanced scorecards in the organization requires CIOs to take important steps to ensure their success, including preparing the organization for change, devising the right metrics, getting buy-in from employees at all levels, and following through the implementation plan to its completion (Berkman, 2002). Preparing the organization for change includes identifying four or five value drivers that are specific to the organization: for example, financial performance, customer service, efficient business processes, innovation, and learning and growth. Armed with the right metrics, the company's successful progress toward its organizational goals can be tracked. A balanced scorecard approach requires using it within IT to promote alignment of new strategically aligned technology initiatives, and eliminating those that contribute little or no strategic value. Also, the organization should appoint a champion, someone who typically oversees the IT budget, who will be accountable for the balanced scorecard implementation within the IT department. Getting employee buy-in requires extensive training across the organization, and redefining jobs in terms of how they fit within the strategic business goals.

(continued)

> Companies that have been able to capitalize on their successful balanced scorecard deployments include Exxon Mobil, who leaped from 1993 to 1995 from last to first in profitability among its industry peers. Also, Cigna Insurance went from losing $1 million a day in 1993 to the most profitable top quartile within its industry in 1995 (Berkman, 2002).

What is the role of BI in IT governance? BI can provide the necessary measurements to any good governance design. Business intelligence can also be used to design the performance measures that will be used to monitor the effectiveness of IT governance. Figure 6.4 illustrates the role of BI in IT governance. We discuss the impact of BI on corporate performance in Section 6.7.

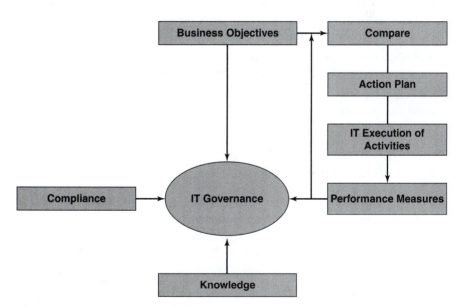

FIGURE 6.4 The Role of BI in IT Governance.
(Source: Adapted from Basco et al., 2005, and COBIT, 2000)

► 6.7 IMPACT OF BUSINESS INTELLIGENCE ON CORPORATE PERFORMANCE

As we described above in the application to IT governance, both performance dashboards and balanced scorecards can be instrumental in helping organizations communicate their strategic objectives, by providing the infrastructure for members of the organization to measure, monitor, and manage the key activities and processes that the organization must pursue in order to meet its goals, or its **key performance**

indicators (KPIs). For a manufacturing manager, for example, the KPIs may include performance measures related to production capacity, and sales forecasts that become inputs for the manager's production schedules, inventory management, operational costs, and profitability levels. For a call center manager, KPIs may include customer churn ratios, customer satisfaction, and customer loyalty.

The goal of using BI to develop KPIs is to provide decision makers with the following capabilities (Whiting, 2006):

1. *Detect* events within a process, such as flagging potentially fraudulent activities in a procurement process.

2. *Prompt* managers to take corrective action—for example, substituting a manufacturing component that may be out of stock by another similar component from another vendor.

3. *Analyze data* in real time, such as in using the current currency values or manufacturing delays to define the best options when deciding where to provision a manufacturing component in order to minimize costs.

4. *Collect data* about the operational processes themselves, for the continuous improvement of the organization's business processes.

When designing performance dashboards for the organization, it's important to avoid ten common mistakes (Eckerson, 2006):

1. Failing to apply the "Three Threes" described in Section 6.4: three applications, three layers, and three types.

2. Overrating the importance of dashboards and scorecards: The purpose of scorecards and dashboards is the same: to convey critical performance information at a glance. The purpose of the performance dashboard system (described in Section 6.4) is to display the status of key performance indicators, with dashboards monitoring operational processes and balanced scorecard dashboards (described in Section 6.5) typically monitoring the progress of tactical and strategic indicators.

3. Failing to deliver three applications:

   i. Access: Monitoring critical information at a glance, using data that are both timely and relevant, and presenting the information via graphical interfaces;

   ii. Analyze: Allowing users to analyze the performance data at different levels of detail in order to get to the root cause of the performance issue at hand; and

   iii. Management: Allowing users the opportunity to communicate the current situation and act on information.

4. Failing to deliver three layers: That is, not presenting the layers of information necessary to get to the root cause of a performance issue at hand. Users typically start looking at performance indicators at a high level, and drill

down to continue to explore the details of the issue. At the bottom level, performance dashboards present a transactional view of the operational data. The middle layer is usually supported by OLAP and interactive reports that present a multidimensional view of the metrics. Finally, the top layer is a graphical summarized view, which is supported by dashboards, scorecards, and portals that are used to monitor KPIs using graphics, text, and numbers.

5. Failing to create the right type of performance dashboard: Dashboards are used to track the following:

   i. Operational metrics, using real-time or "right-time" data to primarily monitor metrics;

   ii. Tactical metrics, to primarily analyze the progress of departmental projects and processes; and

   iii. Strategic metrics, to manage primarily according to strategic objectives.

6. Falling prey to glitz: Dashboards are useless without an adequate under-pinning information infrastructure. Glitzy interfaces could minimize the impact of the dashboard. As a rule or thumb, a maximum of seven KPIs should be presented together.

7. Building a dashboard with a lightweight architecture: A performance dashboard must be build on a robust enterprise architecture, as described in Section 3.4, leading to an agile BI environment that may include information sources from multiple diverse systems.

8. Delivering real-time data without context: In order for dashboards to be effective they must provide sufficient context for users to make accurate and efficient decisions. Often, users must see how the metric has progressed over time to understand when it's appropriate to take action, which may require a significant data integration effort.

9. Failing to design effective KPIs: A KPI measures business performance with respect to a set of business goals. In order to be effective, KPIs must be designed so they are aligned with strategic objectives, are easy to understand, predict future performance, and support other KPIs.

10. Failing to apply KPIs correctly: Finally, in order to effect change, organizations must assign ownership to an individual for each KPI, empower the individual accountable for the KPI, ensure that the organization stands behind the importance of the metric, and continuously review the KPI over time.

In short, BI can support the implementation of dashboards and scorecards for the creation of KPIs that enable the organization to:

1. Communicate and refine its business strategy—through the use of tools like the balanced scorecard for management.

2. Increase visibility of the organization's strategic goals—through the use of scorecards and performance dashboards for effective IT governance.

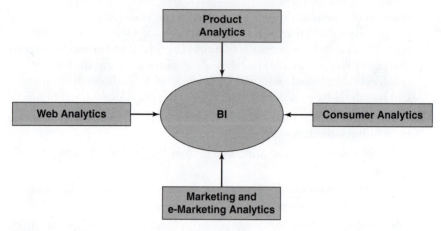

FIGURE 6.5 Impact of BI on Corporate Performance

3. Increase enterprise-wide coordination of activities that together contribute to the firm's competitiveness, as demonstrated by the financial success achieved by those organizations with an effective IT governance.

4. Increase motivation and morale and empower users—by giving knowledge workers the appropriate tools to empower them to work proactively and make better decisions through the use of relevant actionable information.

5. Provide a consistent view of the business—in short, the right information given to the right decision maker at the right time translates into effective and optimized decisions, enhanced efficiency, and increased bottom-line results.

This is in summary the essence of BI, and Figure 6.5 depicts the central role that BI plays on corporate performance. In Section 6.8 we present a case study on how one organization, Western Digital Corporation, built a vigilant information system using BI to revamp its business processes and improve its competitiveness.

CASE STUDY 6-8

DESIGNING VIGILANT INFORMATION SYSTEMS WITH REAL-TIME DASHBOARDS[3]

Western Digital (WD), a $3 billion U.S. designer and manufacturer of high-performance hard drives, was facing business challenges related to its fiercely competitive industry, changing customer requirements, short product lifecycles, demand for reliable products,

(continued)

---

[3] The authors wish to acknowledge Omar El Sawy and his collaborators Robert Houghton, Paul Gray, Craig Donegan, and Ashish Joshi for contributing this section. For a review of the complete case study, refer to Houghton et al., 2004.

and the need to prevent any manufacturing disruptions. Since WD relied on multiple sources of data, ERP reports often produced different results, data were not accurate across the organization, trend data were hard to observe, and in essence management lacked the necessary information to quickly respond to business needs. The leadership at WD recognized the need to be able to have real-time data in order to respond to events and KPIs as they occurred. Furthermore, this information needed to be available across the enterprise and organizational levels. In order for the organization to react more quickly to changes and integrate the enterprise information, it embarked on the implementation of a vigilant information system.

Vigilant information systems (VIS) refer to a new family of information systems that "integrate and distill information and business intelligence from various sources to detect changes, initiate alerts, assist with diagnosing and analyzing problems, and support communication for quick action" (Houghton et al., 2004, p. 20). VIS differ from traditional information systems in that in VIS the system initiates the process (versus the user), and the database is active (versus passive). Each time the data are updated, preset conditions are checked and if met, the system alerts the user. In this sense, a VIS provides sense-and-respond capabilities. Thus VIS must fulfill the following four capabilities, known as the OODA loop (Walls, Widmeyer, and El Sawy, 1992; Houghton et al., 2004):

1. Observing: They provide visibility into the enterprise's most important business processes and capture KPIs in real time, integrating various information sources and systems.
2. Orienting: They provide graphical dashboards to display data, send alerts to managers when preset conditions are met, allow slicing/dicing/drilling down data, and report trends.
3. Deciding: They provide analytics to help answer what-if questions, and include descriptive statistics and time series comparisons.
4. Acting: They provide an infrastructure to communicate decisions quickly to allow quick action and follow-up tracking.

The architecture of the VIS at WD is represented in Figure 6.6. At the bottom layer of the VIS architecture are the raw data coming from various sources, including customer transactions, customer payments, and so on. The raw data flow into different applications residing in the second layer, including ERP systems, several manufacturing and logistic systems. The third layer represents the BI systems, which perform the analysis to ensure that the business is operating within the expected limits. The results of the BI system flow into the dashboards at the fourth layer. As we can see in layer 4, two sets of real-time dashboard information were deployed, one for the factory and one for corporate. The factory dashboards were used to monitor manufacturing variables, including yield, material, production output, station monitoring, and quality. Figure 6.7 depicts the Yield Dashboard. The corporate dashboards were used to monitor management information, including among other variables billings, finished goods inventory, point of sale, planned shipments, and revenue recognition.

The implementation of the VIS at WD demonstrated seven lessons (Houghton et al., 2004):

1. Design the VIS as the "nerve center" for managing the enterprise.
2. The VIS can serve as the basis for team coordination across the enterprise.
3. The VIS OODA loops can foster organizational learning across the enterprise.
4. Real time in the VIS should match the organization's ability to respond; zero latency is not always the goal.

(*continued*)

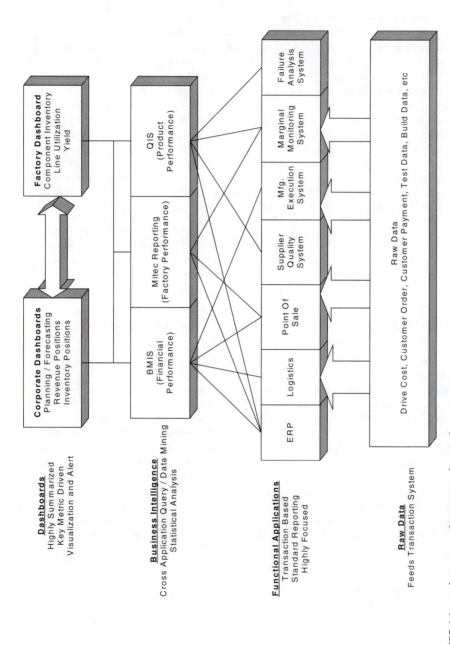

FIGURE 6.6 Architecture of WD's Vigilant Information Systems
(Source: Houghton et al., 2004)

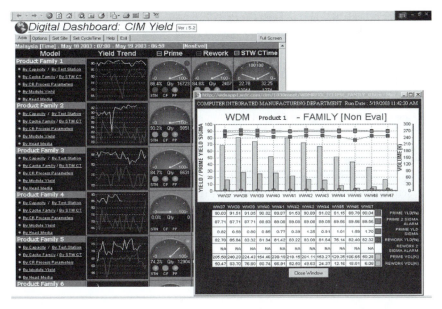

FIGURE 6.7 Yield Dashboard
(Source: Houghton et al., 2004)

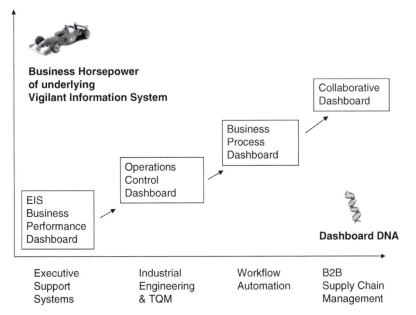

FIGURE 6.8 Four Types of Real-Time Management Dashboards
(Source: Houghton et al., 2004)

5. VIS can provide the infrastructure for an organization's ability to sense and respond.
6. Investment in VIS should be justified not only by return-on-investment but also on the impact of not having them.
7. VIS implementations should not be a technology initiative, but instead a management initiative supported by the leadership of the enterprise.

In summary, real-time management performance dashboards can fall into one of the four categories shown in Figure 6.8 (Houghton et al., 2004):
1. EIS Business Performance Dashboards—used as the basis for decision making at the corporate level, based on business goals and KPIs. They replace prior executive information systems.
2. Operations Control Dashboards—used as the basis for decision making at the manufacturing or services operations level. They replace previous total quality management and industrial engineering systems.
3. Business Process Dashboards—used as the basis for decision making at the enterprise transactional level. They replace previous workflow automation systems.
4. Collaborative Dashboards—used as the basis for interorganizational decision making, such as business-to-business or supply chain management systems.

▶ 6.9 SUMMARY

In this chapter we described those technologies that support the presentation of insights supporting operational and tactical decision making, including *online analytical processing (OLAP)* and *visualization*. OLAP supports the presentation of data in a multidimensional format called a cube, which essentially enables the DW data to be viewed across a set of dimensions that serve to categorize the numeric facts in the DW known as the measures. Visual analytics (which is related to the terms data visualization, information visualization, scientific visualization, and knowledge visualization) refers to the use of computer graphics to create a visual representation of large collections of information. In addition, technologies such as *digital dashboards* and *scorecards*, in particular *performance dashboards* and *balanced scorecards*, provide needed support to operational, tactical, and strategic decision making. The difference between performance dashboards and scorecards is that a dashboard presents multiple numbers in various ways, whereas a scorecard compares a given outcome metric with a target. Those insights are required to support adequate *IT governance* and *corporate performance management*. Finally, we ended the chapter with a case study of how one organization, Western Digital, effectively built a vigilant information system based on a BI infrastructure and management dashboards.

▶ KEY TERMS

balanced scorecard	measures	pivot
cube	online analytical	vigilant information
dimensions	processing (OLAP)	systems
IT governance	online transaction	
key performance	processing (OLTP)	
indicators (KPIs)	performance dashboard	

▶ REVIEW QUESTIONS

1. Describe how OLAP and visualization are used to support operational decision making.

2. Explain how performance dashboards are used to manage tactical metrics.

3. Describe how balanced scorecards are used to monitor the strategic performance of an organization.

4. How can an organization define effective IT governance?

5. How can an organization use BI to develop key performance indicators for competitive corporate performance?

▶ APPLICATION EXERCISES

1. Create a balanced scorecard model for your organization. First, review and clarify its business strategy: Is it fostering customer intimacy, being a low-cost producer, providing innovation-based leadership? What capabilities are needed within the company to actually pursue the strategy? Set up a simple diagram that reflects how you think the business works. Then select the measures for the scorecard in the four quadrants: financial, customer, internal business process, and learning and growth.

2. Access the Web site for Enterprise Performance Management (EPM) http://www.epmreview.com/kpi-library and review the library of KPIs listed there. Describe your organization, and select the appropriate KPIs for your organization from each of the four categories listed there.

3. Research the literature (or the EPM Review Web site http://epmreview.com) to identify for a case study that describes the metrics for their balanced scorecard. Contrast their scorecard with your own organization's scorecard.

4. Review the list of dashboard vendors at http://www.dashboardzone.com/dashboard-vendors and download at least two of the different software tools and compare their functionalities. Which one would you pick to develop your organization's performance dashboard and why?

▶ REFERENCES

Amo, W. 2000. *Microsoft SQL Server OLPA Developer's Guide* (New York: John Wiley).

Berkman, E. 2002. "Balanced Scorecard Demonstrated IT Value." *CIO Magazine*, May 15.

Busco, C., Frigo, M., Giovannoni, E., Riccaboni, A., and Scapens, R. 2005. "Beyond Compliance: Why Integrated Governance Matters Today." *Strategic Finance*, August 1.

COBIT, 2000. 3rd Edition Control Objectives. COBIT Steering Committee and the IT Governance Institute.

Codd, E. 1970. "A Relational Model of Data for Large Shared Data Banks." *CACM*, 13(6), 377–387.

Eckerson, W. 2005. "What Are Performance Dashboards?" *DM Review*, 15(11), 26–29.

Eckerson, W. 2006. "Ten Mistakes to Avoid When Creating Performance Dashboards." *Business Intelligence Journal*, 11(1), 66–71.

Houghton, R., El Sawy, O., Gray, P., Donegan, C., and Joshi, A. 2004. "Vigilant Information Systems for Managing Enterprises in Dynamic Supply Chains: Real-Time Dashboards at Western Digital." *MIS Quarterly Executive*, 3(1), 19–35.

Howson, C. 2008. "Beyond Metrics and Dashboards." *Teradata Magazine*, June.

Kaplan, R., and Norton, D. 1996. *The Balanced Scorecard* (Boston: Harvard Business School Press).

Kaplan, R., and Norton, D. 2004. "The Strategy Map: Guide to Aligning Intangible Assets." *Strategy & Leadership*, 32(5), 10–17.

Kohavi, R., Rothleder, N., and Simoudis E. 2002. "Emerging Trends in Business Analytics." *Communications of the ACM*, 45(8), 45–48.

Morrison, L. 2006. "Visual Business Intelligence Can Drive Performance Improvement." *Journal of Medical Marketing*, 6(2), 119–125.

Thomas, J., and Cook, K. 2005. *Illuminating the Path: The Research and Development Agenda for Visual Analytics*. IEEE.

Walls, J., Widmeyer, G., and El Sawy, O. 1992. "Building an Information Systems Design Theory for Vigilant EIS." *Information Systems Research*, 3(1), 36–59.

Weill, P., and Broadbent, M. 1998. *Leveraging the New Infrastructure: How Market Leaders Capitalize on IT* (Boston: Harvard Business School Press).

Weill, P., and Ross, J. 2004. *IT Governance: How Top Performers Manage IT Decision Rights for Superior Results* (Boston: Harvard Business School Press).

Whiting, R. 2006. "BPM Gets Smarter With A Little Help from BI." *Information Week*, November 6.

Wrembel, R., and Koncilia, C. (Eds.). 2007. *Data Warehouses and OLAP: Concepts, Architectures and Solutions*. (Hershey, Pa.: IGI Publishing.).

PART **III**

MANAGEMENT AND FUTURE OF BUSINESS INTELLIGENCE

CHAPTER 7

BUSINESS INTELLIGENCE TOOLS AND VENDORS

▶ 7.1 INTRODUCTION

In Chapters 3 through 6, we have examined the four key BI capabilities in detail. This chapter focuses on BI tools and vendors, and will be followed in Chapter 8 by a discussion of BI solutions and how they can be developed.

In this chapter, we first introduce BI tools in Section 7.2. This is followed in Section 7.3 by a classification of BI tools into four types based on the four kinds of BI capabilities. Some BI tools within each category are discussed in this section, and each category of BI tools is illustrated using a case example. We then examine selection of BI tools by an organization in terms of customization and standardization in Section 7.4. Subsequently, we discuss some leading BI vendors in Section 7.5. The tools available from the major BI vendors are summarized in the Appendices.

▶ 7.2 WHAT ARE BUSINESS INTELLIGENCE TOOLS?

In Chapter 1, we defined BI as the leveraging of a variety of sources of data as well as structured and unstructured information to provide decision makers with valuable information and knowledge. Such sources of information and data reside within or outside the organization, and the information and data could be quantitative or qualitative. Later, in Chapter 2, we pointed out that the term BI is sometimes used to refer to the **process** through which an organization obtains, analyzes, and distributes such information and knowledge, and it sometimes refers to the **product** of this process, or the information and knowledge that is useful to organizations for their business activities and decision making.

In Chapter 2, we also distinguished between BI tools, BI capabilities, and BI solutions. Figure 7.1 depicts the relationships among these aspects of BI.

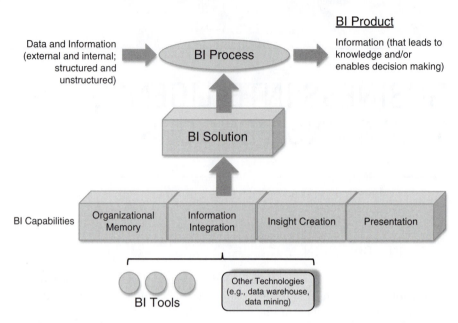

FIGURE 7.1 BI Tools in Relation to BI Capabilities, Solution, Product, and Process

BI tools include application software that enables BI by facilitating access and analysis of data and presentation of results. Several **BI vendors** have developed a variety of BI tools, which complement more traditional information technologies (such as data warehouses, data mining technologies, and transaction processing systems) to enable four types of ***BI capabilities***: organizational memory capability (discussed in Chapter 3), information integration capability (discussed in Chapter 4), insight creation capability (discussed in Chapter 5), and presentation capability (discussed in Chapter 6).

The four BI capabilities come together in **BI solutions**, which are developed for, and deployed within, client organizations. BI solutions utilize the BI tools acquired by the organization, and draw upon the vast amounts of data from existing data warehouses and transaction processing systems, as well as structured and unstructured information from these and other sources (such as e-mail messages) to support the BI process by delivering information and knowledge to facilitate decision making.

In this chapter, we focus on BI tools. The development of BI solutions will be discussed in detail in Chapter 8. Business Intelligence in Practice 7.1 describes a government agency's use of BI to evaluate the impacts of its public diplomacy efforts. It illustrates how BI tools can be used to enable BI capabilities, such as the use of Business Objects' Xcelsius data visualization software to facilitate presentation capability through the creation of a Public Diplomacy Impact dashboard, and the use of Excel and SAP Business Objects XI applications to facilitate insight creation.

Business Intelligence in Practice 7.1: Use of BI Tools to Evaluate Public Diplomacy

The U.S. State Department spends considerable resources on diplomacy programs aimed at improving the image of the United States in other countries. For example, it spent $357 million on diplomacy programs in 2007 through its Public Diplomacy office. These programs include the American Corners information libraries at various U.S. embassies, summer camps for children in the Middle East, and speaking arrangements for celebrities from the U.S.

The large investment in diplomacy programs makes it important to evaluate their effectiveness. This has been emphasized by the Office of Management and Budget (OMB), which, in 2006, gave the State Department a low rating in its ability to measure the effectiveness of diplomacy programs. According to Cherreka Montgomery, Acting Director of the Evaluation and Measurement Unit in the Office of the Under Secretary for Public Diplomacy and Public Affairs, "The OMB has been very clear that performance measurement is something they're placing an emphasis on."

The first step taken by the Public Diplomacy office was to reduce 898 short-term performance measures down to 15 measures, and to develop six outcome measures such as "initiation of positive change to local communities" and "reduced anti-Americanism." In 2007, the State Department's staff members visited Japan, Israel, Germany, Nigeria, Ecuador, Palestinian territories, and India. They surveyed about 1,800 foreign audience members, including some participants in a diplomacy program and some who had not participated in such a program, and compared their attitudes about the United States. Those results were then used to develop focus groups to get more detailed qualitative data. This produced a comprehensive, 300-page report.

To better disseminate the results of this survey and other measures, the Public Diplomacy office used Business Objects Xcelsius data-visualization software to create a Public Diplomacy Impact dashboard. Accessible through the State Department's intranet, the dashboard provides executives with budget details and identifies how well it has achieved its six outcome measures based on survey data. The dashboard indicates that public diplomacy is having a tangible and measurable effect abroad.

With the OMB satisfied with the change in public diplomacy measurements, the Public Diplomacy office is now expanding its use of BI to demonstrate the need for additional resources. It has started a pilot program to obtain more detailed information on expenditures through its various foreign outposts. Its objective is to show, for instance, why youth summer camps in the Middle East may require more funding than camps elsewhere,

(*continued*)

due perhaps to greater costs associated with transportation, staffing, and translation.

This pilot program aims to develop algorithms that better highlight the relationship between expenditures and the six outcome measures, using SAP Business Objects XI business intelligence platform and planning applications. The data for this Business Objects planning application are entered through an Excel interface. The results of the algorithms will then appear under a tab, called What-If Analysis, on the Public Diplomacy Impact dashboard. This would indicate what the State Department could do if it was provided greater funding for diplomacy efforts.

(Compiled from Armstrong, 2008; Essex, 2008; Weier, 2008)

▶ 7.3 TYPES OF BUSINESS INTELLIGENCE TOOLS

A large variety of BI tools have been discussed in the business and academic literature. Some of these tools and technologies are depicted in Figure 7.2. For each tool or technology shown in Figure 7.2, there are numerous specific products from different vendors.

In the light of this diversity of BI tools, several authors have previously classified them into categories. Let us examine a few illustrative examples of how other authors have classified BI tools.

Baars and Kemper (2008) highlight the fact that BI literature has largely emphasized tools targeted toward the analysis and presentation of quantitative business data. Specific tools discussed by Baars and Kemper include *reporting*, *data mining*, and *OLAP tools*. Reporting tools prepare quantitative reports containing numbers, charts, or business graphics. OLAP, or online analytical processing tools, represent tools for interactive, multidimensional analysis of aggregated quantitative business facts (e.g., revenues, costs, and profit), while providing the user with flexibility regarding the choice of dimensions that describe the focal aspects (e.g., customer, product), the selection to be looked at (e.g., April to July), and the level of detail (e.g., global, region, country, ZIP code, or store). Data mining tools enable the identification of hidden patterns in

Text Mining tools	Knowledge Repositories
Web Mining tools	Data Warehousing
Visualization tools	Enterprise Resource Planning systems
Business Analytics tools	Environmental Scanning
Scorecarding tools	Real-time Decision Support tools
Digital Dashboards	
BPM tools	OLAP tools
Document Management tools	RFID
Digital Content Management tools	Data Mining

FIGURE 7.2 A Variety of BI Tools and Technologies

large amounts of structured data using statistical methods. Data mining tools have been drawn in the BI literature from the literature on data mining (as discussed in Chapter 1).

Keydata[1] focuses on a few BI tools and lists them in the order of increasing cost, increasing functionality, increasing business intelligence complexity, and decreasing number of total users as follows: (1) Microsoft Excel, (2) reporting tools, (3) OLAP tools, and (4) data mining tools. This view of BI tools combines a specific tool (i.e., Excel), two categories of BI tools (reporting, OLAP), and a set of BI tools that originate from a technology other than BI but can facilitate BI (i.e., data mining tools).

Olszak and Ziemba (2007) view BI tools in terms of the chain from data to information to knowledge to decisions. They consider databases, data warehouses, and ETL tools (i.e., tools to extract, transform, and load data from transaction systems and the Internet into data warehouses) as supporting data, OLAP tools as supporting information, and data mining tools as supporting knowledge. They also discuss tools for reporting and ad hoc inquiries and the presentation layer (applications that include graphic and multimedia interfaces providing information in a user-friendly form), and seem to imply (without explicitly stating it) that these tools support decisions.

According to Wikipedia,[2] BI tools include spreadsheets, reporting and querying software, OLAP tools, digital dashboards, data mining tools, process mining tools (which focus on the analysis of business processes based on event logs), and business performance management tools (which focus on organizational use of key performance indicators (KPIs) to monitor efficiency of projects and employees relative to operational targets.

As highlighted by Olszak and Ziemba (2007), much of the prior focus in BI has been on tools oriented toward structured, quantitative data, but BI also helps with qualitative and unstructured information. We discussed a variety of tools and technologies earlier, focusing on the tools and technologies enabling each BI capability in detail in Chapters 3, 4, 5, and 6. In doing so, we have examined tools that help with qualitative and unstructured information as well, including document management systems, digital content management systems, text mining, and Web mining. Figure 7.3 maps the BI tools and technologies onto the four BI capabilities. Of these BI tools and technologies, some technologies (data warehousing, ERP, knowledge repositories, environmental scanning, RFID, data mining, decision support, OLAP tools) have been drawn from other arenas to support BI capabilities, whereas other tools (digital content management, document management, text mining, Web mining, business analytics, visualization, digital dashboards, and BPM tools) have emerged along with the development of BI. These tools and technologies have been discussed in Chapters 3 to 6, and are summarized next.

---

[1] http://www.1keydata.com/datawarehousing/business-intelligence-tools.php; accessed on May 1, 2009

[2] http://en.wikipedia.org/wiki/Business_intelligence_tools, accessed on May 1, 2009.

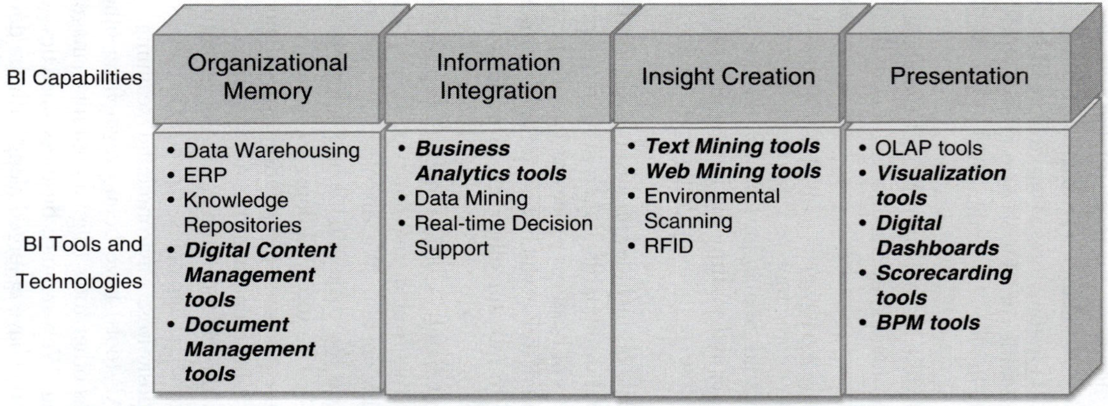

BI Capabilities	Organizational Memory	Information Integration	Insight Creation	Presentation
BI Tools and Technologies	• Data Warehousing • ERP • Knowledge Repositories • *Digital Content Management tools* • *Document Management tools*	• *Business Analytics tools* • Data Mining • Real-time Decision Support	• *Text Mining tools* • *Web Mining tools* • Environmental Scanning • RFID	• OLAP tools • *Visualization tools* • *Digital Dashboards* • *Scorecarding tools* • *BPM tools*

Note: The highlighted tools have emerged along with development of BI, whereas the others have been adapted from other technologies to support BI.

FIGURE 7.3 Classifying BI Tools and Technologies Based on Supported Capability

7.3.1 Tools Supporting Organizational Memory Capability

Organizational memory capability represents an organization's historically accumulated intellectual resources, including data, information, and explicit knowledge. It focuses on the storage of these intellectual resources in such a form that they can be later accessed and used. Tools and technologies enabling organizational memory capability, which were described in Chapter 3, include the following:

- Transactional systems, which are also called "operational systems," "transaction processing systems," or "source systems" (Howson, 2008)
- ERP systems and tools, which lead to consistent standardized processes across the organization and are broader in scope than traditional transactional systems
- Data warehousing tools, which enable the collection of data extracted from various transactional systems, transformed to enable data consistency, and loaded for analysis
- Technologies that support the capture of unstructured information (e.g., document management systems), retaining explicit knowledge (i.e., knowledge repositories), and archiving audio and video files (i.e., digital content management systems)

Business Intelligence in Practice 7.2 describes one illustrative tool for enhancing organizational memory capability: Microsoft's SQL Server 2008.

Business Intelligence in Practice 7.2: Microsoft's SQL Server 2008 Facilitates Organizational Memory Capability

The journey to an effective BI initiative often begins with the capture and storage of intellectual resources (data, information, and explicit knowledge) in such a form that they can be later accessed and used for insight creation. These resources are, in many instances, held in transaction-based systems and broader ERP systems. As these systems continuously churn out data about different aspects of a business and often are unrelated to each other, it becomes difficult to see any meaningful patterns without first storing the data in a central place. In other words, creating a central repository of data that is continuously and dynamically updated based on source systems is a key component of a BI system. Data warehousing tools enable the creation of such repositories, called data warehouses. Existing and newly available data are extracted from various transactional systems, transformed to enable data consistency, and loaded for subsequent analysis and insight creation.

Microsoft's SQL Server 2008's data warehouse component of the overall BI solution is a good example of a tool supporting organizational memory capability. According to Microsoft, SQL Server 2008 is a scalable and reliable

(continued)

data warehouse platform for BI. It enables actionable business decisions at lower costs through seamless integration with the Microsoft BI platform.

SQL Server 2008's design and features enable quick creation of a data warehouse and make updates and maintenance easy. Its fast extract, transform, load (ETL) tool makes consolidation of data from all types of data sources possible. For example, one is able to connect to an Oracle database or a DB2 mainframe without much difficulty. Moreover, support for both relational and nonrelational data, including new data types such as spatial data and FILESTREAM data and Spatial is available. Its multi-threaded 64-bit platform allows concurrent workloads even in large data volumes. It also provides a large number of built-in transformations to help consolidate data from numerous systems, reduce data duplication, and maintain quality. Such prebuilt transformation routines enable fast deployment. Also, its profiling tasks enable one to easily profile source and target data. Furthermore, its *change data capture* functionality (which enables the capture of changes in data in a table) allows identification of operational changes quickly.

The platform is also quite scalable. Its data compression feature reduces storage costs while improving performance. Large tables can also be partitioned, enabling growing volumes of data and users. In terms of management of the data warehouse, SQL Server 2008 provides an integrated management environment, to monitor and manage all databases and associated services across the enterprise. It also provides what are called SQL Management Objects (SMO), which allow administrators to customize and extend the management environment by building additional management tools.

In sum, organizational memory capability is critical toward the creation of an effective BI solution, and SQL Server data warehouse platform's scalability, manageability, and performance make it a desirable option. This is evident in its use by a very large health maintenance organization (HMO) in Israel. The HMO upgraded its 2.7-terabyte Enterprise BI Data Warehouse to SQL Server 2008 to take advantage of new features including data compression, star join for the data warehouse, resource governor, and support for spatial data types. With close to 3.8 million members and having to engage in 70 million customer interactions per year, the HMO relies heavily on its data stores to help the organization provide better care for its members through valuable BI. With more than 1,000 clinics, the HMO was particularly interested in using SQL Server 2008's spatial capabilities to incorporate geographic information into its Enterprise BI Data Warehouse. Microsoft reports that it was able to achieve 50% to 60% data compression rates along with improved decision support and enhanced query performance.

(Compiled using information from the SQL Server 2008 BI page and the case studies section of Microsoft's Web site).[3]

[3] http://www.microsoft.com/sqlserver/2008/en/us/business-intelligence.aspx; http://www.microsoft.com/casestudies/Case_Study_Detail.aspx?CaseStudyID=4000002453, accessed on June 16, 2009.

7.3.2 Tools Supporting Information Integration Capability

Information integration capability represents the ability to link the past structured and unstructured content (i.e., data, information, or knowledge) from a variety of sources that comprise organizational memory with the new, real-time content, including both structured and unstructured information as well as external information and knowledge. Tools and technologies enabling information integration capability, which we described in Chapter 4, include:

- Environmental scanning, which refers to the acquisition and utilization of information about trends, events, and relationships in the environment, which would help management in planning the organization's future course of action
- Text mining tools, which help mine the content of unstructured data, by automatically "reading" large documents of text written in natural language
- Web mining tools, which help search the Web and mine online text
- Radio-frequency identification devices, which help obtain information regarding the location of goods, and transmit it so that it can be stored and used along with other relevant information regarding the item being tracked.

Business Intelligence in Practice 7.3 describes one illustrative tool for enabling information integration capability: Oracle's Data Integrator Enterprise Edition.

Business Intelligence in Practice 7.3: Oracle's Data Integrator Enterprise Edition Facilitates Information Integration Capability

Organizations rely on BI systems for decision making and planning. The quality, consistency, and accuracy of data and information feeding into these systems are crucial to an organization's ability to derive benefits from its BI investments. However, data are often stored across different sources with varying technical platforms and in disparate structures. This lead to potential dangers of data inaccuracy, unreliability, redundancy, and an overall inability to discern meaningful patterns based on these out-of-sync data sources.

Oracle's Data Integrator Enterprise Edition (ODI-EE) is a good example of a tool that enhances an organization's information integration capability by effectively tackling such issues. According to Oracle, ODI-EE is a comprehensive data integration platform that handles a variety of data integration requirements, delivers next-generation extract, transform, and load (ETL) technology, reduces data integration costs, and works even across heterogeneous systems.

(continued)

ODI-EE's more advanced version of the ETL architecture allows it to work with different relational database management systems (RDBMS) to process and transform data. Instead of requiring a separate server to perform the ETL services, this platform leverages the existing RDBMS' capabilities to do all the work. By telling these disparate database systems what needs to be done in their own native language, and by integrating the outputs to feed into other BI tools, it improves performance and allows organizations to retain their existing database systems. Moreover, all this is done in real time based on its *Change Data Capture* capabilities. In this way, ODI-EE is able to perform three styles of data integration: data based, event based, and service based.

To make it easier for users to integrate data and to shorten implementation times, ODI-EE uses what Oracle calls a *Declarative Design* approach. In essence, users specify what they want to accomplish with their data, and the tool generates details of how it could be done. Once the rules for integration are specified, the tool automatically generates data flows from source to target systems, all the while applying robust data integrity controls to ensure consistency and accuracy. With a declarative design approach, automatic code generation reduces learning curves, and the whole process is quicker and simpler. In addition, ODI-EE provides a comprehensive library of what are called *Knowledge Modules*. These are essentially modular, flexible, and extensible templates for generating code across multiple systems. These are hot-pluggable and enable users to easily implement organizational best practices pertaining to data integration.

ODI-EE comes both as a stand-alone product and as part of a bigger Oracle Data Integration Suite. It is especially optimized for the Oracle Business Intelligence Suite of products but can work with any BI system.

Overall, it is a high performance data integration engine and has proved to be a critical component of BI initiatives at many organizations. For example, a large Turkish bank with close to $5 billion in assets was challenged with errors and anomalies in databases. Poor reliability and quality made things difficult, as data were being stored in multiple databases across different platforms. Using Oracle's data integrator, the bank was able to significantly improve data quality, allow analysts to mine data without slowing the system, dramatically reduce processing times, and improve its overall ability to draw on divergent data sources to help make business decisions.

(Compiled from information obtained from the ODI-EE page of Oracle's Web site).[4]

7.3.3 Tools Supporting Insight Creation Capability

Insight creation capability focuses on the utilization of the integrated data, information, and knowledge to produce valuable new insights and enable effective

---

[4] http://www.oracle.com/products/middleware/odi/enterprise-edition.html, accessed on June 16, 2009

decision making based on continual rather than periodic analysis. It produces a description of what happened, an understanding of what happened, and prediction of future behavior. Tools and technologies enabling insight creation capability, which were described in Chapter 5, include:

- Data mining tools, or tools enabling knowledge discovery in databases, which are tools that help extract useful knowledge from the identification of previously unknown relationships among variables
- Business analytics tools, which are similar to data mining tools although more user-friendly in nature, as compared to the historically more technical nature of data mining tools
- Real-time decision support, which is the use of models based on data mining or business analytics to support operational decisions in a real-time fashion

Business Intelligence in Practice 7.4 describes one illustrative tool for facilitating insight creation capability: SAS Analytics.

Business Intelligence in Practice 7.4: SAS Analytics Facilitates Insight Creation Capability

It is now well accepted that organizations use insights created from data to guide their decision making. Decision makers are interested in describing and understanding what has happened and why it has happened, and predicting what could possibly happen. Hence, an organization's insight creation capability, which focuses on the utilization of the integrated data, information, and knowledge to produce valuable new insights, is critical for its BI efforts. Tools facilitating an organization's insight creation capability help detect hidden patterns and trends, describe and predict fluctuations, identify strengths, weaknesses, opportunities and threats, and answer complex business questions. SAS Analytics is one such tool.

According to SAS, SAS Analytics provides an integrated environment for predictive and descriptive modeling, data mining, text analytics, forecasting, optimization, simulation, experimental design, and more. It provides a range of techniques and processes for the collection, classification, analysis, and interpretation of data to reveal patterns, anomalies, and key variables and relationships to create new insights.

Its data and text mining components allow building and deployment of descriptive and predictive models across the enterprise. The easy-to-use graphical user interface (GUI) eases model deployment and scoring processes while enhancing the accuracy of predictions. The *Text Miner* tool makes discovering and extracting knowledge from text documents possible. It

(*continued*)

transforms textual data into a usable and understandable format that facilitates classifying documents, finding explicit relationships or associations between documents, and clustering documents into categories. It also integrates text-based information with structured data for improved analyses and decision making. Support for multiple languages is also available.

The forecasting components help with both operational and strategic decision making. One is able to analyze and predict future outcomes based on historical patterns. Its *Time Series Forecasting* tool integrates time series and econometric techniques for modeling, forecasting, and simulating business processes. The *Forecast Server* generates large quantities of high-quality forecasts quickly and automatically, allowing more effective planning.

Its operations research component *SAS/OR* enables organizations to leverage optimization, project scheduling, and simulation techniques to identify the actions that will produce the best results. It allows consideration of alternative actions and scenarios. Functionality that enables experimentation with the effects of changes to underlying data helps determine the best allocation of resources.

Its quality improvement component, *SAS/QC*, helps identify, monitor, and measure quality processes over time. It incorporates statistical process control (SPC) and allows designing of experiments to improve process or product quality. Another key component of SAS Analytics pertains to its tools for statistical analyses. The focus is on using statistical data analysis to drive fact-based decisions. SAS is known for its statistical offerings and the tools enable a wide range of analyses—from the more traditional analysis of variance to exact methods and dynamic data visualization techniques. It also allows more advanced users to interact with the system using an interactive matrix programming language.

SAS Analytics has become the insight creation tool of choice for many organizations due to its data/text mining capabilities and strong statistical analysis and forecasting functionalities. For example, a large competitive electricity retailer in Canada needed a better way to understand and predict demand for electricity. Given the nature of the industry, customer demand varies by the minute. Weather and other variables can affect hourly, daily, and monthly demand patterns. The retailer wanted to optimize its approach to balancing supply and demand. It chose SAS Business Analytics because of its efficiency, speed, usability, and capacity to analyze and use enormous amounts of data. The results were optimized decision making and forecasting and executive confidence in the ability to manage price and commodity risks.

(Compiled from information obtained from the SAS Analytics and customer stories pages of SAS's Web site).[5]

[5] http://www.sas.com/technologies/analytics/index.html#section=1; http://www.sas.com/success/ Enmax.html, accessed on June 16, 2009

7.3.4 Tools Supporting Presentation Capability

Presentation capability, which is the point of contact between the BI solution and the user, focuses on presenting appropriate information in a user-friendly fashion based on the user's role, the specific task, and the user's inputs regarding nature of presentation. Tools and technologies enabling presentation capability, which were described in Chapter 6, include:

- Online analytical processing (OLAP) tools, which focus on exploring and analyzing multidimensional data in a highly interactive fashion, and with varying levels of aggregation
- Visualization tools, which involve the use of advanced graphics to present information so that it is easier to understand and interpret
- Digital dashboards, which display metrics in various ways (e.g., tables, charts, graphs, maps, colors, and speedometers), in a customizable interface and a navigable layout, so that users can interactively obtain pertinent information about the current state
- Scorecards, which are also graphical displays, but monitor and show progress by focusing on certain metrics and comparing them to a target, threshold, or forecast
- Corporate performance management, or business performance management, which focuses on the monitoring and managing of organizational performance using certain carefully selected key performance indicators (KPIs) such as a measure of customer loyalty

Business Intelligence in Practice 7.5 describes one illustrative tool for enhancing presentation capability: SAP's Business Objects Xcelsius Enterprise.

Business Intelligence in Practice 7.5: SAP's Business Objects Xcelsius Enterprise Facilitates Presentation Capability

The insights created from BI tools are often complex. In order to truly derive maximum benefits from BI, the information and insights generated through BI need to be presented in a simple, clear, easy to understand, yet comprehensive manner. If users are not able to interpret and comprehend the insights and interact with data dynamically, then the efforts of data storage, integration, and insight creation may not go too far in helping the organization. Hence, proper presentation is very important.

There is a variety of data visualization products that augment other BI tools by simplifying the presentation of insights to users. SAP's Business Objects Xcelsius Enterprise is one such effective product.

(continued)

According to SAP, its BusinessObjects Xcelsius Enterprise is a point-and-click data visualization tool designed specifically to create interactive analytics and dashboards. Data visualization offers users simple and effective ways to quickly understand, collaborate with, and act on key business information. More important, it is seamlessly integrated with SAP's other BI products such as SAP BusinessObjects Enterprise and SAP BusinessObjects Edge BI, via secure, live connections. One is either able to use a utility that enables querying as a Web service to directly connect to the underlying data, or connect to a report in Crystal Reports, other documents, or queries, via SAP's BusinessObjects Live Office software. This means the users interact with the same data the other systems use or previously generated insights, in real time and in a secure manner.

Not only does this tool allow creation of highly interactive and intuitive visualizations to help decision makers, but also its drop-down menus and sliders allow clear presentation of complex business data and testing of future business scenarios. Its intuitive design environment enables dashboard designers to quickly create professional-looking models using prebuilt components, 'skins', maps, charts, gauges, and selectors—all this with an easy-to-use point-and-click interface. The users are able to personalize their dashboards according to their particular needs, access them securely from anywhere, and conduct powerful what-if analyses. Since the visualizations thus created are *Adobe Flash*-based files, they can be easily shared in real time with other applications, via Microsoft Office, Adobe PDF, the Web, Crystal Reports, or the SAP BusinessObjects BI portal. Easy-to-use integration kits are provided to allow users from other environments such as Microsoft's SharePoint or IBM's WebSphere portal to easily integrate the dashboards and models from BusinessObjects Xcelsius Enterprise.

Overall, its simple and intuitive design, ability to personalize the dashboards for each individual user, secure access, and powerful what-if analysis capability make it an attractive choice for organizations. For example, when Volvo and Renault car dealers in Sweden and Norway needed to enhance their existing integrated financial and business management system, they turned to SAP's BusinessObjects Xcelsius. The car dealers needed more control and a better overview of the level of service and profitability on each and every work order per dealer, and also at the local and regional levels. They needed a visual, easy-to-use application that would quickly show the status of each individual work process, so that workshop technicians and supervisors could compare and aggregate work order information. The BusinessObjects Xcelsius seamlessly integrated with their existing systems, and allowed the dealers to create a workshop "barometer" based on 12 key business ratio figures. A quick look at the various speedometers with green, yellow, and red areas would reveal the

(continued)

current status of the workshop. A green indicated everything was well, a yellow indicated that performance targets may not be met, and a red indicated a problem that needed to be addressed immediately.

(Compiled from information obtained from the BusinessObjects Xcelsius page of SAP's Web site)[6]

▶ 7.4 CUSTOMIZATION VERSUS STANDARDIZATION OF BI TOOLS

As discussed above, there are multiple BI tools supporting each capability and several alternative vendors for each BI tool. The kinds of BI tools that are best suited for an individual depends on the individual's role within the organization, abilities, and preferences, as well as existing vendor investments. For example, users could be classified into "power users," "business users," and "middle class" (Scheps, 2008). "Power users," who include analysts and others with a good understanding of BI tools, benefit from the advanced features of BI tools by studying the data architecture and identifying where to obtain needed data, developing their own reporting tools, and developing more innovative techniques for developing and applying insights from BI tools (Scheps, 2008). In contrast, "business users" are information consumers lacking BI expertise, who comprise as much as two-thirds of the user base in most organizations. They utilize BI as the means to a desired goal, focus on standardized outputs, do not develop new ways of viewing the data, and rely on others (usually, "power users") to obtain information that goes beyond the standard reports. Finally, "middle class" comprises users who are similar to "business users" in that they are also primarily consumers of information. However, they have some BI skills that they can use when needed. Consequently, "middle class" users generally behave like "business users," but occasionally design reports and queries or perform additional analyses.

Numerous options exist within each tool in terms of the user interface, accessibility to data, and so on. The same BI tool may need to be set up differently in varying situations, especially for different kinds of roles (e.g., for the top executives, middle managers, and customer-service personnel), different kinds of tasks (e.g., when a middle manager is planning for the future versus evaluating past performance), and for different individuals (e.g., one individual may prefer use of color to highlight differences, whereas another may prefer varying shapes to highlight differences).

Consequently, two important and interrelated issues are encountered in the adoption of BI tools: (1) To what extent should BI tools be customized for specific users, roles, and tasks? (2) To what extent should BI tools be standardized across the organization? Some authors (e.g., Scheps, 2008) recommend providing different levels of tools to different type of users, especially providing "middle

[6] http://www12.sap.com/solutions/sapbusinessobjects/large/intelligenceplatform/bi/dashboard-visualization/xcelsius-enterprise/index.epx, accessed on June 16, 2009.

class" users with tools they can use to draw upon their latent BI skills to develop ad hoc queries. However, this could lead to these users spending valuable time on BI tools rather than their business tasks, and developing queries that may not be available to others for reuse. Moreover, customization of BI tools for specific users, roles, and tasks could be inefficient (due to the time taken for customization and potential reduction in users' ability to help each other). On the other hand, standardization of all BI tools could be overly restrictive, and could inhibit some of the major benefits from BI.

We recommend a balanced approach between customization and standardization. More specifically, we recommend greater customization and lower standardization of BI tools as we move from tools supporting organizational memory capability toward tools supporting presentation capability. Tools supporting organizational memory capability should be standardized as they focus on data that are useful across the organization, and should be standardized so as to avoid inconsistency, redundancy, and inaccuracy. At the other extreme, tools supporting presentation capability are the ones users most directly interact with, and this is where customization is most beneficial. Tools supporting information integration and insight creation capabilities are between these extremes, with some customization and personalization in aspects such as the kind of data that are accessible and the kind of analyses that are available. Moreover, whereas tools supporting presentation capability should be customized with respect to roles, tasks, and individuals (i.e., personal preferences and abilities), tools supporting information integration need to be customized only with respect to roles, and tools supporting insight creation capabilities need to be customized with respect to roles and tasks. We have depicted these recommendations in Figure 7.4.

▶ 7.5 LEADING BUSINESS INTELLIGENCE VENDORS

During the past few years, considerable consolidation has occurred within the BI industry as a result of mergers and acquisitions. Most notably, four large vendors—IBM, Microsoft, Oracle, and SAP—have been acquiring a number of companies to strengthen their BI offerings (Wailgum 2008a, 2008b; Kellen, 2007). Through these acquisitions, the four companies (now known as the "**mega-vendors**") have staked their claims in the BI market, spending billions on top-tier BI vendors such as Cognos, Business Objects, and Hyperion (Wailgum 2008a, 2008b; Kellen, 2007). According to a Gartner report in February 2008 (Richardson et al., 2008), the acquisitions in 2007 enabled the big four to move from owning a quarter of the BI market in December 2006 to owning two-thirds of it in December 2007.

We now review some of the leading BI vendors, while recognizing that the situation could change over time as more acquisitions and mergers take place. The vendors are classified into three categories: the four "mega-vendors" (Oracle, SAP, IBM, Microsoft), six major **independent vendors of BI** (SAS, Microstrategy, Information Builders, TIBCO Software, Inc., QlikTech, and Actuate), and other

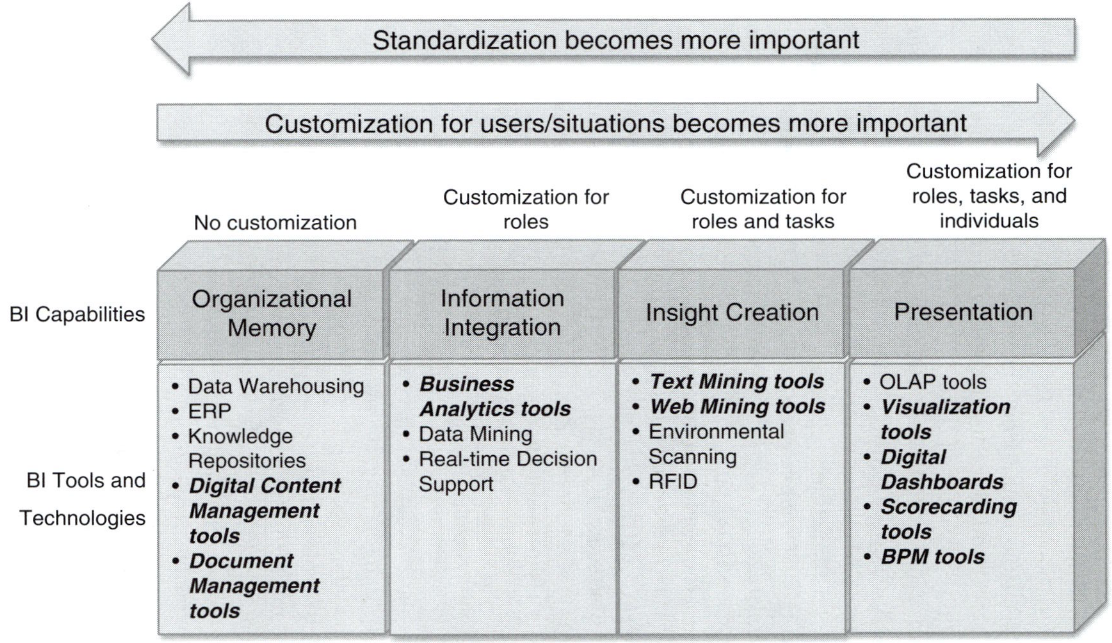

FIGURE 7.4 Customization and Standardization of BI Tools and Technologies

Standardization becomes more important

Customization for users/situations becomes more important

BI Capabilities	Organizational Memory	Information Integration	Insight Creation	Presentation
	No customization	Customization for roles	Customization for roles and tasks	Customization for roles, tasks, and individuals
BI Tools and Technologies	• Data Warehousing • ERP • Knowledge Repositories • *Digital Content Management tools* • *Document Management tools*	• *Business Analytics tools* • Data Mining • Real-time Decision Support	• *Text Mining tools* • *Web Mining tools* • Environmental Scanning • RFID	• OLAP tools • *Visualization tools* • *Digital Dashboards* • *Scorecarding tools* • *BPM tools*

Note: The highlighted tools have emerged along with development of BI, whereas the others have been adapted from other technologies to support BI.

191

notable BI vendors (Teradata, HP, arcplan, Board International, and Panorama Software). Hyperion, Business Objects, and Cognos—which were three of the leading independent BI vendors—have been acquired by Oracle, SAP, and IBM, respectively, as discussed above, and are examined below in the context of their new parent mega-vendors.

The following discussion is based on our knowledge of the BI industry, relevant articles in the business literature (e.g., *FinanceWeek*, 2008; Wailgum 2008a, 2008b), information available online from the vendors' Web sites, and several industry reports by Gartner and Forrester Research. The industry reports include Gartner's 2008 report on BI platforms (Richardson et al., 2008), Gartner's 2009 report on BI platforms (Richardson et al., 2009a), Gartner's 2009 report on BI reporting capabilities (Richardson, Schlegel, and Sallam, 2009b), and Forrester's 2008 report on enterprise BI platform vendors (Evelson et al., 2008). Gartner's 2008 and 2009 reports on BI platforms classified vendors into four types based on ability to execute (ATE) and completeness of vision (COV): Leaders (strong in ATE, strong in COV), Challengers (strong in ATE, limited in COV), Visionaries (limited in ATE, strong in COV), and Niche Players (limited in ATE, limited in COV). However, none of the vendors in the 2008 and 2009 reports was classified as a Challenger. Gartner's 2009 report on BI reporting capabilities evaluated each of nine BI platforms in terms of 10 key major capabilities using a five-point scale, with 5.0 being the best possible score. Forrester's 2008 BI report (Evelson et al., 2008) classified vendors into Leaders, Strong Performers, and Contenders.

Oracle (including Hyperion): Oracle (including Hyperion) was named as a leader in BI platforms by Gartner in 2008 and 2009, and as a leader in enterprise BI platforms by Forrester in 2008. In the context of Gartner's 2009 report on BI reporting capabilities, Oracle was invited to submit its BI Publisher for evaluation, but was unable to participate and was therefore not included in that report.

Oracle has been strengthening its presence in the BI industry through acquisitions. In March 2007, Oracle acquired Hyperion Solutions for $3.3 billion. Hyperion focused on BI tools and financial applications, was itself a combination of Essbase, Hyperion, and Brio, and had also acquired predictive analytics vendor Decisioneering in January 2007. Oracle had earlier acquired Siebel Systems (which was a leading customer relationship management software vendor and had a significant analytics business) for $5.85 billion in September 2006, Sigma Dynamics (provider of real-time predictive analytics technology) in August 2006, and PeopleSoft for $10.3 billion in 2005. More recently, Oracle has acquired Microsystems (a pioneer in enterprise computing with software assets including Java and the Sun Solaris operating system) in April 2009.

Oracle has a variety of BI-related tools and solutions, including Oracle Business Intelligence Suite, Oracle Business Intelligence Publisher, Oracle Business Activity Monitoring, Oracle Crystal Ball, Oracle Data Integrator, and Oracle Business Intelligence on Demand. Oracle's combination of BI platform (e.g., Oracle BI Enterprise Edition, or OBIEE) and analytic applications (e.g., Oracle Financial Analytics, Oracle Sales Analytics) is considered to be one of the better sets of offerings available. According to the 2009 Gartner report (Richardson et al., 2009): "The availability of more than 70 functional and industry-specific packaged BI applications built on the Oracle BI Enterprise Edition Platform attests to Oracle's understanding of how to leverage the market interest in domain-specific and prepackaged solutions as a growth driver for its platform." Another important strength of Oracle is the federated query capability for sourcing data into BI applications from multiple sources, rather than just a data warehouse. However, Oracle seems to be lagging behind the competition in introducing emerging technologies, such as in-memory processing and interactive visualization and search.

SAP (including Business Objects): Like Oracle, SAP (including Business Objects) was named a leader in BI platforms by Gartner in 2008 and 2009 and a leader in enterprise BI platforms by Forrester Research in 2008. SAP significantly strengthened its presence in the BI industry by acquiring Business Objects, which was considered to be the world's leading provider of BI solutions. SAP announced the acquisition of Business Objects for $6.78 billion in October 2007. Business Objects itself had bought Cartesis (a specialist in finance and performance management software with more than 1,300 corporate customers, 600 employees, and 200 consultants worldwide) in April 2007. Earlier, Business Objects had bought Firstlogic, Inc. (a global provider of enterprise data quality software and services) and Nsite (an on-demand process management platform that creates Web-based routing and approval workflows) in 2006 and Crystal Decisions (which was best known for its widely deployed report-generator Crystal Reports) in 2003. SAP also bought corporate performance management software company, OutlookSoft, in May 2007 and Pilot Software, a privately-held company specializing in strategy management software, in February 2007.

SAP Business Objects has a number of BI-related products, including SAP Business Objects Enterprise, SAP Business Objects Xcelsius Enterprise (focusing on data visualization), Netweaver BI, and Crystal Reports. According to Gartner's 2009 report, SAP Business Objects is the most commonly used BI platform standard. The reporting and ad hoc query capabilities of SAP Business Objects and the OLAP tools for Netweaver BI are mentioned as its major strengths. Crystal Reports was evaluated in the context of Gartner's 2009 report on BI reporting capabilities, and received a best possible score of 5.0 for financial reporting and a score of 4.0 for data volume scalability and complex, interactive reporting. Moreover, SAP Business Objects provides leading-edge capabilities in several areas of BI, including text analytics and OnDemand BI (SaaS). Gartner's 2009 report on BI platforms also indicated that the SAP BI Accelerator is facilitating performance improvement to the SAP installed base of NetWeaver BI customers. In May 2009, SAP Business Objects announced SAP Business Objects Explorer, which integrates search and navigation capabilities from the SAP Business Objects portfolio with NetWeaver Accelerator software. The co-CEO of SAP compared SAP Business Objects Explorer to an "iTunes" for BI, allowing any business user to search and find BI information very quickly. He remarked: "It enables you to do one very important thing—you can look at any quantity of data—we're talking about terabytes, hundreds of terabytes, and get an answer in less than a second in normal language" (Montalbano, 2009). However, SAP's acquisition of Business Objects could cause confusion among its NetWeaver BI users. Also, Gartner's 2009 report indicates dissatisfaction with SAP Business Object's customer support and with its OLAP capabilities.

IBM (including Cognos): IBM announced the acquisition of Cognos (a large developer of BI tools and solutions) for $4.9 billion in November 2007. IBM had earlier announced the acquisition of Telelogic AB (which focuses on enterprise software development tools) in June 2007, and Solid Information Technology (a privately held company that provided in-memory database software) in December 2007. More recently, in July 2009, IBM announced the acquisition of SPSS, which focuses on predictive analytics and is closely tied to Business Objects (a part of SAP), for about $1.2 billion.

The 2008 Gartner Report included Cognos as a leader in BI platforms in 2008 and IBM Cognos as a leader in BI platform in 2009. IBM Cognos was named by Forrester Research as a leader in enterprise BI platforms in 2008.

IBM Cognos offers IBM Cognos 8, which delivers a range of BI capabilities on a single service-oriented architecture (SOA), including reporting, analysis, scorecarding, dashboards, and extending BI through mobile access and other means. In the 2009 Gartner survey, IBM Cognos 8 was the highest scoring BI platform, with particular areas of strength including infrastructure, metadata management, workflow and collaboration, reporting, ad hoc query, advanced visualization, and scorecarding. IBM Cognos 8's Web services-based SOA was considered to be much better integrated than some competing products, with shared metadata across the platform facilitating transfer from report to query to analysis. In Gartner's 2009 report on BI reporting capabilities, Cognos 8 BI Report Studio received a best possible score of 5.0 for complex, interactive reporting and other scores of 4.0 or above for data volume scalability, integration, and mobile device support. However, the majority of Cognos 8 deployments continue to be report-centric, with a much lower usage for ad hoc analysis and discovery. Gartner's 2009 study of BI platforms also found performance problems with IBM Cognos 8 attributed to the lack of robust caching, which leads to users accessing the database each time a report is refreshed.

Microsoft: Microsoft has been classified by Gartner as a leader in BI platforms since 2008, and was classified as strong performer (just behind leaders) in enterprise BI platforms in the 2008 Forrester report. As compared to IBM, SAP, and Oracle, Microsoft has made smaller but potentially strategic acquisitions. In July 2008, Microsoft announced the acquisition of DATAllegro, a leading vendor of data warehouse appliances, and plans to re-architect DATAllegro's solutions around a Microsoft SQL Server stack. Microsoft also acquired FAST (or Fast Search & Transfer ASA, which focused on enterprise search technologies) in April 2008, and 90 Degree Software (a BI vendor) in March 2008. Earlier, Microsoft bought ProClarity in April 2006 for its analytics server.

Microsoft's BI strategy relies to a considerable extent on Excel, SQL Server, and SharePoint Server. Microsoft SQL Server Reporting Services was included in Gartner's 2009 report on BI reporting capabilities, but its score reached 4.0 in only one of the ten evaluation criteria (complex, interactive reporting), whereas it scored 2.7 or below in five of the other criteria. A strong leverage of the installed base of these products enables continued adoption, which is also facilitated by the low-price point and packaging of Microsoft's BI platform. However, as compared to its large competitors, Microsoft's product vision is considered to be somewhat limited, concentrating on reporting and Excel analyst-driven BI along with some strategic BI (through Microsoft Office Performance Point Server), but lacking the operational BI vision of Oracle and SAP, which will push BI further into business processes and closer to decision-making points (Richardson et al., 2009). Gartner's 2009 survey on BI platforms also indicated concerns regarding Microsoft's long development cycles that inhibit innovation and regarding Microsoft's metadata management being considerably poorer than its competitors.

Table 7.1 summarizes the above discussion of BI mega-vendors.

Leading Independent BI Vendors

SAS: Like Oracle and SAP Business Objects, SAS was named by Gartner as a leader in BI platforms in 2008 and 2009, and by Forrester Research as a leader in enterprise BI platforms in 2008. SAS' BI products include SAS Analytics, SAS Enterprise BI Server, SAS Visual BI, and SAS Web Report Studio. In Gartner's 2009 report on BI reporting capabilities, SAS Web Report Studio received scores of 4.0 or above on four of the ten criteria: sophisticated SQL support, data volume scalability, integration, and complex interactive reporting.

SAS leverages its expertise in advanced data analyses in focusing on the analytics aspect of BI, especially in SAS Analytics. Whereas most other BI vendors in the report focus on historical analysis, SAS's approach to BI is based on forecasting, predictive modeling and optimization, and embedding them in industry-specific and cross-functional applications oriented toward specific business problems, such as risk management and warranty analysis. According to the company's Web site:[7] "Other vendors provide business intelligence solely in the form of historical reports that give you hindsight but limited insight. SAS Business Intelligence enables you to understand the past, monitor the present, and predict outcomes as you move your business ahead."

Gartner's 2009 survey of BI platforms found SAS to be the only BI vendor whose customers extensively utilize data mining or predictive modeling. SAS derives a large percentage of its revenue from the financial services industry, and an increasing percentage of its revenue from packaged analytic applications built on its BI platform. This is consistent with Gartner's 2008 assessment: "SAS dominates in advanced analytic solutions." However, despite SAS BI Server having been deployed in hundreds of organizations, few organizations consider SAS to be their enterprise

---

[7] http://www.sas.com/technologies/bi/; accessed May 31, 2009.

Table 7.1 A Comparison of BI Mega-Vendors*

Vendor	Evaluation in industry surveys	Illustrative BI-related products	Strengths	Weaknesses
Oracle (including Hyperion)	G'08: Leader G'09: Leader F'08: Leader	Oracle BI Suite Enterprise Edition Plus; Oracle BI Suite Standard Edition One; Oracle BI Publisher; Oracle Business Activity Monitoring; Oracle Crystal Ball; Oracle Data Integration Suite; Oracle BI on Demand	• Good combination of BI platform and analytic applications • Federated query capability for sourcing data from multiple sources	• Lags behind competitors in introducing emerging technologies, e.g., in-memory processing and interactive visualization and search
SAP (including Business Objects)	G'08: Leader G'09: Leader F'08: Leader	SAP Business Objects Enterprise; SAP Business Objects Xcelsius Enterprise; Crystal Reports; Netweaver BW (Business Warehouse)	• SAP Business Objects is the most commonly used BI platform standard • SAP Business Objects' excellent reporting and ad hoc query capabilities • Leading-edge capabilities in several areas of BI, including text analytics and OnDemand BI	• Dissatisfaction with SAP Business Object's customer support • Concerns about OLAP capabilities of SAP Business Object • SAP's acquisition of Business Objects may cause confusion among NetWeaver BI users

Vendor	Ratings	Products	Strengths	Weaknesses
IBM (including Cognos)	G'08: Leader G'09: Leader F'08: Leader	IBM Cognos 8, delivering numerous BI capabilities on a single service-oriented architecture: reporting, analysis, scorecarding, dashboards, and extending BI	• IBM Cognos 8 considered strong in infrastructure, metadata management, workflow and collaboration, reporting, ad hoc query, advanced visualization, and scorecarding	• Report-centric nature of IBM Cognos 8, with much lower usage for ad hoc analysis and discovery • Performance problems with IBM Cognos 8, attributed to the lack of robust caching
Microsoft	G'08: Leader G'09: Leader F'08: Strong performer	Microsoft SQL Server; Microsoft SharePoint Server Microsoft Office Performance Point Server; Microsoft Excel	• A strong leverage of the installed base of Microsoft's products enables continued adoption, which is also facilitated by the low-price point and packaging of Microsoft's BI platform	• Seemingly limited product vision, concentrating on reporting and Excel, but lacking operational BI • Long development cycles may inhibit innovation • Considered weak in metadata management

* Industry reports include Gartner's 2008 (G'08) and 2009 (G'09) surveys on BI platforms, and Forrester's 2008 survey on enterprise BI platforms (F'08).

BI standard. Moreover, SAS has acquired a reputation of being more difficult in terms of usability. SAS is trying to address this concern by integrating JMP, an in-memory analytics tool with data discovery and visualization capabilities, into SAS Visual Data Discovery. Also, SAS acquired Teragram, a leader in natural language processing and advanced linguistic technology, in March 2008, to strengthen its text mining capabilities and add enterprise and mobile search to its BI offerings.

MicroStrategy: Like Microsoft, MicroStrategy was classified by Gartner as a leader in BI platforms in both 2008 and 2009, and by Forrester as a strong performer (just behind leaders) in enterprise BI platforms in 2008. MicroStrategy's BI-related products include MicroStrategy Intelligence Server, intelligence server extensions (e.g., MicroStrategy Report Services, MicroStrategy OLAP Services), user interfaces (i.e., MicroStrategy Web, MicroStrategy Mobile, MicroStrategy Desktop, and MicroStrategy Office), and development and administration tools (e.g., MicroStrategy Architect, MicroStrategy Object Manager).

MicroStrategy's strengths in BI include outstanding BI metadata management (which was found to be highest in the 2009 Gartner survey of BI platforms), parameterized reporting, and excellent technical performance even when used with large enterprise data warehouses. In Gartner's 2009 report on BI reporting capabilities, MicroStrategy Report Services performed extremely well, receiving a perfect score of 5.0 in terms of four criteria (data volume scalability; complex, interactive reporting; sophisticated SQL support; and high-quality, portable output) and above 4.0 on two other criteria (ease of use for end users and financial reporting). Moreover, "Since MicroStrategy is not bogged down by the integration challenges, overhead and complex operating environment of the megavendors, it has a window of opportunity to forge ahead with innovation" (Richardson et al., 2009a). MicroStrategy offers a Web-based authoring environment for the power user and a more powerful desktop tool oriented toward IT.

MicroStrategy's focus on BI platforms may exclude it from consideration in enterprise BI standardization projects that aim to leverage the existing information infrastructure, especially in comparison to megavendors offering end-to-end BI, packaged analytics, and integration middleware optimized for their enterprise applications (Richardson et al., 2009a). MicroStrategy's report authoring is not aimed at casual business users. Despite MicroStrategy's development environment being robust and flexible, a steep learning curve exists, even for experienced report developers. However, subsequent to the publication of Gartner's 2009 reports on BI platforms and BI reporting, MicroStrategy has addressed these concerns to some extent by releasing MicroStrategy 9 in March 2009. MicroStrategy 9 includes in-memory technology, faster and more user-friendly Web interface including self-service features, and easier and more interactive dynamic dashboards (*ITNews*, 2009). According to the company's Web site,[8] "MicroStrategy 9's powerful enterprise reporting technology is unique because it is

---

[8] http://www.microstrategy.com/9/breakthroughs.asp#Dynamic%20Dashboard%20Creation; accessed May 31, 2009.

entirely metadata-driven and therefore does not require programming, unlike most other BI technologies that address the same requirements."

Information Builders: Like Microsoft and MicroStrategy, Information Builders was classified by Gartner as a leader in BI platforms in both 2008 and 2009, and as a strong performer (just behind leaders) in the 2008 Forrester report on enterprise BI platforms. Information Builders' products related to BI include WebFOCUS BI platform, iWay software suite of prebuilt integration components, and host-based reporting (FOCUS).

WebFOCUS delivers report-centric BI through extranets to a large number of user deployments. Reporting is an integral part of the WebFOCUS BI platform. In the 2009 Gartner survey of BI reporting capabilities, WebFocus was considered the best in terms of ease of use for end users as well as developers, with scores of 4.7 and 3.8, respectively. It scored the best possible 5.0 in two categories (user volume scalability, and complex, interactive reporting), and scored between 4.5 and 4.7 in four other categories (data volume scalability, sophisticated SQL support, integration, and ease of use for end users).

Besides its excellence as a platform for developing custom Web-based BI applications and highly parameterized enterprise reporting for end users, Information Builders' other strengths in BI include its being commonly considered as the BI standard (e.g., by a majority of respondents to Gartner's 2009 BI platform survey) and the ability, through iWay, of integrated extraction, transformation, and loading from disparate systems. However, Information Builders is considered to be limited in terms of OLAP capabilities, and also due to its focus on the financial services industry and on North America.

TIBCO: TIBCO (including Spotfire) was classified as a visionary in the Gartner's 2008 and 2009 reports on BI platforms, and as a strong performer (behind leaders) in the 2008 Forrester report on enterprise BI platforms. TIBCO had earlier focused on business process management, but moved actively into BI when it acquired Spotfire (a company focusing on business analytics, especially dashboards and data visualization) for $195 million in 2007 (Gonsalves, 2007). More recently, TIBCO acquired Insightful Corporation, a provider of statistical data analysis and data mining solutions, for $25 million in June 2008.

TIBCO Spotfire seeks to enable business users across the enterprise to quickly and easily visualize and interact with their data to gain new insights and make better decisions. With a focus on business analytics, from ad-hoc query and interactive reporting to advanced analytics, TIBCO Spotfire offers several BI tools, including TIBCO Spotfire, TIBCO Spotfire DecisionSite, TIBCO Spotfire Analytics Server, and TIBCO Spotfire S+. TIBCO Spotfire also provides BI solutions through the development of analytic applications that span business processes.

According to Gartner's 2009 BI report on BI platforms, TIBCO Spotfire's architecture combines in-memory analytics and interactive visualization, and thereby enables flexibility and ease in developing and using analytic applications, especially for personal and workgroup applications. Moreover, the acquisition of Insightful provides TIBCO Spotfire a set of predictive capabilities including a data mining workbench (Insightful Miner) and the S+ language for quick prototyping of what-if modeling and statistical analysis. Gartner's 2009 study of BI platforms found TIBCO Spotfire to receive the highest rating in terms of customer support. However, this study also found, consistent with TIBCO Spotfire's market positioning, that TIBCO Spotfire is "not used by a large number of users in most of its deployments, nor is it used to analyze particularly large data sets." Moreover, TIBCO Spotfire was considered weak in metadata management and as rarely being used as the enterprise standard BI platform. TIBCO Spotfire was not included in Gartner's survey of BI reporting capabilities.

QlikTech: QlikTech was founded in Sweden as a consulting company in 1993, but moved into BI in 1997 and is now based in Radnor, Pennsylvania. QlikTech was classified as a visionary in the Gartner's 2008 and 2009 reports on BI platforms, and as a contender (behind leaders and strong performers) in the 2008 Forrester report on enterprise BI platforms. QlikTech was not included in Gartner's survey of BI reporting capabilities.

QlikTech focuses on in-memory analytics, an emerging trend that enables the analytics to be performed in random access memory (RAM) rather than on data stored on disk, therefore eliminating the need for time-consuming hard-disk input/output tasks. Enabled by 64-bit computing and declining costs of RAM, in-memory analytics first loads all the information into memory. It provides several benefits: faster response times, consistent response times regardless of the number of tables being accessed, reduced need for pre-calculation, and reduced need for balancing between data size and response time considerations.

According to Gartner's 2009 report on BI platforms, QlikTech's in-memory model, automated data integration, associative technology, and graphical analytical environment cater to an underserved market for work-group-level analytic applications that enable business users to build solutions with little assistance from IT. QuikTech's QlikView has been highly acclaimed both in the Gartner's 2009 report (according to which, "QlikTech's architecture delivers an exceptionally high degree of customer satisfaction") as well as a 2009 study, by Aberdeen, of how the major BI and performance management vendors stacked up across various customer-driven metrics (Woodie, 2009). However, QlikView is perceived to lack the statistical and predictive modeling capabilities of some of its main competitors, including SAS JMP and TIBCO Spotfire.

Actuate: Actuate has been classified as a niche player in Gartner's 2008 and 2009 reports on BI platforms, and as strong performer (behind leaders) in the 2008 Forrester report on enterprise BI platforms. Its major products include Actuate BIRT (Business Intelligence and Reporting Tools, which is an open-source reporting project) tools for creating interactive reports, dashboards, and mashups (Web pages or applications that combine data or functionality from two or more external sources to create a new service); Actuate e.Reports, a tool for producing on-demand reports intended for presentations, and e.Spreadsheet, which auto-mates and centralizes spreadsheet production, maintenance, archiving, and security.

Actuate is considered strong in terms of reporting capabilities, open-source products (related to BIRT), and spreadsheet distribution (through e.Spreadsheet reporting technology). Actuate focuses primarily on reporting, and is the only vendor to have two products included in the 2009 Gartner survey comparing BI reporting components: Actuate BIRT and Actuate e.Reports. Actuate BIRT received a best possible 5.0 in terms of high-quality, portable output, and other scores of 4.0 or greater in ease of use for end users and complex, interactive reporting. Actuate e.Reports received a 5.0 in terms of user volume scalability and complex, interactive reporting, and other scores of 4.0 or greater in ease of use for end users and data volume scalability.

However, Actuate is generally not considered to be an enterprise BI standard, and also ranked low in terms of support for OLAP and ad hoc analysis in Gartner's 2009 report on BI platforms. According to this report: "given that Actuate is making limited investments in enhancing its OLAP capabilities, its niche focus will exclude it from shortlists as more enterprises look to standardize on vendors that can provide end-to-end BI platform capabilities."

Table 7.2 summarizes the above discussion of the major independent BI vendors.

Other Notable BI Vendors

In the above detailed discussion, we have focused on the mega-vendors and major independent vendors of BI. However, a few other vendors need to be mentioned; these are Teradata, HP, arcplan, Board International, and Pano-rama Software. Although HP and Teradata are important in the arena of enterprise data warehouse servers (with products such as HP Neoview enter-prise data warehousing platform and Teradata Active Enterprise Data Ware-house, respectively), they are not yet considered among leading vendors of BI tools (Wailgum, 2008b). Teradata and HP have been excluded from Gartner's 2009 report on BI platforms, as well as the 2008 Forrester report on enterprise BI platforms.

arcplan, Board International, and Panorama Software were included in Gartner's 2009 report on BI platforms. However, they were all considered niche players, and seen as being limited in both ability to innovate and completeness of vision: arcplan seems to position itself as a partner of large BI vendors; Board International is constrained to Windows and primarily to a European user base; and Panorama Software is limited to departmental rather than broad-reach BI, and often encounters performance problems because of being based on data sources over which it has no control (Richardson et al., 2009a). They were all excluded from the 2008 Forrester report and from Gartner's 2009 study of reporting components.

Table 7.2 A Comparison of Major Independent BI Vendors*

Vendor	Evaluation in industry surveys	Illustrative BI-related products	Strengths	Weaknesses
SAS	G'08: Leader G'09: Leader F'08: Leader	SAS Enterprise BI Server; SAS Analytics; SAS Visual BI; SAS Web Report Studio	• Extensive use of data mining and predictive modeling • Powerful analytic solutions	• Few organizations consider SAS to be their enterprise BI standard • Considered more difficult to use
Micro Strategy	G'08: Leader G'09: Leader F'08: Strong performer	Intelligence Server; Intelligence Server extensions; User interfaces; Development/administration tools	• Outstanding metadata management • Good in parameterized reporting • Excellent technical performance • Greater innovation ability	• Generally not considered for enterprise BI standardization • Report authoring is not aimed at casual business users
Information Builders	G'08: Leader G'09: Leader F'08: Strong performer	WebFOCUS BI platform; iWay software suite of prebuilt integration components; host-based reporting (FOCUS)	• Excellent custom Web-based BI • Highly parameterized reporting • Commonly used as BI standard • Capability to extract, transform, and load from disparate systems	• Limited in terms of OLAP capabilities • Limited due to the focus on financial services industry and on North America

Vendor	Ratings	Products	Strengths	Weaknesses
TIBCO (including Spotfire)	G'08: Visionary G'09: Visionary F'08: Strong performer	TIBCO Spotfire; TIBCO Spotfire DecisionSite; TIBCO Spotfire Analytics Server; TIBCO Spotfire S+	• Excellent customer support • Flexibility and ease in developing and using analytics, especially for personal/workgroup applications • Predictive capabilities	• Generally not used by a large number of users, to analyze very large data sets, or as the enterprise standard BI platform • Weak in metadata management
Qliktech	G'08: Visionary G'09: Visionary F'08: Contender	QlikView; QlikView Server; QlikView Publisher	• Excellent customer support • In-memory model and automated data integration capability • Easy for users to build solutions	• Lacks strong statistical and predictive modeling capabilities
Actuate	G'08: Niche player G'09: Niche player F'08: Strong performer	Actuate BIRT tools; Actuate e.Reports; e.Spreadsheet	• Reporting capabilities • Open-source products (BIRT) • Spreadsheet distribution (through e.Spreadsheet reporting technology)	• Generally not considered as an enterprise BI standard • Considered weak in support for OLAP and ad hoc analysis

* Industry reports include Gartner's 2008 (G'08) and 2009 (G'09) surveys on BI platforms, and Forrester's 2008 survey on enterprise BI platforms (F'08).

▶ 7.6 SUMMARY

In this chapter we discussed and illustrated BI tools. We also summarized the major BI vendors and the tools they offer. We compiled further information about these BI tools from the vendors' Web site in two appendices: Appendix A summarizing BI tools offered by mega-vendors, and Appendix B summarizing BI tools offered by large independent BI vendors. This chapter's discussion of BI tools and vendors will be useful in Chapter 8, which focuses on BI solutions and the processes related to their sourcing and development.

▶ KEY TERMS

business intelligence
  tools
business intelligence
  solutions

business intelligence
  vendors
mega-vendors
independent BI vendors

customization of BI
standardization of BI
  tools

▶ REVIEW QUESTIONS

1. Distinguish between a "BI tool" and a "BI solution."

2. Identify and illustrate any two BI tools that facilitate organizational memory.

3. Briefly explain the one attribute you consider important most important for a BI vendor, and illustrate using an example.

4. Distinguish between tools supporting organizational memory and tools supporting information integration.

5. Identify and briefly explain how mergers and acquisitions have affected the BI industry.

6. Distinguish between "power users," "business users," and "middle class" users of BI.

7. What factors affect decisions regarding customization or standardization of BI tools? How?

▶ APPLICATION EXERCISES

1. Select any one of the four "mega-vendors" from Table 7.1. Use the Web to obtain additional information about this vendor and its BI tools. Prepare a review of this vendor and its BI tools, highlighting the strengths and weaknesses beyond the ones identified in Table 7.1.

2. Select any one of the six independent vendors from Table 7.2. Use the Web to obtain additional information about this vendor and its BI tools. Prepare a review of this vendor and its BI tools, highlighting the strengths and weaknesses beyond the ones identified in Table 7.2.

3. Based on Appendices A and B, identify any two BI tools that would be helpful for presentation capability. Obtain more information about these tools using the Web pages identified in the Appendices, and then compare the tools.

4. Visit http://www.sas.com/technologies/bi/entbiserver/. Take the interactive video tour under "Resources," and then review SAS Enterprise BI Server based on the video tour and other information available from this Web page.

5. Using Business Intelligence in Practice examples from the earlier chapters in the book, identify a company that has either already benefited from insight creation capability or can benefit from it in the future. Obtain more information about this company using the Web, and then identify potential BI tools (from Appendices A and B) that might be useful for this company.

▶ **REFERENCES**

Armstrong, M. 2008. "Measuring 'Public Diplomacy'?" *inRunner.us*, March 4, http://mountainrunner.us/2008/03/measuring_public_diplomacy.html.

Baars, H., and Kemper, H-G., 2008. "Management Support with Structured and Unstructured Data—An Integrated Business Intelligence Framework." *Information Systems Management*, 25, 132–148.

Essex, D. 2008. "Get Smart with Your Data." *Government Computer News*, February 14, http://gcn.com/articles/2008/02/14/get-smart-with-your-data.aspx.

Evelson, B., and Hamerman, P. D. 2007. Cognos Acquisition Puts IBM in Thick of BI Race Move Changes Competitive and Partnering Dynamics (Cambridge, Mass.: Forrester Research). http://www.forrester.com/Research/Document/Excerpt/0,7211,44105,00.html (accessed May 21, 2009).

Evelson, B., Karel, R., Kobielus, J., Nicolson, N., and Moore, C. 2008. The Forrester Wave: Enterprise Business Intelligence Platforms, Q3 2008 (Cambridge, Mass.: Forrester Research).

FinanceWeek. 2008. "SPSS: Breaking the Bounds of Business Intelligence." *FinanceWeek*, March 10, http://www.financeweek.co.uk/item/5961 (accessed May 27, 2009).

Gonsalves, A. 2007. "Tibco Plans to Blend BI with BPM in SpotFire Buy." *Intelligent Enterprise*, May 2, http://www.intelligententerprise.com/showArticle.jhtml?articleID=199203107 (accessed May 27, 2009).

Howson, C. 2008. *Successful Business Intelligence: Secrets to Making BI a Killer App* (McGraw-Hill Osborne).

InformationBuilders. 2008. Air Canada Soars with Web-Based Flight-Tracking Application, http://www.informationbuilders.com/applications/airCanada.html (accessed April 5, 2009).

ITNews. 2009. "Media Release: MicroStrategy Announces General Availability of Micro-Strategy 9." *ITNews*, March 27, http://www.itnews.com.au/News/99698,media-release-microstrategy-announces-general-availability-of-microstrategy-9.aspx (accessed May 29, 2009).

Kellen, V. 2007. "The State of BI: An RV Parked in a Cul-de-Sac." *Cutter Benchmark Review*, September, 16–22.

Montalbano, E. 2009. "SAP Expands on Business Intelligence." *InfoWorld*, May 11, http://www.infoworld.com/d/applications/sap-expands-business-intelligence-981 (accessed May 29, 2009).

Olszak, C. M., and Ziemba, E. 2007. "Approach to Building and Implementing Business Intelligence Systems." *Interdisciplinary Journal of Information, Knowledge, and Management*, 2.

Richardson, J., Schlegel, K., Sallam, R. L., and Hostmann, M. 2009a. Magic Quadrant for Business Intelligence Platforms, Gartner RAS Core Research Note G00163529, January 16, http://mediaproducts.gartner.com/reprints/oracle/article56/article56.html (accessed May 26, 2009).

Richardson, J., Schlegel, K., and Sallam, R. L. 2009b. Critical Capabilities for Business Intelligence Reporting, Gartner RAS Core Research Note G00162662, February 14, https://resource.microstrategy.com/ResourceCenter/transmit.aspx (accessed May 31, 2009).

Richardson, J., Schlegel, K., Hostmann, M., and McMurchy, N. 2008. Magic Quadrant for Business Intelligence Platforms, Gartner G00154227, February 1.

Scheps, S. 2008. *Business Intelligence for Dummies* (Indianapolis, Ind.: Wiley).

Wailgum, T. 2008a. "Business Intelligence: A Technology Category in Tumult," *CIO*, March 24, http://www.cio.com/article/202750/Business_Intelligence_A_Technology_Category_in_Tumult (accessed May 25, 2009).

Wailgum, T. 2008b. "Nine Business Intelligence Vendors to Watch," *CIO*, March 25, http://www.cio.com/article/203900/Nine_Business_Intelligence_Vendors_to_Watch (accessed May 26, 2009).

Weier, M. H. 2008. "Government Using BI Software to Measure Public Diplomacy." *InformationWeek*, December 3.

Woodie, A. 2009. "BI Vendor QlikTech Celebrates Success." *ITJungle*, February 24, http://www.itjungle.com/fhs/fhs022409-story07.html (accessed May 29, 2009).

Appendix 7.1 A Summary of BI Products from Mega-Vendors[a]

Product	Description
	Oracle (including Hyperion)
Oracle Business Intelligence Suite Enterprise Edition Plus[b]	"Oracle Business Intelligence Suite Enterprise Edition Plus (Oracle BI EE Plus) is a comprehensive suite of enterprise BI products that delivers a full range of analysis and reporting capabilities. Featuring a unified, highly scalable, modern architecture, Oracle BI EE Plus provides intelligence and analytics from data spanning enterprise sources and applications—empowering the largest communities with complete and relevant insight. Oracle BI EE Plus also bundles key Oracle Hyperion reporting products for integrated reporting with Oracle Hyperion financial applications."
Oracle Business Intelligence Suite Standard Edition One[c]	"Oracle Business Intelligence Standard Edition One (SE One) is a complete, integrated BI system designed for deployments from 5 to 50 users. It includes proven, leading BI and data warehousing technology, including Oracle Interactive Dashboards, Oracle BI Publisher for highly formatted reporting, Oracle Answers for ad hoc reporting and analysis, Oracle Warehouse Builder for ETL, and Oracle Database—all in one easy to install package."
Oracle BI Publisher[d]	"Oracle Business Intelligence (BI) Publisher (formerly XML Publisher) is an enterprise reporting solution for authoring, managing, and delivering all your highly formatted documents, such as operational reports, electronic funds transfer documents, government PDF forms, shipping labels, checks, sales and marketing letters, and much more. Built on open standards, Oracle BI Publisher also allows IT Staff and developers to create data models against practically any data source and build custom reporting applications that leverage existing infrastructure. Oracle BI Publisher can generate tens of thousands of documents per hour with minimal impact to transactional systems. Reports can be designed using familiar desktop products and viewed online or scheduled for delivery to a wide range of destinations."
Oracle Business Activity Monitoring[e]	"Oracle Business Activity Monitoring (Oracle BAM) is a complete solution for building interactive, real-time dashboards and proactive alerts for monitoring business processes and services. Oracle BAM gives business executives and operation managers the information they need to make better business decisions and take corrective action if the business environment changes."

(Continued)

Appendix 7.1 (*Continued*)

Product	Description
Oracle Crystal Ball[f]	"Crystal Ball software is a leading spreadsheet-based software suite for predictive modeling, forecasting, Monte Carlo simulation and optimization. With over 4,000 customers worldwide, including 85% of the Fortune 500, Crystal Ball is used by customers from a broad range of industries, such as aerospace, financial services, manufacturing, oil and gas, pharmaceutical and utilities. Crystal Ball is used in over 800 universities and schools worldwide for teaching risk analysis concepts. The diverse applications for Crystal Ball include financial risk analysis, valuation, engineering, Six Sigma, portfolio allocation, cost estimation, and project management. With Oracle Crystal Ball Enterprise Performance Management, you can apply the power of Crystal Ball to your Oracle Enterprise Performance Management (EPM) and Business Intelligence (BI) applications to improve the strategic decision-making process."
Oracle Data Integration Suite[g]	"Oracle Data Integration Suite includes a comprehensive set of data management components for building, deploying, and managing enterprise data integration solutions. It includes the necessary components for data movement, data quality, data profiling, and metadata management for solving any data integration and data management challenge. Together with service-oriented architecture (SOA), Oracle Data Integration Suite provides the agility needed for service oriented data management. With Oracle Data Integration Suite's open and hot-pluggable components, organizations can easily extend and evolve their architectures instead of replacing existing investments."
Oracle BI on Demand[h]	"Customers who choose Oracle Business Intelligence (BI) On Demand get the advantage of letting Oracle experts manage their Oracle BI solution, gaining access to critical information for their business at a lower total cost of ownership and with faster time-to-value than they get with in-house deployment. Oracle BI On Demand also lets customers shift focus back to their core business and away from supporting technology.

They also get Oracle's end-to-end, hot-pluggable BI technology platform, including market-leading data warehousing, data integration, and portals that deliver actionable intelligence directly to those who need it, when they need it."

SAP (including BusinessObjects)

SAP Business Objects Enterprise[i]	"SAP BusinessObjects Enterprise software is a flexible and scalable information infrastructure that makes it easy for you to discover and share insight for optimal decision making. Built on a service-oriented architecture, the software offers an extensive set of solutions on a single platform—and enables IT departments to extend BI to any application or process in any environment."
SAP Business Objects Xcelsius Enterprise[j]	"SAP BusinessObjects Xcelsius Enterprise is a point-and-click data visualization tool designed specifically to create interactive analytics and dashboards with secure, live connections to SAP BusinessObjects Enterprise and SAP BusinessObjects Edge BI. You can share these meaningful visualizations live via Microsoft Office, Adobe PDF, the Web, Crystal Reports, or the SAP BusinessObjects business intelligence (BI) portal. SAP BusinessObjects Xcelsius Enterprise drop-down menus and sliders allow you to present complex business data clearly, giving your decision makers an easy way to interact with data and test out future business scenarios."
Crystal Reports[k]	"Crystal Reports software enables you to easily design interactive reports and connect them to virtually any data source. Your users can benefit from on-report sorting and filtering—giving them the power to execute decisions instantly."
NetWeaver BW[l]	"With SAP NetWeaver Business Warehouse (SAP NetWeaver BW), you can integrate data from across the enterprise and beyond, and then transform it into information to drive sound decision making, targeted action, and solid business results. Incorporating a business intelligence (BI) infrastructure, a comprehensive set of tools, planning and simulation capabilities, and data-warehousing functionality are delivered through enterprise portal technology."

IBM (including Cognos)

IBM Cognos 8[m]	"IBM Cognos 8 BI delivers the complete range of BI capabilities on a single service-oriented architecture (SOA).

(Continued)

Appendix 7.1 (*Continued*)

Product	Description
	Provides the capabilities and information you need to make better decisions. Use reports, analysis, dashboards and scorecards to monitor business performance, analyze trends and measure results. A service-oriented architecture makes it easy to deploy and manage." Components of IBM Cognos 8 BI include: "Reporting: Write and deliver any type of report, adaptable to any data source, quickly and easily. Analysis: Analyze and report against online analytical processing (OLAP) and dimensionally aware relational sources. Scorecarding: Build scorecards to align teams and tactics with strategy. Dashboards: Communicate complex information quickly with a range of easy-to-build dashboards. Extend BI: Increase BI's reach and user adoption rates through search, mobile access, and more."
	Microsoft
Microsoft Excel[n]	"Excel is the most commonly used business intelligence tool today, and for good reason. It is a powerful application that provides all the functionality you need to create spreadsheets, analyze data, and share information in a manageable environment." With Excel 2007, it is easy to "create and use reports that include rich data visualization, information from inside and outside your organization's data warehouse, PivotTable views, and professional-looking charts."
Microsoft SQL Server (2008 version)[o]	"Microsoft SQL Server 2008 provides a scalable Business Intelligence platform optimized for data integration, reporting, and analysis, enabling organizations to deliver intelligence where users want it. Features provide abilities to: Create high-performance Analysis Services solutions with optimized cube designers, subspace computation, and MOLAP-enabled writeback capabilities Implement enterprise-scale Reporting Services solutions through new on-demand processing and instance-based rendering Build flexible and effective reports with the new Tablix data structure and rich formatting capabilities

Microsoft SharePoint Server[p]

"Microsoft Office SharePoint Server 2007 is an integrated suite of server capabilities that can help improve organizational effectiveness by providing comprehensive content management and enterprise search, accelerating shared business processes, and facilitating information-sharing across boundaries for better business insight. Additionally, this collaboration and content management server provides IT professionals and developers with the platform and tools they need for server administration, application extensibility, and interoperability."

Expand reach, and empower more users through optimized integration with the 2007 Microsoft Office system"

Microsoft Office Performance-Point Server[q]

"Microsoft Office PerformancePoint Server 2007 is a powerful performance management application that enables you to monitor and analyze your business. By providing flexible, easy-to-use tools for building dashboards and scorecards, Office PerformancePoint Server 2007 can help everyone across your organization make informed business decisions that align with companywide objectives and strategy."

---

[a]The material in this Appendix has been obtained from the vendors' Web sites, the URLs for which are identified in the footnotes.

[b]http://www.oracle.com/appserver/business-intelligence/enterprise-edition.html

[c]http://www.oracle.com/appserver/business-intelligence/standard-edition-one.html

[d]http://www.oracle.com/appserver/business-intelligence/bi-publisher.html

[e]http://www.oracle.com/appserver/business-activity-monitoring.html

[f]http://www.oracle.com/crystalball/index.html

[g]http://www.oracle.com/products/middleware/odi/odi-suite.html

[h]http://www.oracle.com/newsletters/information-indepth/on-demand/sep-07/business-intelligence.html

[i]http://www12.sap.com/solutions/sapbusinessobjects/large/intelligenceplatform/bi/information-infrastructure/enterprise/index.epx

[j]http://www12.sap.com/solutions/sapbusinessobjects/large/intelligenceplatform/bi/dashboard-visualization/xcelsius-enterprise/index.epx

[k]http://www12.sap.com/solutions/sapbusinessobjects/sme/reporting/crystalreports/index.epx

[l]http://www.sap.com/platform/netweaver/components/businesswarehouse/index.epx

[m]http://www-01.ibm.com/software/data/cognos/products/cognos-8-business-intelligence/

[n]http://www.microsoft.com/bi/products/excel.aspx

[o]http://www.microsoft.com/sqlserver/2008/en/us/business-intelligence.aspx

[p]http://sharepoint.microsoft.com/Pages/Default.aspx

[q]http://www.microsoft.com/bi/products/performancepoint-server.aspx

Appendix 7.2 A Summary of BI Products From Leading Independent BI Vendors[a]

Product	Description
	SAS
SAS Enterprise BI Server[b]	"SAS® Enterprise BI Server is a comprehensive, easy-to-use business intelligence software solution that integrates the power of SAS analytics and data integration to share insights that power better business decisions. It includes role-based, self-service interfaces for all types of users within a well-defined IT governance framework and a centralized point of administration. This helps organizations simplify and speed business intelligence deployment."
SAS Analytics[c]	"SAS Analytics provides an integrated environment for predictive and descriptive modeling, data mining, text analytics, forecasting, optimization, simulation, experimental design and more. From predictive analytics to model deployment and process optimization, SAS provides a range of techniques and processes for the collection, classification, analysis and interpretation of data to reveal patterns, anomalies, key variables and relationships, leading ultimately to new insights and better answers faster."
SAS Visual BI[d]	"SAS Visual BI, powered by JMP® software, provides dynamic business visualization, enabling business users to interactively explore ideas and information, investigate patterns and discover previously hidden facts through visual queries. Business users gain instantaneous insight into relationships and patterns in data by viewing and interacting with information in ways that static charts and Excel spreadsheets cannot match."
SAS Web Report Studio[e]	"SAS Web Report Studio provides fast, simple access to query and reporting capabilities on the Web. It empowers business users and decision makers across the enterprise with self-sufficient access to consistent data and the predictive power of SAS analytics for more accurate decisions. At the same time, it enables IT departments to minimize administrative overhead, maximize resources and free IT staff to focus on more strategic issues."
	Micro Strategy
Intelligence Server[f]	"MicroStrategy Intelligence Server™ is the industry's most advanced, scalable, secure and robust business intelligence server. MicroStrategy Intelligence Server provides the core analytical processing and job management for all reporting, analysis and monitoring applications. Employing a Services-Oriented Architecture (SOA), MicroStrategy Intelligence Server makes it easy to

	standardize on a single, open platform for all your enterprise reporting and analysis needs through a number of access channels: Web browsers, Microsoft® Office, Desktop clients, and email."
Intelligence server extensions[g]	"MicroStrategy Report Services: The enterprise reporting engine that delivers the full range of report formats, including scorecards and dashboards, financial reports, customer invoices and statements, and highly detailed operational reports"
	"MicroStrategy OLAP Services: Enables MicroStrategy Web, Office, and Desktop users to perform intuitive OLAP analysis with Intelligent Cubes"
	"MicroStrategy Distribution Services: Enables high volume, managed report distribution through email, printers, and file systems on a scheduled basis"
	"MicroStrategy MultiSource Option: Enables users to seamlessly report, analyze, and monitor data across multiple data sources through a single business model"
	"MicroStrategy Data Mining Services: A fully integrated component that delivers data mining predictive models to all users"
	"MicroStrategy SAP® Services: A fully integrated component that delivers SAP certified NetWeaver™ integration"
User interfaces[h]	"MicroStrategy Web: An interactive environment for reporting and analysis through an all-HTML and zero-footprint web client
	MicroStrategy Desktop: An integrated development, administration, and run-time business intelligence environment on the personal computing desktop
	MicroStrategy Office: Delivers the full power and sophistication of the MicroStrategy industrial-strength business intelligence platform to the Microsoft Office Productivity suite
	MicroStrategy Mobile: An interactive user interface for monitoring, reporting, and analysis for BlackBerry® devices"
Development & administration tools[i]	"MicroStrategy Architect: A rapid development tool that maps the physical structure of the data warehouse into a logical business model
	MicroStrategy Object Manager: Manages BI applications between development, testing, and production systems
	MicroStrategy Command Manager: Enables the creation and execution of text-based commands from a command line and a graphical interface
	MicroStrategy Enterprise Manager: A monitoring tool that provides usage and resource information about the BI environment

(Continued)

Product	Description
	MicroStrategy Integrity Manager: A report comparison tool that provides automated information integrity assurance and regression analysis MicroStrategy SDK: Exposes the functionality of the MicroStrategy architecture via an open API for customization of the Web interface and integration with third-party applications"
	Information Builders
WebFOCUS BI platform[j]	"WebFOCUS is a comprehensive and fully integrated enterprise BI platform whose architecture, integration, and simplicity permeate every level of the global organization—executive, analytical, and operational—and make any data available, accessible, and meaningful to every person or application who needs it, when and how they need it."
iWay software suite of pre-built integration components[k]	"iWay Software's integration methodology is simple: We use a single, integrated set of graphical design tools to assemble powerful pre-built components for enterprise-class business-to-business (B2B), business process automation (BPA), or enterprise information management (EIM) integration scenarios – without the use of custom code. Integration configurations can be deployed in a standalone manner to any environment supporting a JVM – or to Web application servers from any vendor." Pre-built integration components are categorized into: Service Enablement (e.g., Application System Adapters); Message Processing (e.g., Event Processing); Data Integration (e.g., Data Transformation); Business Integration (e.g., Partner Management; Management (e.g., Validation).
Host-based reporting (FOCUS)[l]	"FOCUS application development and reporting tools provide maximum functionality for non-technical business managers to business analyst/power users to professional developers. FOCUS can create reports from virtually any database, relational or legacy. FOCUS reports and applications are portable and scalable to more than 35 operating systems, including IBM mainframes, Compaq OpenVMS and NonStop™ systems, AS/400s, and an array of UNIX platforms, such as HP-UX, AIX, Solaris, and others. So users on multiple computer platforms throughout an enterprise can run the same consistent reports. FOCUS users in every major industry are finding it easier than ever to build and maintain custom applications and reports in Windows, Windows NT, even the Internet."

TIBCO (including Spotfire)

TIBCO Spotfire[m]

"The TIBCO Spotfire Enterprise Analytics platform offers a radically faster business intelligence experience and is far more adaptable to specific industry and business challenges than traditional alternatives.
Unlike traditional BI, the Spotfire Enterprise Analytic platform equips every employee to quickly discover new insights in the information they work with every day. Spotfire's interactive, visual capabilities for data analysis empower individuals to easily see trends, patterns outliers and unanticipated relationships in data with unprecedented speed and adaptability."

TIBCO Spotfire DecisionSite[n]

"DecisionSite allows engineers, researchers, and analysts to visualize, analyze, and explore attribute-rich data in real time. Across drug discovery, process engineering, energy exploration, and national safety, Spotfire greatly increases the speed of decision-making in the face of increasing data volume and complexity. Unlike niche tools, custom spreadsheet solutions and other static data reports, DecisionSite's interactive, visual capabilities for data analysis empowers individuals to quickly and easily see trends, patterns, outliers, and unanticipated relationships in data."

TIBCO Spotfire Analytics Server[o]

"The Spotfire Analytics Server provides the enterprise with a centralized platform for the integration, deployment and administration of next generation business intelligence applications.
The Spotfire Analytics Server gives your organization complete control over the configuration and security of the entire Spotfire Enterprise Analytics platform. This single point of integration makes it simple to leverage your existing corporate information, user directory and authentication infrastructure and assets. It enables distributing Guided analytic applications throughout the enterprise and provides unmatched scalability while reducing the cost of managing applications."

TIBCO Spotfire S+[p]

"TIBCO Spotfire S+ products enable decision makers across the organization to benefit from the power of advanced analytics by integrating statistical modeling and data mining into existing business processes and solutions. Statisticians and business analysts can prototype, test, and deploy analytics much faster than with alternative statistical modeling environments.
Based on the flexible S language, Spotfire S+ is the de facto standard for flexible statistical analysis from academia to commercial research, providing commercial support to scale cutting-edge statistics across the organization."

(Continued)

215

Appendix 7.2 (*Continued*)

Product	Description
Qliktech	
QlikView[q]	"With an in-memory data model, QlikView allows data to be analyzed at both an aggregate and a detailed level without the time-consuming and costly step of building multidimensional OLAP cubes. In addition, associations between data are automatically mapped in QlikView and respond instantly to user selections. Since data is kept in-memory, the response time of any calculation is lightning fast, even on extremely large data sets analyzed by multiple concurrent users."
QlikView Server[r]	"QlikView Server is the central source of truth in an organization. With today's distributed workforce, QlikView Server provides a simple way for organizations to ensure everyone has access to the latest data and analysis, independent of their location. Regardless of the client chosen—zero-footprint Web browser clients, Windows, Internet Explorer plug-in, or Java—QlikView Server provides secure access to the latest version of each QlikView application."
QlikView Publisher[s]	"QlikView Publisher, an optional module for QlikView Server, is an administration and management tool that provides a single control point for the company's QlikView analytics applications and QlikView reports. Administrators can schedule, distribute and manage security and access for QlikView applications and QlikView reports across the enterprise. With QlikView Publisher, companies can balance the business need for widespread distribution of analytics functionality and reports with the requirement to maintain centralized control and synchronization of sensitive corporate data."
Actuate	
Actuate BIRT tools[t]	"Actuate BIRT Interactive Viewer: Ad-hoc web reporting tool that enables end users to modify their report views to suit their needs. Actuate BIRT Report Studio: Ad-hoc web reporting tool that enables business users to develop their own reports, based on templates created by IT and/or developers. Actuate BIRT Report Designers: Both BIRT Designer and BIRT Designer Pro enable IT and developers to create templates and reports that can be accessed within the Actuate framework and used by both business and end users.

Actuate BIRT Flash and Dashboards: BIRT reports can arrive in any format, including (Flash) dashboards that users can customize to meet their own reporting needs."

Actuate e.Reports[u] "e.Reports, Actuate's pixel-perfect report production tool, provides the most discerning users with brochure-quality, on-demand reports designed for presentation. e.Report products create every business report imaginable, from annual reports to internal operational reports, and from banking and credit card statements to wealth management portfolio reports."

e.Spreadsheet[v] "Actuate e.Spreadsheet automates and centralizes spreadsheet production, maintenance, archiving, and security, eliminating version discrepancies and curbing the proliferation of multiple silos of Excel® workbook data."

[a] The material in this Appendix has been obtained from the vendors' Web sites, the URLs for which are identified in the footnotes.
[b] http://www.sas.com/technologies/bi/entbiserver/index.html
[c] http://www.sas.com/technologies/analytics/index.html
[d] http://www.sas.com/technologies/bi/visualization/visualbi/index.html
[e] http://www.sas.com/resources/asset/sas-web-report-studio-factsheet.pdf
[f] http://www.microstrategy.com/Software/Products/Intelligence_Server/
[g] http://www.microstrategy.com/Software/
[h] http://www.microstrategy.com/Software/
[i] http://www.microstrategy.com/Software/
[j] http://www.informationbuilders.com/products/webfocus/index.html
[k] http://www.iwaysoftware.com/products/prebuilt.html
[l] http://www.informationbuilders.com/products/focus/overview.html
[m] http://spotfire.tibco.com/Products/Info.aspx
[n] http://spotfire.tibco.com/products/decisionsite_features.aspx
[o] http://spotfire.tibco.com/Products/Analytics-Server.aspx
[p] http://spotfire.tibco.com/Products/S-Plus.aspx
[q] http://www.qlikview.com/contents.aspx?id=10396
[r] http://www.qlikview.com/product/QV%200320%20Product%20Data%20Sheet%209%20eng%20US%20ltr.pdf
[s] http://www.qlikview.com/product/QT%200320%20QlikView%20Publisher%209%20eng%20US%20ltr.pdf
[t] http://www.actuate.com/products/birt/
[u] http://www.actuate.com/products/e-reports/summary/
[v] http://www.actuate.com/products/e-spreadsheet/

CHAPTER 8

DEVELOPMENT OF BUSINESS INTELLIGENCE

▶ 8.1 INTRODUCTION

In Chapter 7, we described BI tools and vendors. In this chapter, we focus on BI solutions and the processes associated with developing them. The chapter begins by examining BI solutions (Section 8.2) and their desired characteristics (Section 8.3), and then discusses sourcing of BI solutions and tools (Section 8.4), the overall methodology for developing BI solutions (Section 8.5), and then the specific steps in developing BI solutions (Section 8.6).

▶ 8.2 BUSINESS INTELLIGENCE SOLUTIONS

In Chapters 3 to 6, we described the four BI capabilities—organizational memory capability, information integration capability, information integration capability, and presentation capability—in detail. We then examined in Chapter 7 how these four BI capabilities could be obtained through BI tools available from several vendors. These four BI capabilities come together in a BI solution, which is developed for, and deployed within, a client organization. A BI solution utilizes the BI tools that are either acquired from vendors or developed internally by the organization, and draws upon the vast amounts of data from existing data warehouses and transaction processing systems, as well as structured and unstructured information from these and other sources (such as e-mail messages) to deliver the information and knowledge that facilitate decision making. Thus, a BI solution can benefit from a variety of BI tools. Business Intelligence in Practice 8.1 illustrates this using the example of Haggen, Inc.

Business Intelligence in Practice 8.1: Haggen Deploys a BI Solution Using Multiple Technologies

Haggen, Inc., a grocery retailer that opened its first store in 1933, has grown to 15 food and pharmacy locations in Washington and Oregon. Employing over 3,700 employees, Haggen is one of the largest privately owned

(continued)

---

companies in the state of Washington and one of the nation's 75 largest grocery chains.

When Harrison Lewis joined Haggen in September 2005 as Vice President and Chief Information Officer, he was already recognized in the retail industry as a process innovator and a result-oriented visionary. He found that the company had a lot of information scattered across several systems that focused on point-of-sale transactions, planning, finance, and human resources functions. But it had no way of effectively integrating this information into useful reports, despite having attempted to organize the information in various ways, including Excel spreadsheets, Access databases, and query reports for information residing on the company's AS400. Lewis remarked: "You name it, we had it. We needed a way to provide visibility of this information for our business users to allow them to make better decisions." It was impossible to report complex merchandise and category performance analysis due to the need to connect multiple levels of granularity (including department, category, subcategory, and SKU levels) and several source systems. Another major issue was that access to operational data was usually delayed by seven to ten days. This inhibited day-to-day operational capabilities, stifled innovation, and curtailed managers' ability to optimize offerings.

The problems associated with the integration, transformation, and maintenance of quality data were attributed to the absence of a data warehouse and business intelligence (BI) solution. Therefore, one of Lewis's first responsibilities was to find a BI and data warehouse solution. Rather than being based on quantified return-on-investment, the decision to seek a data warehouse and BI solution was based on the company leaders' "shared vision" that having timely, integrated information was critical to the company's future.

Over the last couple of years, Haggen has developed a BI solution that resides on an enterprise data warehouse and benefits from a number of BI tools. In doing so, Haggen has depended on an enterprise-level data warehouse from Teradata,[1] the ARC retail business intelligence solution[2] from Manthan Systems,[3] and GoldenGate software for Real-Time Business Intelligence[4].

Haggen's BI solution converts data from point-of-sale devices, in the form of the transaction logs, into an XML (extensible markup language) file that is sent to an ODS (operational data store). The company uses Microsoft's SSIS (SQL Server integration service) to translate its data into XML format.

GoldenGate Software helps to make the data available in near real time by capturing transactional data from the POS system and a variety of other

(*continued*)

---

[1] http://www.teradata.com/t/ accessed June 10, 2009.

[2] http://www.arc-bi.com/, accessed June 10, 2009.

[3] http://www.manthansystems.com/, accessed June 10, 2009.

[4] http://www.goldengate.com/, accessed June 10, 2009.

sources, and continuously feeding the data into the Teradata data warehouse for immediate access and easy analysis. According to Lewis, "With Golden-Gate in place, we have not only seen a dramatic decrease in data latency and errors, we have obtained visibility throughout the sales day in record time. This allows us to make important decisions about the business that have a positive effect on that day's sales and operations."

The ARC retail business intelligence solution analyzes data from the data warehouse into the desired reports or key performance indicators (KPIs) and disseminates relevant customized data to employees at all levels of the organization. It enables category managers to discern trends in any given day or week and identify items that are contributing to the growth of the category, as well as items that are not contributing. ARC reports also help Haggen to profile its customers based on purchasing trends, thereby facilitating targeted marketing strategies.

Although the implementation process encountered a few problems, it was completed in seven months. The most significant problem arose when business managers disagreed with the IT managers' plan to load only six months of historical data into the data warehouse for the initial rollout. Instead, the business stakeholders argued that a full year of data was essential for making useful comparisons. IT leaders agreed to load the additional data, although this extended the project by two months. Another challenge was in finding the data and then mapping it into ARC's data model. After this had been achieved, Haggen managers identified its KPIs, which determine the way in which ARC analyzes and displays the information. Eventually, almost all critics of the project were satisfied through involvement in the KPI development process and being able to see for themselves how the improved information availability would benefit their jobs as well as the entire company. Teradata's professional services consultants helped guide this process to completion.

Haggen's top brass is delighted at how well the components of the BI solution align to meet the firm's business needs. "We have metrics that we report out on a regular basis to each of the business areas and to senior management," he says. "The reports detail usage metrics and trends by individual and by KPI. The system has been very much internalized, and the usage has been pretty incredible."

(Compiled from Amendola, 2007; *Business Wire*, 2007; Janies, 2008; Zarrello, 2008)

Over the course of time, as technology evolves and needs change, an organization could adopt multiple BI solutions. Business Intelligence in Practice 8.2 illustrates this evolution by examining the adoption of BI solutions over time by Air Canada. This illustration focuses on BI solutions intended primarily for internal purposes.

Business Intelligence in Practice 8.2: Air Canada's Adoption of Internal BI Solutions Management

Air Canada, which is among the world's 20 largest commercial airlines and the largest airline in Canada, has benefitted considerably from BI over the years. Chantal Berthiaume was given the charge of BI at Air Canada in 1999, when the airline was generating reports from mainframe data. Since then, Air Canada has standardized on Information Builders' tools and migrated most of its data from legacy applications. Air Canada's IT infrastructure has largely been outsourced to IBM through a deal originally signed in the 1990s, but it continues to manage its BI internally.

In 2002, Air Canada selected WebFOCUS from Information Builder due to its reporting capability, lower price, usability, and easy integration with the existing portal, Excel spreadsheets, and PDFs. Berthiaume wanted to provide the users with as much functionality as possible, without requiring them to be knowledgeable or overly technical. Air Canada's first WebFOCUS project involved replacing a legacy revenue management reporting system that ran on the mainframe.

In December 2005, Air Canada started beta-testing Information Builders' WebFOCUS Active Reports, which combine data and interactive controls into a single, self-contained HTML file that can be transmitted through e-mail. Recipients are then able to analyze the data offline, without any connection back to the databases. Over 70 sales managers, from Asia to Australia, and with different levels of access to information technology and Internet access, began using it. Prior to Active Reports, the sales managers could all access an intranet portal for sales data, but viewing the information was difficult for some of them due to infrastructure issues. This problem was addressed by providing the information using Active Reports, which is delivered through e-mail. However, the main issue that was addressed through Active Reports was to meet the diverse information requirements in a timely fashion. For example, sales needed to be tracked by agency, country, and sales region. Ticket sales could arrive via one of Air Canada's partners or in the form of paper-based tickets that need to be scanned. Moreover, Air Canada did not want its sales office in one country to know what its office in another country was generating, so reports needed to be customized. Air Canada found Active Reports to be sufficiently flexible to address these requirements.

Following the beta test, Air Canada adopted Active Reports in 2006. At that time, Chantal Berthiaume's department, which was responsible for BI, included five developers: two for the WebFOCUS suite (including Active Reports), one for Oracle, one business analyst who was acting as liaison with IBM, and one developer for maintenance and to handle ad hoc requests. This

(*continued*)

group has been managing training and access, and guidance of users who encounter problems in interpreting reports. The group also frequently answered unrelated IT questions.

In 2007, Berthiaume indicated that her unit would be looking at visualization and would use visual dashboards for analysis. Since then, Air Canada has used data visualization in revenue management. Managers in Air Canada's Commercial branch, which is responsible for understanding how revenue is generated for the airline, had created an Advance Booking Report (ABR) that computes yield and revenue for each major market, sorted by time. This report has been used to answer questions such as the following: Does decrease in bookings represent a trend? Are the flights likely to be over-booked, or do we have excess capacity? The ABR is useful to people familiar with the information, but it was difficult for revenue management and sales personnel to identify problems, drill down into the data, and take timely decisions to improve bookings. Now, thanks to data visualization, they can drill down simply by highlighting a field. The data visualization tool uses geographic displays to reveal point-of-sale data on a world map, with multiple views being a click away by highlighting the relevant specific data element. Linking interactive graphs also helps detect correlations in the data. For example, users can select a time period and display a scatter plot of routes grouped by profitability (e.g., low bookings with low fares). Another click produces a report that identifies the issue in a single page. This leads to better comprehension of the issues, more productive meetings, and well-defined follow-up activities. "It's the same data but it is interactive, so users can isolate a certain aspect of the data, drill down, and spot problems with bookings and sales," says Berthiaume. "With this much data, it is easy to overlook anomalies and discrepancies without a visualization tool," she explains. "If you know you have a problem in a particular market, you can drill down into that data, but if you don't know there is a problem, you might miss it." The new revenue management system has been key to managing the business, helping Air Canada to understand the areas to focus on, and developing a more resilient business model.

Air Canada has used WebFOCUS to create a BI solution that helps its maintenance staff to identify deviations, which, in the airlines industry, refer to aircraft maintenance issues, including tracking parts for repairs. Air Canada's maintenance personnel uses this BI solution to list all the deviations that require attention, and produce standard or customized reports listing the type, location, and destination of each affected airplane, along with a catalog of available parts. This BI solution also facilitates the identification of the required parts and performance tracking of each maintenance crew, including its success in identifying, classifying, and closing deviations.

(Compiled from Corcoran, 2008; InformationBuilders, 2008; Smith, 2007; itbusiness.ca, 2006).

▶ 8.3 CHARACTERISTICS OF GOOD BUSINESS INTELLIGENCE SOLUTIONS

A BI solution should have the following characteristics for it to be valuable to the organization. These are all desired attributes of a BI solution, and compromising on them would reduce the BI solution's contributions, at least in the long term. The first five characteristics—alignment, intelligence, usability, accuracy, and connectivity—are essential in both the short and long term. The last three characteristics—flexibility, portability, and scalability—could be compromised somewhat without adverse short-term effects, but they are also crucial for sustained performance in the long term.

1. *Alignment:* The BI solution should be aligned to the organization's business strategy as well as the processes that help create business value (Williams and Williams, 2004). Moreover, the BI solution should provide the appropriate context in which it presents information. For example, it is not enough that the BI solution reports that the sales revenue was X yesterday and Y a year ago that same day. The BI solution should also identify changes in important factors that may have caused sales to be X one day and Y on the same date the previous year. If the BI solution is aligned to the organization's business strategy, processes, and context, it will provide greater benefits to the organization.

2. *Intelligence:* The BI solution should provide insights that are valuable and would not otherwise be available. In this regard, insight creation capability, discussed in Chapter 5, is especially relevant.

3. *Usability:* The BI solution should be easy to use. Usability is an important requirement, because a potentially valuable (in terms of alignment and intelligence) BI solution would fail if it is not easy to use, and poor usability cannot be addressed through training. In enhancing usability, presentation capability, discussed in Chapter 6, is especially relevant.

4. *Accuracy:* The BI solution should be based on clean data, because otherwise it would produce inaccurate reports and insights. It is important to ensure that the data feeding the BI solution are consistent and accurate. In enhancing accuracy, organizational memory capability, discussed in Chapter 3, is especially relevant.

5. *Connectivity:* The BI solution should have effective interfaces with the various other information technologies in the organization, such as ERP systems, data warehouses, and so on. In enhancing the BI solution's connectivity with the other technologies, information integration capability, discussed in Chapter 4, is especially relevant.

6. *Flexibility:* The BI solution should be flexible. In the current dynamic environment, business changes are inevitable. The BI solution should be such that it can be easily and quickly modified to adapt to the changing

business context. For this reason, dashboards and their link to business agility and strategy, discussed in Chapter 6, are especially relevant.

7. *Portability:* The BI solution combines software and hardware, but the software should be developed so it is easily portable to other hardware platforms. Moreover, the BI solution should work with different database servers and across leading operating systems (Olszak and Ziemba, 2007). For this purpose, innovative technologies—in particular, mobile BI, discussed in Chapter 10, are especially relevant.

8. *Scalability:* Finally, the BI solution should be scalable. It should be possible to expand the usage of the BI solution to a larger number of users and larger volumes of data without comprising performance. For this purpose, innovative technologies—in particular, mobile BI and Enterprise 2.0, discussed in Chapter 10, are especially relevant.

▶ 8.4 SOURCING OF BUSINESS INTELLIGENCE SOLUTIONS

The sourcing of BI solutions can be examined in terms of two major aspects, as shown in Figure 8.1. One aspect concerns the source of tools and technologies that are used in the development of the BI solution. This aspect is depicted along the horizontal axis, with three underlying possibilities: internal sourcing of the tools, with the tools being created by the organization's own IT staff; external sourcing of tools from vendors, such as the ones discussed in Chapter 7; and a combination of the two, with some tools being internally developed and the others being obtained from external vendors. A combination of external and internal sourcing also involves BI solutions being procured and then tweaked. The other aspect focuses on how the BI solution is developed. This aspect is shown along the vertical axis, and incorporates similar three possibilities: internal development of the BI solution by the organization's own IT staff; outsourcing of the development to an external vendor (again, such as the ones discussed in Chapter 7, since most of those BI vendors also build BI solutions for organizations); and joint development of the BI solution by the organization's own IT staff and an external vendor.

Combining the two aspects of sourcing, with each including three possibilities, produces nine cells as shown in Figure 8.1. However, two of these, internal sourcing of BI tools and technologies along with either external development or joint development, are highly unlikely because organizations with the internal ability to create BI tools would also develop the BI solution internally. The other seven cells represent five situations that are fairly common:

I. Completely in-house development. In this situation, the organization creates the BI tools internally, and also develops the BI solution internally.

II. Utilization of tools acquired from vendors (possibly with some internal tools) in in-house development. In this situation, the organization develops the BI

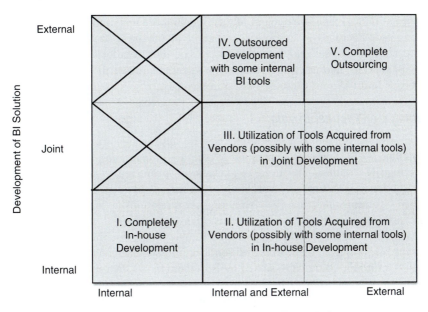

FIGURE 8.1 Broad BI Approaches to Sourcing of BI Solutions

solution internally but utilizes at least some tools obtained from external vendors.

III. Utilization of tools acquired from vendors (possibly with some internal tools) in joint development. In this situation, the organization and an external vendor jointly develop the BI solution, using at least some tools obtained from external vendors.

IV. Outsourced development with some internal BI tools. In this situation, the organization outsources the development of the BI solution to the external vendor, with some of the BI tools existing within the client organization being used to develop the BI solution along with tools obtained from an external vendor, usually the same vendor that is developing the BI solution.

V. Complete outsourcing. In this situation, the organization outsources the development of the BI solution to the external vendor, and the BI tools needed for the BI solution are also obtained from an external vendor, usually the same vendor that is developing the BI solution. This situation is completely in contrast to the first situation—complete in-house development.

Except for completely in-house development (situation I), all the above situations involve external vendors, who either only provide BI tools (situation II) or provide BI tools as well as participate in the development of the BI solution (situations III, IV, and V). Therefore, the selection of vendors and tools is an important part of the development of the BI solution. Organizations need to make three major decisions in this regard: whether to pursue a strategic or a tactical approach to vendor selection, whether to focus on mega-vendors or to use independent BI vendors, and whether to focus on a few standardized BI tools or to adopt a variety of tools. We next discuss these three considerations in greater detail.

Strategic or Tactical Buying

Organizations pursue two distinct types of approaches to vendor selection (Howson, 2007). Some organizations pursue a strategic, long-term approach to selecting BI vendors. In these organizations, preferred vendors are usually identified at the enterprise level. Such organizations identify a few (usually one to three) vendors, and then develop a long-term relationship with them, and this relationship generally spans BI as well as other information technologies, such as data warehousing and ERP solutions. This does not imply that these customers will only buy BI tools from their preferred vendors, but it does mean that other vendors would find it more difficult to sell BI tools to them or obtain a contract from them for the development of a BI solution.

Other organizations adopt a more tactical approach to vendor selection. Instead of forming strategic vendor relationships, these customers carefully decide on each individual BI tool and BI solution, examining the functionality, price, and ease of deployment of various alternatives from different vendors. Whereas strategic buyers would need a strong justification not to buy BI tools or solution from their preferred vendors, tactical buyers look for the vendor who seems to offer the best options for each individual tool or solution. Such organizations are either medium in size or their technology acquisition decisions are made at the departmental level. However, in some organizations, success with departmental BI can eventually lead to an enterprise-level BI solution (Howson, 2007).

Mega-vendors or Independent BI Vendors

We discussed a number of mega-vendors and independent BI vendors in Chapter 7. Whereas the mega-vendors—IBM, Microsoft, Oracle, and SAP—offer a large variety of information technology products, including BI tools and solutions, the independent vendors (e.g., SAS, Microstrategy, Information Builders, TIBCO Software, Inc., QlikTech, Actuate, Teradata, HP, arcplan, Board International, and Panorama Software) focus primarily on BI. An organization should decide whether to go with a mega-vendor or an independent BI vendor. Usually, this decision is combined with the strategic or tactical approach discussed above, with strategic buyers more commonly (but not always) going with mega-vendors and tactical buyers more commonly going with independent BI vendors.

Mega-vendors offer several advantages over independent BI vendors. First, they usually offer integrated suites with a family of components, which minimizes problems in integrating the BI solution with other information technologies. Second, the customer organization can perform a single contractual negotiation, long term and across information technologies, with the mega-vendor instead of multiple contracts and negotiation processes with different vendors, thereby leading to efficiency benefits for the customer. Third, the customer organization would not need to mix and match BI and other technologies, as such choices would be facilitated by the mega-vendor based on its portfolio of products. Fourth, mega-vendors may be expected to offer greater financial stability, thereby reducing the risk associated with the vendor encountering financial problems. Finally, the customer organization can more easily find people with expertise with the BI tools offered by mega-vendors.

On the other hand, independent vendors provide several benefits as well (Cuzzillo, 2008). One major benefit is the ability to mix and match BI tools and solutions for the organization's own unique needs, instead of leaving the decision to the vendor. This also allows the customer organization to get the best possible tool for each BI capability, which may not be possible with the mega-vendors because a mega-vendor may be strong in some technologies but not in others. Second, buying from independent vendors provides the customer greater leverage with the vendors, and the ability to switch customers across BI tools and solutions, instead of the risk of becoming a captive customer upon signing a long-term contract with a mega-vendor. Third, customers have greater influence over independent vendors with respect to the direction of their future products. Finally, mega-vendors may not be suitable for smaller organizations because the complex capabilities, vast set of features, and complicated licensing associated with their product offerings may not be needed by small customers, and may in fact inhibit their flexibility.

Standardization or Multiple Options

Another related decision for organizations concerns whether they should standardize on one tool to deliver a BI capability or instead incorporate multiple options. Standardization offers consistency across the organization, reduces redundancy and maintenance costs, and may be less expensive. On the other hand, incorporating multiple options enables greater customization and therefore potentially greater utilization and greater benefits. For example, a senior executive might benefit most from a dashboard, whereas an IT-savvy user might benefit most from a query tool.

The extent to which an organization standardizes in selecting BI tools depends considerably on the organization's context, including factors such as prior experience with BI, competence of the internal IT staff, and available resources. Moreover, as we move from tools supporting organizational memory to tools supporting presentation capability, standardization and use of one large vendor becomes less important, and providing multiple alternatives and mixing several niche vendors becomes more important. This comparison is depicted in Figure 8.2.

Business Intelligence in Practice 8.3 illustrates vendor selection using the example of PhoneWorks, which we examined earlier, in Business Intelligence in Practice 2.3 on BI's insight creation capability.

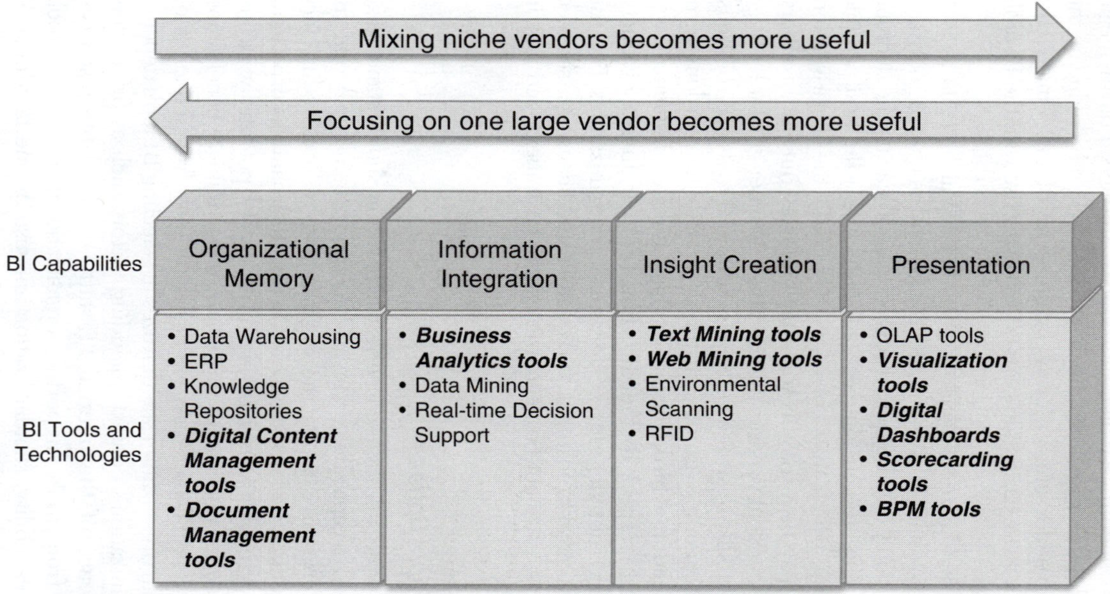

Selecting BI Tools and Technologies 227

Note: The highlighted tools have emerged along with development of BI, whereas the others have been adapted from other technologies to support BI.

FIGURE 8.2 Selection of One or Multiple Vendors for BI Tools and Technologies

Business Intelligence in Practice 8.3: PhoneWorks Selects LucidEra's Sales Analytics Solution

As discussed in Business Intelligence in Practice 2.3, PhoneWorks is a professional services firm that helps organizations to develop and implement sales strategies. It does so through the creation of new inside sales teams or the optimization of existing inside sales groups, and considerably enhanced its insight creation capability through the use of a sales analytics-as-a-service solution from LucidEra.

As a smaller organization that did not have an internal IT infrastructure, PhoneWorks lacked a large budget and internal technical resources to deploy a full-scale BI solution. Therefore, it preferred to seek an on-demand solution. Also, it had previously used the Software as a Service (SaaS) model in its relationship with Salesforce.com, and wanted to keep the same model for its analytics.

The above considerations, along with the desire for a simple user interface, analytic templates, and the ability to quickly identify and eliminate duplicate data, led PhoneWorks to LucidEra. LucidEra's sales analytics-as-a-service solution was also a natural choice for PhoneWorks because it had been developed to enhance the capabilities of Salesforce.com by adding BI functionality on top of Salesforce.com's Customer Relationship Management offerings.

PhoneWorks had a previous relationship with LucidEra's CEO, by which it did not require a formal evaluation process. Phoneworks was able to use a simplified overall evaluation process and solution selection because of LucidEra's preference for SaaS, the connection between LucidEra's sales analytics-as-a-service solution and SalesForce.com, and familiarity with LucidEra's CEO. These factors also led to a quick buy-in as the employees recognized the value of adding the LucidEra solution to their organization.

Due to the nature of SaaS, the implementation process was seamless for Phone Works. From the end-user perspective the main areas of involvement were granting LucidEra access to the Salesforce.com information and making sure they added all the information they wanted to track and measure to their Salesforce.com data.

(Compiled from dssresources.com, 2008, and Wise, 2008)

Organizations also often switch BI tools, sometimes during the development of a BI solution, either due to problems with current BI tools or due to the availability of important functionality in new tools. This might involve moving to a different vendor as well. For example, while developing a BI solution, Ace Hardware encountered problems with the BI tool it was using. According to Brian Cook, software engineering consultant of IT at Ace:

"In the past, it was hard to keep the development moving forward with the tool because of its inflexibility. . . . People were getting tied in knots trying to develop reports in that tool. The tool was very rigid and had a lot of requirements as far as the way you did reporting. There was one way to do development and you had to figure it out."

Consequently, Ace Hardware evaluated BI tools from several vendors, including Information Builders, Business Objects, Cognos, Hyperion, and Microsoft. Eventually, Ace Hardware selected Information Builders' WebFOCUS, which seemed to offer the needed flexibility for its developers and strong integration with Microsoft Excel "even stronger than Microsoft's own reporting tools" (Havenstein, 2007).

▶ 8.5 METHODOLOGY FOR DEVELOPING BUSINESS INTELLIGENCE SOLUTIONS

Two distinct approaches to software development—waterfall development and agile development—are relevant in the context of development of BI solutions (Upton and Fuller, 2005; Howson, 2008). These two approaches differ considerably from each other, as discussed below. In addition, intermediate or hybrid approaches that combine the features of these two approaches are also frequently used for system development. The **waterfall** approach[5] views software development as a sequential process, in which the tasks in the development process are performed in a specific order, and one task is completed before starting the next task. For example, all the analysis needs to be completed before design starts, and all the design needs to be completed before development begins. In this approach, progress is viewed as flowing steadily downward (hence the name "waterfall") through the phases of development, such as planning, analysis, design, development, testing, deployment, and review. Figure 8.3 depicts this approach, with seven steps (plan, analyze, design, build, test, deploy, and review) performed sequentially, and once each without feedback, so that the project is completed following the review.

By contrast, the **agile development** approach is based on iterative development, wherein requirements and solutions evolve through iterations based on frequent inspection and adaptation. Thus, the agile approach breaks the development process into small increments over short time frames. Each iteration involves the complete software development cycle including planning, analysis, design, development, testing, deployment, and review. This process helps reduce risk and enables changes to be incorporated quickly. Multiple iterations are usually needed to release a new product or novel features. Figure 8.4 depicts this approach, wherein the project goes through multiple iterations, with the seven steps (plan, analyze, design, build, test, deploy, and review) performed quickly, and each set of steps in the multiple iterations feed back to subsequent iterations.

[5] See: http://en.wikipedia.org/wiki/Waterfall_model

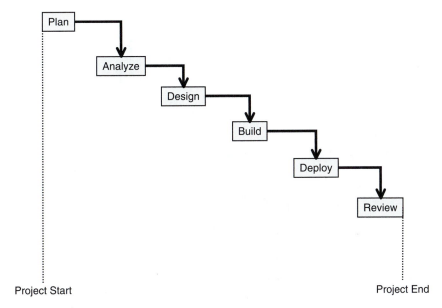

FIGURE 8.3 Waterfall Approach to the Development of a BI Solution

The two approaches differ in several ways. The waterfall approach emphasizes comprehensive documentation, whereas the agile approach seeks quick development of working software. The waterfall approach focuses on contracts, and the agile approach emphasizes collaboration. The waterfall approach focuses on planning, whereas the agile approach emphasizes flexibility. Finally, the waterfall approach focuses on processes, and the agile approach emphasizes people. Consequently, the waterfall approach is sometimes described as "heavy" because the various steps are strictly documented and adhered to, whereas the agile approach is described as "thin" or "light" because it is usually more flexible (Upton and Fuller, 2005).

The agile development approach is better suited for the development of BI solutions (Moss and Atre, 2003; Adelmen and Moss, 2007; Howson, 2008). BI projects are characterized by ambiguous and dynamic requirements, with uncertain technology components and other obstacles. Moreover, they involve considerable data integration challenges. Therefore, agile development, involving the use of prototyping and the breaking up of the scope and deliverables into multiple releases, is recommended for developing BI solutions. The agile approach relies on close collaboration between business users and IT developers, with some project teams establishing specific forums where "business users and IT developers routinely meet to review prototypes and hash out requirements" (Howson, 2008, p. 143).

In light of the above benefits, as well as existing literature and research on BI, we recommend development of a BI solution using an agile development

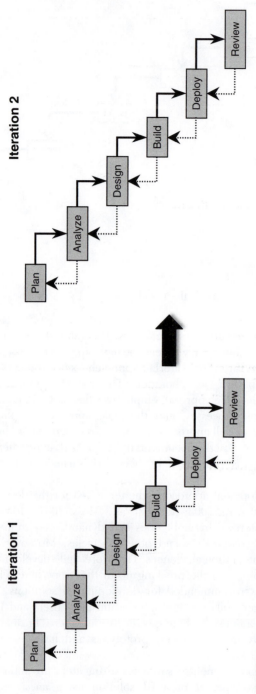

FIGURE 8.4 Agile Approach to the Development of a BI Solution

PRIMARY DEVELOPMENT STEPS

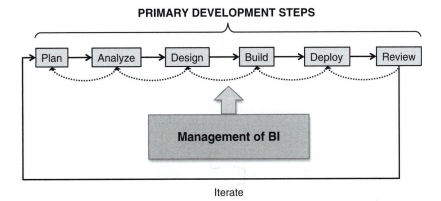

Iterate

FIGURE 8.5 Development of a BI Solution

approach. Our recommended process for BI development includes six primary steps that are performed in multiple iterations (as indicated through the long feedback loop from review to planning). Each of these steps relies on inputs from the preceding step, as they proceed sequentially, albeit with the possibility of feedback to the preceding step, as indicated by the dashed, curved arrows. Figure 8.5 summarizes this process for the development of a BI solution.

We next examine, in Section 8.6, the primary steps in the development of a BI solution. As shown in Figure 8.5, these steps in the development of a particular BI solution benefit from the selection of BI tools and vendors, which we discussed in Section 8.4, and from the other aspects of the management of BI in the organization, which we will discuss in Chapter 9.

▶ 8.6 STEPS IN THE DEVELOPMENT OF THE BUSINESS INTELLIGENCE SOLUTION

In this section, we describe the seven primary steps in the development of a BI solution, which are shown in Figure 8.5. These steps—plan, analyze, design, build, deploy, and review—are performed sequentially, although with the possibility of feedback to the preceding step (Moss and Atre, (2003); McAfee and Wagonfield, 2004). Following review, another iteration including these six steps is continued as discussed above in the context of agile development, and as indicated using the feedback arrow labeled "Iterate" in Figure 8.5.

8.6.1 Plan

Appropriate planning for BI development is critical. As we have discussed and illustrated throughout the book, BI solutions can provide major strategic benefits. However, if a company does not plan adequately for the BI solution, it risks basing decisions on inaccurate or incomplete data. Moreover, acquiring BI tools and developing and maintaining BI solutions vary considerably, but can be quite expensive. A company might spend only thousands of dollars on BI software or as much as millions of dollars. According to Forrester Consulting, a typical BI deal in a large company with a large vendor is in the range of $150,000 to $300,000, including only the software licenses and the first year of maintenance (King, 2009). Including other essential services, a company might spend considerably more on BI than on other types of software. According to Boris Evelson, principal analyst at Forrester, "For every dollar you spend on business intelligence software, you better expect to spend five to seven times as much on services, such as ensuring it works with the company's other software" (King, 2009).

In planning for the BI project, it is important to begin by focusing on the information the BI solution would provide and how that information would help the business. The organization should not start the BI project, or purchase BI software, only because people think they need it. Instead, it is important to identify, at a broad level, the information requirements that need to be addressed, and to examine why a BI solution would be most helpful. In fact, planning for BI projects is very much the purview of either the BI steering committee (which we will discuss in Chapter 9), if the organization has one, or the IT governance committee (which we discussed in Chapter 6). Some of the key issues to consider in planning for the BI project are as follows (Moss and Atre, 2003):

- *Project Objectives and Alignment*: What are the objectives of the proposed BI project? Have the project objectives been clearly stated? How well are the project objectives aligned to the business strategy?

- *Project Scope and Deliverables*: Has a formal request been submitted for this BI project? What deliverables have been requested? Can we implement the needed scope within the expected schedule and with the available resources?

- *Cost-Benefit Analysis*: What are the major expected costs associated with the project? What are the expected benefits? What is the expected return on investment (ROI)? By when would the ROI materialize?

- *Infrastructure*: Does our infrastructure have any gaps? Which infrastructure components need attention, and can they be included as a part of the BI project? Which technical infrastructure components need attention, and which nontechnical infrastructure components?

- *Staffing and Skills*: Do the team members have the necessary skills to perform their assigned roles? Should we schedule any training prior to the project kickoff? Has a full-time project manager been assigned to this project?

- *Organizational Involvement*: Do we have a senior executive sponsoring the project? Do we have important stakeholders with whom we should communicate regularly? How much time are business executives committing to this project?

When planning for second and later iterations of the BI solution, the above questions need to be addressed in light of the prior history of the development process. For example, it is important to consider whether the project is moving to a different department, and what implications that has for the BI solution and its development.

8.6.2 Analyze

During this step, the focus is on identifying the business requirements that need to be addressed through the BI solution. The objective here is to use the business requirements to facilitate identification of the functional and technical requirements related to the infrastructure, data, reporting, and training aspects. In conducting the analysis for the BI project, it is useful to do the following (Williams and Williams, 2004):

- Map business strategies to core business processes.
- Capture and model the key business and decision processes that create organizational value.
- Identify process metrics for the key business and decision processes and determine the potential business value of incorporating BI into those processes.
- Explicitly and formally seek inputs from relevant business users. This may begin by focusing first on senior executives and identifying their information needs that would be addressed through the BI solution, and then incorporating the needs of lower hierarchical levels.
- Encourage participation and debate so that the requirements are more completely identified in the earlier iterations.
- Assess organizational readiness to exploit BI, and identify infrastructure changes that may be needed.

8.6.3 Design

During this step, the focus is on using the requirements identified through analysis to create detailed design specifications. The detailed design specifications pertain to the following:

- Specifications regarding how organizational memory capability would be utilized in the BI solution. These specifications concern the identification of the data to be sourced from the organization's existing information systems and databases. The extract, transform, and load processes for moving information from the source data systems to the BI solution also need to be designed.
- Specifications regarding how information integration capability would be utilized in the BI solution. Any inconsistencies in existing data sources, and ways of addressing them within the context of the BI solution, need to be identified to ensure effective information integration. The nature, timing,

and utilization of additional information flows beyond the existing information systems, through aspects such as Web mining and data mining, to be included in the BI solution, should also be specified.

- Specifications regarding how insight creation capability would be utilized in the BI solution. These specifications focus on analytics and need to be designed based on the information that will need to be provided to the users. It is important to identify the processes that will be used to describe the past, summarize the current situation, and identify prediction regarding the future. This needs to be done for the various situations, such as for different areas (e.g., sales, inventory, manufacturing), roles (e.g., vice president of marketing and sales, sales supervisor, or a salesperson), and tasks (e.g., sales forecasting, sales transaction, return of purchased item).

- Specifications regarding how presentation capability would be utilized in the BI solution. These specifications focus on the form (e.g., dashboards, reports, ad hoc queries), timing (e.g., at regular intervals, on demand), and media (e.g., computer workstations on the company's intranet, Internet, and/or mobile phones) through which various types of information would be provided to the users. In addition to designing the individual interfaces, it is also important to make sure that the entire BI solution is consistent and that users are provided a single access point to all the needed information.

In addition to producing the above specifications, three other aspects are important during the design phase. First, the security mechanisms and levels for various kinds of information are identified. Second, a detailed test plan is created. Finally, the BI tools that could potentially be used to develop the BI solution are identified.

8.6.4 Build

During this step, the design specifications are used to create the complete BI solution. Thus, the BI solution (or a pilot or preliminary version of it to begin with) is available at the conclusion of this step. The major tasks that are performed during this step include the following:

- Install and configure the data model.
- Create the needed analytics software.
- Create the needed reports and dashboards.
- Implement and load the data model.
- Incorporate relevant BI tools.
- Test the reports and dashboards while involving some of the intended users.
- Identify and develop the support processes that would be needed once the BI solution is deployed.
- Create test scripts for testing the complete BI solution.

- Develop a training program for users, including the identification of the specifics of training and the resources needed.

8.6.5 Deploy

During this step, the users are trained, and the BI solution is tested and implemented. The major tasks that are performed during this step include the following:

- Complete testing of the current iteration of the BI solution, including the associated security, backup, and recovery procedures as well as support processes.
- Training of the users involved in the current iteration of the BI solution and training of the associated support staff, including operations and help-desk personnel.
- Rollout of the BI solution to some users in the first iteration and to an increasing number of users in subsequent iterations.

The deployment, implementation, or rollout of the BI solution could differ in three important aspects. First, in some situations, the BI solution is deployed so that its adoption is voluntary or mandatory for the concerned users. In the former case, potential users are motivated, but not forced, to adopt the BI solution. This is done by making the BI solution a useful but not required part of the users' desktops and providing them soft training (seminars, presentations, etc.). In the latter case, the organization enforces the adoption of the BI solution, by making it the corporate standard for performing business tasks, communicating important messages to employees, and completing performance evaluations of individuals.

Second, the BI solution could be rolled out throughout the entire organization in one step or incrementally across the organization. Consistent with the agile development approach, incremental rollout is recommended. It is best to start with a small group of business users including some "power users," with considerable information technology expertise, as well as some less technically savvy business users (Moss and Atre, 2003).

Third, if the BI solution is rolled out incrementally, as recommended here, a decision needs to be made regarding which group to use as the first adopters. One useful approach is to begin with a focus on top executives as the users, with salespeople the next group of users. Once support from the salespeople has been obtained, it can be used to help move the remainder of the organization onto the BI bandwagon. Given their sales abilities, if salespeople serve as evangelists for BI, highlighting the power of the tools and how BI is improving their performance, others within the organization are more likely to follow quickly.

8.6.6 Review

During this step, the results of the deployment of the BI solution are evaluated. The project managers, users, sponsors of the BI solution, individuals involved in supporting the BI solution, and relevant IT personnel should be involved in this review process. The major questions that are addressed during the review include the following (Moss and Atre, 2003):

- How satisfied are the sponsors of the BI solution? What are their main concerns at this point?
- Do the users in this iteration like the BI solution? What aspects do they like? Do they find the BI solution easy to use? What aspects are they concerned about?
- How well are the associated security, backup, and recovery procedures working? How can they be improved?

The subsequent iteration of the BI solution would depend on the above review. As discussed earlier, and indicated using the feedback arrow labeled "Iterate" in Figure 8.5, another iteration including the above six steps may be performed.

Although BI solutions often have high costs associated with them, the development of a BI solution is not necessarily expensive. Business Intelligence in Practice 8.4 illustrates the development of a BI solution by one organization, Associate Grocers, Inc., in an inexpensive fashion.

Business Intelligence in Practice 8.4: Developing a BI Solution for Less than $25,000

Although the ability of business intelligence (BI) to deliver valuable and meaningful data in a dashboard environment is now well recognized, it is criticized for being too expensive and/or too complex. However, Associated Grocers, Inc. (AG), which is based in Baton Rouge, Louisiana, effectively addressed both these concerns and successfully got a BI system up and running for less than $25,000, according to Steven A. Miller, the company's senior vice president of strategic planning, projects, and information services.

CIO and *DM Review* magazines highlighted the benefits of BI for companies in 2006. Upon discovering that companies implementing BI had found information that enabled targeted investment and growth, Miller sought to examine what was hidden within their corporate data. However, estimated costs of enterprise-level BI tools were well over $100,000. Even if the lowest possible cost was negotiated for a turnkey implementation, the cost would still be excessive for AG. A BI presentation from a local vendor at a trade show in Baton Rouge, Louisiana, in October 2006 revealed to the company's leadership that they could develop a BI solution using Excel as the means for display by using tools such as SQL 2005, report services, and

(continued)

analysis services. Having recently standardized on Microsoft products through an enterprise agreement, this was considered to be the most effective way for AG to begin with BI.

A few weeks later, the accounting department had some questions concerning profitability, and especially on variations in margins on freight and gross sales. Armed with their newly acquired expertise on BI capabilities, AG's leadership recognized that if they cubed (a cube is a data structure that extends two-dimensional spreadsheets and enables fast data analysis) up the data in SQL and enabled users to connect to the data through Excel, they could generate reports without requiring time-consuming access queries.

AG hired a local vendor for $5,000 for instruction on how to cube data and build reports in Microsoft Excel through pivot tables, also known as a "mini data mart." The Excel interface was beneficial because AG had recently signed a Microsoft Enterprise Agreement.

During the next few weeks, the vendor began learning AG's business and assisted in creating cubes that analyzed the sources of margin fluctuations on sales and freight. The gross margin analysis proved too difficult, but the freight revenue analysis was more straightforward and the resulting report is now one of AG's standard reports. The successes of cubing up data for sales and freight produced interest in other information that could be displayed. The marketing team, which works closely with AG's member stores, started creating pivot tables in Excel that displayed, in both chart and graph, sales over time relative similar stores in the area, thereby helping identify opportunities for growth, greater efficiency in ordering, or reduced markup rates.

Following this largely successful experiment with several reports generated in this fashion, AG needed a more robust graphical interface that could be used by a larger number of employees. Another local vendor in Baton Rouge recommended a product called Report Portal, which enables adding cubes to a Web-based portal, where business users can easily access them. Report Portal could be downloaded online and used for free for 60 days. AG paid the local vendor for assistance in getting this system to work. AG's team soon began to understand how to connect to the portal, and many other cubes have subsequently been added, including operational statistics, order processing metrics, and help desk requests.

Numerous reports have been created and added for easy access by users. For experienced users, reports can be created on the fly from data that are no more than one day old at any time. By clicking a BI report, presented in a chart format that can be modified in various different ways, users can manipulate sales data for different time frames, departments, or stores.

For AG, the greatest benefit of this approach is the flexibility it provides the firm for learning and adopting desired capabilities. However, the BI system has a few shortcomings: it does not include "void reporting" capabilities; it

(*continued*)

lacks forecasting tools, which would allow AG to conduct predictive analyses of data; and large data sets occasionally cause cubes to freeze when trying to drill down to the item level.

By implementing BI incrementally, AG was able to limit its financial exposure: "Initially, AG had very little understanding of the scope, requirements and benefits, which is why justification was so difficult. If we had been able to justify an enterprise-level tool early in the project, it would still have taken years to implement. Our current mode of implementation allows us to learn at a very small cost and create a desire and appetite for more capability over time" (Miller, 2008).

At AG, BI have cost less than $25,000, including approximately $10,000 for professional services, less than $5,000 on licensing, and $10,000 on Report Portal. However, the costs do not include any internal labor costs related to the contributions by AG's employees, such as the time spent by AG's infrastructure team and database analysts.

(Compiled from All, 2008; Miller, 2008)

▶ 8.7 SUMMARY

In this chapter we examined BI solutions and their desired characteristics. We also described the process associated with the sourcing of BI solutions and tools, the overall approach to developing BI solutions, and the development of BI solutions. We also provided four examples to illustrate these aspects of BI development. In Chapter 9, we discuss the overall management of BI.

▶ KEY TERMS

agile development	business intelligence	outsourced development
analysis	solutions	planning
business intelligence	deployment	review
vendors	design	sourcing
business intelligence	development	waterfall development
development	internal development	

▶ REVIEW QUESTIONS

1. How does the agile approach to system development differ from the waterfall approach?

2. Why is the agile approach appropriate for the development of a BI solution?

3. Identify and briefly explain any four characteristics of a good BI solution.

4. Distinguish between strategic and tactical buying in the context of BI. When is each approach more commonly used?

5. Identify and briefly explain the steps involved in the development of a BI solution.

6. It may not be easy to develop a BI solution that is good in terms of all the characteristics identified in Section 8.3. Why?

7. Identify and briefly explain the five situations regarding the sourcing of BI solutions.

► **APPLICATION EXERCISES**

1. Using Business Intelligence in Practice examples from the earlier chapters in the book, identify a company that has adopted a BI solution, and examine how the company (a) decided to adopt BI and (b) selected an external vendor.

2. Download the case study titled "Integrated Insight," published in *Teradata Magazine* in September 2007, from http://www.teradata.com/tdmo/v07n03/pdf/AR5378.pdf. Analyze this case study to address the following questions: (a) What factors led to UnumGroup's moving to "enterprise intelligence"? (b) Which BI capability or capabilities did UnumGroup focus on? (c) What has been UnumGroup's experience (in terms of benefits obtained, problems encountered, etc.) with BI thus far?

3. Visit http://www.sap.com/solutions/sapbusinessobjects/customers/index.epx, and download the case study on Forbes (titled "Forbes: SAPBusinessObjects Software Provides New Marketing Insights"). Analyze the case study to address the following questions: (a) What factors led to Forbes moving to BI? (b) Which BI capability or capabilities does this case focus on? (c) What major benefits has Forbes obtained from BI?

4. Visit http://www.pentaho.com/. Use the information available from this Web site to review Pentaho BI Suite Enterprise Edition. Also use the case study on Unionfidi (available from http://www.pentaho.com/products/demos/Pentaho_Case_Study_Unionfidi.php) for your review.

5. Select any one of the Business Intelligence in Practice examples from this chapter, and identify an alternative approach, such as using a different sourcing arrangement (e.g., using internal development instead of outsourcing, or using a different vendor, or even going without BI) that might have helped the concerned organization to achieve the kind of benefits it obtained according to the Business Intelligence in Practice.

► **REFERENCES**

Adelman, S., and Moss, L. 2007. "Is the Development Methodology for BI Different than Operational Development Methodology?" *Information Management Online*, July 2.

All, A. 2008. "BI on a Budget: Associated Grocers Shows It Can Be Done." *ITBusinessEdge*, April 29, http://www.itbusinessedge.com/cm/blogs/all/bi-on-a-budget-associated-grocers-shows-it-can-be-done/?cs=11603.

Amendola, V. 2007. "Data Warehousing Meets Business Intelligence." *Integrated Solutions for Retailers*, December. http://ismretail.com/index.php?option=com_jambozine&layout=article&view=page&aid=7252&Itemid=99999999 (accessed April 6, 2009).

Armstrong, M. 2008. "Measuring 'Public Diplomacy'?" *inRunner.us*, March 4, http://mountainrunner.us/2008/03/measuring_public_diplomacy.html.

Business Wire, 2007. "Haggen's Business Managers Get an Analytic Edge with Manthan's ARC Business Intelligence Suite." *Business Wire*, July 4.

Corcoran, M. 2008. "The Value of BI in a Weak Economy." *Enterprise Systems*, http://esj. com/Articles/2008/12/03/The-Value-of-BI-in-a-Weak-Economy.aspx? (accessed April 5, 2009).

Cuzzillo, T. 2008. "How to Select the Right Business Intelligence Vendor." eWeek.com, October 20. http://www.eweek.com/c/a/Enterprise-Applications/How-to-Select-the-Right-Business-Intelligence-Vendor/ (accessed June 15, 2009).

dssresources.com. 2008. "LucidEra's on-demand sales analytics allow Phone Works to track pipeline progression throughout the sales cycle," April 2. http://dssresources.com/news/2475.php.

Essex, D. 2008. "Get smart with your data." *Government Computer News*, February 14, http://gcn.com/articles/2008/02/14/get-smart-with-your-data.aspx.

Glaser, J., and Stone, J. 2008. "Effective Use of Business Intelligence: Leveraging Your Organization's Business Data Could Improve Financial and Operational Performance— and Quality of Care." *Healthcare Financial Management*, February, pp. 68–72.

Havenstein, H. 2007. "Ace Hardware Shifts BI Tools After Early Struggles." *Computer World*, April 23, p. 11.

Howson, C. 2007. "How Buying Changes in the New BI Landscape." *Intelligent Enterprise*, November 21.

Howson, C. 2008. *Successful Business Intelligence: Secrets to Making BI a Killer App* (McGraw-Hill Osborne).

Howson, C. 2009. "Four Business Intelligence Resolutions for 2009." *Intelligent Enterprise*, January 26.

InformationBuilders. 2008. Air Canada Soars with Web-Based Flight-Tracking Application. http://www.informationbuilders.com/applications/airCanada.html (accessed April 5, 2009).

itbusiness.ca. 2006. Air Canada Puts Browser-Based BI into Pilot Mode. http://www. itbusiness.ca/it/client/en/home/News.asp?id=39202 (accessed April 5, 2009).

Janies, L. 2008. "Marketplace of Ideas." *Teradata Magazine*, December.

King, R. 2009. "Business Intelligence Software's Time Is Now." *Business Week*, March 2.

McAfee, A., and Wagonfield, A. B. 2004. Business Intelligence at SYSCO. *Harvard Business School Publishing Case*, 9-604-080, July 19.

Miller, S. A. 2008. "Business Intelligence (BI) for Less than $25k." *CIO*, April 27.

Moss, L., and Atre, S. 2003. *Business Intelligence Roadmap* (Boston: Addison-Wesley).

Olszak, C. M., and Ziemba, E. 2007. "Approach to Building and Implementing Business Intelligence Systems." *Interdisciplinary Journal of Information, Knowledge, and Management*, p. 2.

Smith, B. 2007. "Air Canada Uses BI as Excel Exit Strategy." *IT World Canada*, July 25.

Swartz, N. 2007. "Gartner Warns Firms of 'Dirty Data'." *Information Management Journal*, May/June, p. 6.

Upton, D. M., and Fuller, V. A. 2005. Wipro Technologies: The Factory Model. Harvard Business School Publishing Case, 9-606-021, October 25.

Wailgum, T. 2008. "Business Intelligence: A Technology Category in Tumult." *CIO*, March 24.

Weier, M. H. 2008. "Government Using BI Software To Measure Public Diplomacy." *InformationWeek*, December 3.

Williams, N., and Williams, S. 2004. "Capturing ROI through Business-Centric BI Development Methods." *Information Management Magazine*, August.

Zarrello, C. 2008. "No More Day Old Bread." *RIS News*, May 1.

CHAPTER 9

MANAGEMENT OF BUSINESS INTELLIGENCE

▶ 9.1 INTRODUCTION

In Chapter 8, we discussed the sourcing of BI solutions and tools and the development of BI solutions, including the overall methodology and the specific steps in the development process. In this chapter, we examine the management of BI.

Overall, the **management of business intelligence** refers to the set of actions needed to obtain the most value from the organization's various BI efforts. It incorporates a variety of actions such as educating employees regarding BI, evaluating benefits from BI, building organizational support for BI, developing and sourcing BI solutions, and so on. The importance of management of BI is well recognized. For example, Ian Bertram, Gartner global BI manager, remarks:

> "Organizations tend to throw technology at BI problems. You could have the right tool, but it could be doomed to failure because of political and cultural issues, an absence of executive support so the message doesn't get out, and poor communication and training." (Pauli, 2009)

The various actions related to management of BI can be viewed in terms of three broad categories: (a) enhancing the quality of the infrastructure related to BI, so that it best supports BI tools and solutions; (b) developing the structures needed for the management of BI; and (c) establishing and using appropriate processes for the day-to-day management of BI. These three aspects—infrastructure, structures, and processes—mutually affect each other, as shown in Figure 9.1. We discuss these three aspects in detail in this chapter. We begin by examining the infrastructure (Section 9.2), and then discuss the structures (Section 9.3), and finally the processes (Section 9.4).

▶ 9.2 INFRASTRUCTURE

Two aspects of the infrastructure—data infrastructure and organizational culture—have considerable effects on the impacts of BI tools and solutions, as well as the structure and processes associated with the management of BI. We first

243

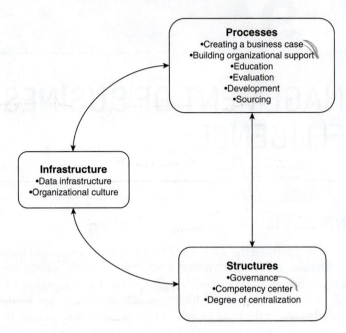

FIGURE 9.1 Overview of the Management of Business Intelligence

examine data infrastructure (Section 9.2.1) and then organizational culture (Section 9.2.2).

9.2.1 Data Infrastructure

The success of BI depends to a considerable extent on the data available in the organization. Indeed, data quality is considered to be the most important technical factor for successful BI (Howson, 2008). This is not surprising, because the information contained in reports from a BI solution is directly based on the available data. Therefore, the organization's data, including the data being provided by transactional systems, enterprise resource planning systems, and so on, and the data that reside in the data warehouse, should be of the highest quality. Data quality itself is multidimensional in nature. According to Gartner (Swartz, 2007, p. 6), organizations should consider several aspects of data quality, including:

- Existence (whether the organization has the data)
- Validity (whether the data values fall within an acceptable range or domain)
- Consistency (whether the same piece of data stored in multiple locations contains the same values)
- Integrity (the completeness of relationships between data elements and across data sets)

- Accuracy (whether the data describes the properties of the object they are meant to model)
- Relevance (whether the data is the appropriate data to support the business objectives).

A 2007 survey of BI adoption and use (Sabherwal, 2007) indicated that although the respondent firms appeared to be well prepared for BI in terms of the needed culture and the recognition of BI's importance, their prior data warehouses seemed to be letting them down. Similar concerns about data infrastructure were revealed in a survey by the Data Warehouse Institute (Preston, 2007) in which 81% of the respondents complained about inaccurate data reporting, 78% complained about arguments concerning which data is appropriate for "master data" repositories, and 51% complained about poor decisions due to incorrect definitions. That BI is constrained by poor quality of data in data warehouses seems reasonable; a data warehouse is usually the foundation upon which a BI solution is based. Therefore, most organizations that have succeeded with BI—for example, Cardinal Health (Carte et al., 2005) and Continental Airlines (Watson et al., 2006)—first enhance the quality of the data in their data warehouses before embarking upon BI solutions.

9.2.2 Organizational Culture

Organizational culture refers to the norms and beliefs that guide the behavior of the organization's members. As noted earlier, the success of BI depends not only on technology. It also depends on people who actively seek and utilize new opportunities and aim to make decisions based on the best possible information (Howson, 2008). Thus, BI depends on an organizational culture that values data and their utilization to pursue opportunities. Such a culture has previously been called an "analytics culture" (Davenport, 2006) and a "data-driven decision style" (Carte et al., 2005). For successful BI, organizational members should recognize the importance of collecting and utilizing quantitative evidence and making decisions based on reliable data.

Such an organizational culture is more likely in organizations where senior executives set an example by consistently exhibiting a desire for facts and analysis. For example, Barry Beracha, the former CEO of Sara Lee Bakery, was considered a "data dog" because he hounded his employees for data to support any conclusion (Davenport, 2006). Indeed, a sign on his desk stated: "In God we trust, all others bring data" (this quote has been originally attributed to W. Edwards Deming) (Davenport and Harris, 2007).

Although an organizational culture that emphasizes data-based decisions is likely to lead to greater success with BI, the reverse effect could occur over time as well. In other words, higher success with BI could also lead to greater emphasis on data; as business users recognize that the BI solutions lead to improved decisions, they are more likely to base their decisions on facts and analysis rather than intuition (Howson, 2008).

On the other hand, an organizational culture where employees are reluctant to share data might make BI less effective, as the employees might be afraid that the BI solution would make information *too transparent*. However, empirical studies (Sabherwal, 2007; Howson, 2008) indicate that this is not a significant problem. For example, in one survey (Sabherwal, 2007), almost 15% of the respondents indicated that the fact that BI may make business information too transparent poses no problem at all with respect to BI adoption and use in their respective organizations.

▶ 9.3 STRUCTURES

Three structural aspects—governance, competency center, and degree of centralization—play an important role in the management and impacts of BI. We examine these three aspects next, starting with BI governance.

9.3.1 Business Intelligence Governance

BI governance is defined as the guiding principles, decision-making bodies, decision areas and decision rights, and oversight mechanisms that are used to encourage desirable behavior in the management, development, and use of BI (Leonard, 2009). This definition of BI governance[1] is broader than the earlier view as a resource rationalization exercise (Gutierrez, 2006), which focused only on the prioritization mechanisms for approving, rejecting, and sequencing BI. The components of BI governance are as follows (Leonard, 2009):

1. *Guiding principles*, which are the overall beliefs for guiding the BI vision and goals, and developing criteria for the approval of BI projects. For example, a guiding principle might state: "BI ensures that information is managed as a corporate asset—standardized, integrated, shared, and reused across the organization."

2. *Decision-making bodies*, which identify the individuals or groups that make the BI decisions, the individuals or groups that provide inputs and sponsorship, and the ways these individuals or groups interact. The individuals or groups may be a subset of the IT governance group discussed in Chapter 6. Membership of decision-making bodies usually includes business and IT, and spans functional areas and hierarchical levels so as to achieve a balanced view of organizational needs and interests and facilitate communication links and feedback mechanisms. One important decision-making body is the **BI steering committee**, which includes senior representatives from the various functions and businesses, and focuses on aligning the organizational strategic initiatives and processes with

---

[1] This definition is consistent with the following definition of information technology (IT) governance: "Specifying the decision rights and accountability framework to encourage desirable behavior in the use of IT" (Weill and Ross, 2004).

investments in BI solutions and tools. The individual in charge of BI, such as the BI Program Manager or Director of BI, and other relevant IT directors should serve on the BI steering committee, which meets on a regular basis (usually, every month or every two weeks) to resolve any conflicting priorities, discuss new opportunities, and address any issues related to ongoing BI projects (Howson, 2008).

3. **Decision areas and decision rights**, which focus on the identification of key types of decisions and allocation of rights for making those decisions to specific organizational roles or decision-making bodies. Three types of decision areas are commonly used: investments in BI solutions and tools, BI project status, and BI adoption and utilization. For each decision area, responsibility and accountability are assigned to stakeholders for either decision making or input. Moreover, it is important to involve both business managers from various departments or subunits as well as technical experts from IT in processes related to BI, such as those involved in project management. Organizations having problems with BI often tend to involve only IT people, thereby leading to an inappropriate focus on the "intelligence" aspect of "business intelligence" while ignoring the "business" aspect.

4. **Oversight mechanisms**, which are the formalized policies and procedures for implementing BI governance and evaluating progress. They include procedures for the approval of business cases and budgets, mechanisms for tracking BI projects, procedures for evaluating BI utilization, training procedures, and the plan for communications about BI. The templates and tools related to BI mechanisms are usually developed during BI projects as needs arise, and are subsequently refined and institutionalized over time.

9.3.2 Business Intelligence Competency Center

Gartner Research defines the **BI competency center**, which is sometimes called a BI center of excellence, as "a cross-functional team with specific tasks, roles, responsibilities and processes for supporting and promoting the effective use of business intelligence across the organization" (Miller, Brautigam, and Gerlach, 2006). The BI competency center serves as a center for expertise related to BI and promotes and facilitates the usage of BI throughout the organization. The BI competency center provides a central location for driving and supporting a company's overall information delivery strategy. It coordinates an organization's BI solutions and tools, helps share best practices across the organization, and thereby helps raise implementation effectiveness while lowering redundancy. It also helps with data stewardship (including metadata management, data standards, data quality, and data architecture), data acquisition (including extraction, transformation, and loading of data), vendor contracts management, development of analytical skills, and user support and training (LeVoyer, 2009). The BI competency center could also help develop a standardized set of models across the organization, using existing BI tools. For example, BI dashboards developed for one department can be extended to other departments. In this way, new groups can be up and running more quickly, without having to reinvent the wheel (Mitchell, 2009).

A BI competency center differs from a BI project in that the BI competency center is a permanent organization whereas the BI project is specifically aimed at the development of a BI solution. The BI competency center provides staff and resources to support BI projects. The center could include a combination of some dedicated members and some members who may also have other responsibilities, such as a database administrator from a central IT department who spends a certain proportion of his or time at the center (Howson, 2008). Potential roles associated with a BI competency center include a manager of the center, a business analyst, a chief data steward, and a technical consultant. Representatives from each unit participate in the center and help in deciding how BI can best serve their units, including defining its governance, appropriate architecture and metrics, and staff training (Pauli, 2009).

We next illustrate the use of a BI competency center at an Italian organization, CSI-Piemonte, in Business Intelligence in Practice 9.1.

Business Intelligence in Practice 9.1: BI Competency Center Helps CSI-Piemonte Share Solutions

CSI-Piemonte is an Italian consortium of public bodies that promotes innovation in public administration through information technologies. It has more than 80 associated groups and over 1,200 employees. It coordinates activities performed by local bodies in order to modernize processes and enable improvements in operational efficiency within and between administrative bodies. It helps these organizations to analyze demographic and other data to better serve the citizens. For example, it uses the SAS Enterprise Intelligence Platform to help local doctors in integrating and analyzing prescription data to make sure that the World Health Organization guidelines are being followed.

CSI-Piemonte has over 30 years of experience in planning, developing, and managing information systems related to various areas, such as health (e.g., regional medical system), agriculture (e.g., farm and food production), environmental control (e.g., the registry of electromagnetic sources and industrial hazards), territory management (e.g., an information system for the management of water resources), population and land registries and taxes (e.g., a tax data warehouse), and welfare services (e.g., an integrated information system for social services in the Piemonte region).

(continued)

As necessitated by the above vast array of information systems, CSI-Piemonte has a highly complex set of data sources and analytic applications. When the SAS Institute Inc. released a new version of its core BI software (SAS 9) in 2003, Paola Leproni, Manager at CSI-Piemonte, recognized that upgrading the technology throughout her organization would be a daunting task. To address this problem, she decided to create a BI competency center to streamline the front-end and back-end BI functions, including data quality, metadata management, and report writing. Leproni hoped a BI competency center could centralize BI-related tasks instead of assigning them in a haphazard way, and thereby help improve operational efficiency and facilitate sharing of best BI practices throughout her organization. She also hoped a BI competency center would prove "useful and very flexible to move all our technology to the new version." This would help address problems they had faced in the past. "Because we have a big number of applications, every time we had to move these applications from an older release to a new one, we had some difficulties," Leproni said.

CSI-Piemonte set up a BI competency center in 2004 with the help of SAS. As a result of the formation of the center, the SAS upgrade progressed faster and more smoothly than expected. Impressed with the group's merits, CSI-Piemonte soon expanded its BI competency center.

With about 80 members, the center now comprises four main groups. One group focuses on developing and maintaining front-end BI applications and reports, and the other three groups focus on back-end data management tasks, such as ensuring data quality and metadata management.

For example, the BI competency center assists with the reuse of code developed for a specific BI application for one customer, which could also be applicable for another customer with similar requirements. CSI-Piemonte now has a BI-related organizational memory that can be drawn upon to address new problems. "It is easier than in the past to share solutions in the organization," Leproni remarked. "Many different users have the same issues."

Overall, the BI competency center has made BI processes run more smoothly. "With the BI competency center, we manage all the BI applications in a way that is centralized, that is more orderly than in the past. . . . It is very useful to have a BI competency center because the technology that we have is very complex and can be used in a very powerful way. So it is very important to have a BI competency center that helps to use the technology in the best ways." (Compiled from Kelly, 2008; Leproni, 2008)

9.3.3 Degree of Centralization of Business Intelligence

Degree of centralization of BI in an organization may be viewed in two different ways. First, it could refer to whether the BI solutions at the organization are focused at the enterprise level or at the departmental level, with a focus at the enterprise level implying greater centralization and a focus at the departmental level implying greater decentralization. Departmental BI focuses on the needs of individual business units, utilizes the best available technology, focuses on short-term success, and requires dedicated resources. On the other hand, enterprise BI focuses on the needs of the entire company, utilizes technology specified by corporate standards, focuses on longer-term success, and involves shared resources (Howson, 2008). Enterprise BI— that is, the more centralized approach—is generally recommended, except for small organizations or those in the early stages of BI adoption.

Second, centralization of BI could refer to the extent to which the development of BI reports is centralized—that is, included within BI solutions—rather than allowing users to develop their own reports and spreadsheets. Encouraging user-developed reports is helpful as it encourages greater adoption of the BI solution. However, encouraging user-developed reports might lead to the problem of "spreadmarts" (derived from the combination of "spreadsheet" and "data mart") in which valuable data resides in desktop spreadsheets that are not shared across the organization. Moreover, increased user development of reports may also imply inefficiency (because business users would be more productive in other arenas) and redundancy (due to the nonreusability of these reports by others). Recognizing the positive and negative effects of decentralized development of reports, a balanced approach is recommended. Business users should be provided the ability to develop their own reports, but with two additional measures: (a) users should be encouraged, and motivated through incentives, to share their creative reports with others; (b) the BI solution should itself contain desired reports to the extent possible, and should be enhanced over time to incorporate frequently requested additional reports. The BI competency center can play an important role in enabling business users to create their own reports as well as to disseminate information about such user-developed reports.

▶ 9.4 PROCESSES

Several processes—creating the business case for BI, building organizational support, education, evaluation, development, and sourcing—play important roles in the management and impacts of BI. We discussed two of these processes, development and sourcing, in Chapter 8. We examine the remaining four processes next, starting with creating the business case.

9.4.1 Building the Business Case for Business Intelligence

In order to obtain resources needed for BI, a business case justifying these investments is important. Several benefits of BI have been highlighted and illustrated throughout this book. In Chapter 1, we discussed how BI produces four direct contributions—dissemination of real-time information, creation of new knowledge based on the past, support for responsive and anticipative decisions, and improvement in organizational planning for the future—which, in turn, produces a variety of benefits in terms of organizational performance. The organizational benefits we discussed in that chapter include enhanced responsiveness to industry trends, improved decisions based on the latest developments, increased efficiency, improved customer service, and greater innovativeness.

In addition to the benefits highlighted in Chapter 1, BI can help a company in several ways. Some examples are as follows:

- BI can help a company to avoid falling behind competitors who are investing in BI. Otherwise, those competitors would be able to manage their business better, more quickly respond to market changes, and consequently produce better earnings (Kelly, 2008).

- BI can improve cross-selling and up-selling by helping identify the additional products that an organization might be able to sell to each of its customers, based on the customers' history and characteristics (McAfee and Wagonfield, 2004).

- BI can help maximize customer satisfaction based on the aggregated information about the customer's interactions with the company across various contact points and over time.

- BI can help a company in identifying which of its current customers it might lose (McAfee and Wagonfield, 2004).

- BI can help an organization produce faster and more accurate compliance and regulatory reporting. By providing a detailed view of the company's performance, BI allows the company to identify trends and other behaviors that may not comply with federal compliance regulations (Kelly, 2008).

Expectation regarding organizational benefits such as the ones mentioned above, if appropriately justified, can be a valuable component of the business case for BI. Furthermore, if the expected ROI for a BI investment can be reliably estimated, it would help strengthen the business case. However, ROI computation may not be appropriate for all BI investments, especially for enterprise-level BI investments, which often have longer-term payoffs that are difficult to quantify with reasonable accuracy. Traditional ROI assessment is difficult for BI, as indicated by the fact that nearly half of the respondents in an *InformationWeek* survey (Weier, 2007) had difficulty in evaluating ROI associated with BI because its benefits are often intangible or long term in nature.

Instead of ROI, managers should therefore focus on the fundamental value proposition offered by BI, which can rarely be quantified but is instead based on an understanding of the problems that might be holding the company back. Several companies have followed this approach successfully.

- The CIO of Union Pacific Corp. remarked: "I am using BI to really understand what value we as a company derive from different assets. At the end of the day, the most expensive asset is people, and if people can be involved in lowering the costs of other, less intelligent assets, it helps preserve their jobs. That's the value proposition." (King, 2005)

- The Chief Technology Officer for Maricopa County, Arizona, looked at "the value proposition of better decisions," and therefore did not do a formal ROI study (Havenstein, 2007).

- The CIO at Energizer Holdings, Inc., remarked: "It's as simple as, good decisions are better than bad decisions. You start with that premise and scale your effort. At some point in time, it becomes a little like e-mail. Did you do an ROI when you put in e-mail?" (Havenstein, 2007)

According to Bill Hostmann, vice president at Gartner Inc., "It's not easy to persuade someone to go to college based on a purely financial or numbers game, and the same thing goes for BI. You just have to believe that BI is absolutely essential for you as an organization to invest, that this is a fundamental core competency that you have to have" (Kelly, 2008). Although cost/benefit analysis is useful for the implementation of BI tools, solutions, and infrastructure, investment decisions regarding BI are often based on intuition as much as on quantitative data. For example, despite operating in an industry that functions based on quantitative data, Brinker International made major decisions, such as whether to start a BI effort and which vendor to select, based largely on intuition and reputation. Business Intelligence in Practice 9.2 describes this in greater detail.

Business Intelligence in Practice 9.2: Brinker International Makes Major BI Decisions

Brinker International, Inc., is one of the world's leading casual dining restaurant companies that serves over one million guests every day. It has 125,000 team members and operates over 1,700 restaurants in 27 countries, including Macaroni Grill, Chili's Grill & Bar, On The Border Mexican Grill & Cantina, and Maggiano's Little Italy.

Information technology plays an important role at Brinker's restaurants. For example, once a waiter enters the information about the order from a group of, say, five individuals into a restaurant's point of sale system, the order appears in the kitchen on overhead display screens. The software behind the system, which knows the theoretical cook times of each of the meals on the restaurant's menu, identifies the schedule that should be followed in placing items into the ovens or on the grill, so that all five meals for the group will be ready at the same time. After the cook begins each meal, he or she taps a bar on the display screen so that the next order to be prepared appears.

The following morning, analysts at Brinker International in Dallas go through detailed reports on the operations at the more than 1,800 restaurants Brinker operates. They seek insights into how they can improve the dining experience for customers and improve the company's bottom line, by looking

(continued)

at such information as which meals are leading to the greatest customer satisfaction, and which restaurants have greater average bills.

The director of business intelligence (BI) at Brinker, remarked: "In the restaurant business, people like to work on gut feelings. But when you operate 1,800 restaurants you can't rely on gut feelings—there's too much going on, too many variables. There has been an explosion of technologies in recent years that allow us to see and analyze the business in new ways. What we have been able to do is put hard facts in front of our executives so they can have more confidence in the decisions they are making."

Such hard facts, which are powered by a 1.2 terabyte Teradata data warehouse and BI tools from Information Builders, enable Brinker's executives make better decisions on such issues as which new locations to invest in and which restaurant practices produce the greatest customer satisfaction levels and profit margins.

Prior to BI, Brinker's system focused on operational data. The chain's SQL Server 2000 database had been online for about five years. Although it was reasonably successful in capturing data, it did not meet Brinker's needs for analyses and reporting. Moreover, the company was facing difficulty in providing direct access to data to all individuals who needed it. Moreover, Brinker had become more strategic in its thinking over the preceding several years, but lacked the information to support strategic analysis, something that the organization has a stronghold of today.

From the beginning of the inception of the BI platform, Brinker's goals were clear: it needed a reliable platform that could evolve with the business, provide data in close to real-time, and support ad hoc analysis, but without much administrative support. By April 2006, the Brinker's BI governance team had decided to go through a vendor selection process that included Microsoft, Oracle, Netezza, and Teradata. They shortlisted Netezza and Teradata, and then selected Teradata, with one major factor being its proven record in the food and retail service industries. The team also received favorable comments about Teradata from peers at Harrah's, which is one of Teradata's leading clients.

The business case proposed to senior executives was based more on soft return on investment projections than on hard ROI. According to Brinker's CIO, "At the time we couldn't accurately predict what decisions could be made using the system, or the financial impact that would have. We were able to walk through some scenarios, however, and basically say here's what we have to do now to get the information and here's what we would be able to do. Our executives were pretty insightful—they understood the value that improved BI could provide."

Implementation started in August 2006, with the first phase of the project ready about five months later. Some problems were encountered along the

(*continued*)

way, most involving processes for ETL: "We found that we didn't pay a lot of attention in the past to how data was being captured. How, for example, do you accurately capture cook time?" he said. The team decided to replace the tools it was using to ETL data into the Microsoft SQL database with tools from Informatica, because the Microsoft tools were more suitable for SQL.

The Teradata data warehouse went live in January 2007, using Web-FOCUS from Information Builders as the primary front-end tool to run queries. Managers and executives are excited by the early insights that they have been able to obtain from the BI solution, such as the effects of overall market conditions on their bottom line.

BI has also provided Brinker with some surprising insights. Brinker restaurants used to encounter considerable bottlenecks in "To-Go" (or take-out) operations, especially at the peak of the dinner rush, when they found it tough to keep pace with the orders coming in over the phone and at the take-out counter. The gut feeling among managers was that the kitchen staff was unable to keep up with the number of orders being received. However, analyses using the BI solution helped them recognize that this wasn't the situation. Instead, the bottleneck was in the food packaging and take-out counter areas. "The hunch turned out to be wrong. Now, by focusing on the right area our managers have been able to improve their Take Out perform-ance," remarked the CIO (Duvall, 2008).

(Compiled from Lewis, 2007; Duvall, 2008; King, 2009)

Making a business case for BI investments is not only important at the start of a BI project. It is also important to be able to continually demonstrate the value of BI investments, so that commitment is sustained even in the face of executive turnover and economic problems (Glaser and Stone, 2008).

9.4.2 Building Organizational Support

For continued success of BI in an organization, it is important to build, and maintain, organizational support for BI. **Organizational support for BI** is important for several reasons. First, business users might feel skeptical of the benefits from BI, either to the organization or to themselves, and therefore be reluctant to use them. Second, users might feel threatened by BI, due to the fear that their roles and responsibilities might be affected if BI is implemented effectively. Third, some users may prefer to make decisions based on intuition and gut feeling rather than information and analysis. Fourth, people are typically just resistant to change. Due to these and other reasons, BI projects may not provide adequate returns if organizational support is not maintained. Managers responsible for BI should therefore be extra attentive to users' perceptions and feelings. For example, Ford Parts Supply and Logistics used BI to improve the processes for supplying OEM service parts to 5,900 dealers in North America, achieving a 20% reduction in backorders, a 30% reduction in end-to-end cycle time, and a 20% reduction in safety stock inventory. The major challenge in reaching these achievements was securing the support of business operations for the changes necessary to exploit the BI applications, a change that took over a year to realize (Williams and Williams, 2004).

We now examine some ways in which organizational support for BI can be built and maintained. First, it is important to build a business case for BI based on expected benefits, as discussed in Section 9.4.1. The business case could also help convince users about the importance of BI.

A second way of building organizational support for BI involves following an incremental approach, demonstrating value of BI through small investments, and then using these results to build support for future BI efforts. This was the approach used at Associated Grocers, which we discussed in Business Intelligence in Practice 8.4. According to Associated Grocers' CIO: "We trained a core set of 25 to 30 initial users in the ad hoc capabilities of the new platform, and we have some slow adopters. We've started to change people's mind-sets and the entire culture within our organization. The users have learned they can go directly to the application to get what they need faster rather than funneling every request through IS. Furthermore, the user base is expanding rapidly as more people want to be trained." (Lewis, 2007, p. 3)

A third approach focuses on redefining roles so that individuals would see how they could benefit from BI. For example, Hewlett Packard Mobile Computing used BI to improve its processes for increasing product quality and customer satisfaction, meeting warranty commitments, and managing warranty costs. HP did not accomplish these improvements by pursuing the philosophy of "build it and they will come." Instead, it redefined processes, roles, and responsibilities to support the business improvement opportunities enabled through BI. Consequently, users did not face uncertainty regarding how their roles would be affected by BI (Williams and Williams, 2004).

A fourth approach focuses on explicitly assigning people the responsibility of building organizational support for BI. For example, consider the case of South Wales police (responsible for the two Welsh cities of Cardiff and Swansea), which implemented a BI solution in 2006. To win the support of police officers who would be using the BI solution, a business change manager was assigned the responsibility of facilitating seminars for senior and middle managers. These managers served as "communications champions" and cascaded information down to colleagues and helped them in case they faced difficulties. They also provided insights into the best ways of undertaking the process change (Glaser and Stone, 2008).

Finally, to build and sustain organizational support for BI, it is important to carefully manage expectations. Sometimes, users have a low expectation that projects will be delivered on time and will meet their expectations, and therefore they do not participate enthusiastically in BI projects. Alternatively, users sometimes may have overly high expectations from BI, believing that BI solutions would be delivered almost instantly and do everything for them. Management of user expectations, and the consequently maintenance of organizational support, could benefit from involving users in BI-related processes and meetings from their onset (Glaser and Stone, 2008).

9.4.3 Education

For the continued success of BI at an organization, it is important to keep current as well as potential users of BI educated about its potential benefits, functionality, and use of BI solutions and tools. This is done to some extent during the training associated with a BI development project. However, education about BI is broader than training, as it also includes updating the trained users' knowledge about BI through frequent communication, such as newsletters, user groups, and brown-bag lunches. It is important to ensure that the education provided is ongoing and collaborative. Web-based sessions in which BI users share tips and tricks are especially useful. The BI competency center can also play an important role in educating users and others regarding BI.

According to Nick Millman, senior director for information management services at Accenture, "What's often missing is the explanation of where the data comes from and how you can use it to derive some insight" (Mitchell, 2009). Therefore, education about BI incorporates not just training on how to use BI tools and solution, but also informing users about the value of data and analysis, especially in the context of decisions they themselves need to make. Consistent with this approach, Anthony Abbattista, vice president of technology solutions at Allstate Insurance Co. (and a former BI consultant) remarks: "It's really [about] teaching people to mine for value." Abbattista therefore focuses on building that knowledge one user at a time. "We build out initial capabilities with front-line managers and people in the trenches. They then become the consultant to people around them."

BI users are usually trained either at the start of a BI project or toward its conclusion, but rarely outside the realm of a project. As individuals become more comfortable with BI, they need to expand their use of BI, especially as they better recognize the potential benefits. Moreover, it takes time and considerable learning to become proficient with BI. Ongoing education and support should therefore be provided (Glaser and Stone, 2008).

9.4.4 Evaluation

In Section 9.4.1, we examined the process of building a business case for BI. The focus in that section was on identifying *future* benefits from BI efforts, and using them to either quantitatively or qualitatively justify the expected costs. **Evaluation** is similar in that it focuses on evaluation of benefits and costs, but differs in that here the focus is on the benefits and costs that have been incurred in the *past*.

BI evaluations periodically revisit the expectations as per the business case and utilize them as the baseline to determine whether BI initiatives are progressing as expected. However, unexpected benefits (such as new insights that have been obtained through BI but were not included in the business case, or quicker decisions and the associated savings or competitive advantage) and costs (i.e., comparing budget forecasts to actual spending) should be considered as well. Moreover, BI evaluations could benefit from surveys of users regarding the value of information obtained from BI tools and solutions. Unsolicited inputs from users, such as increased demand for data access and requests for BI training or enhancements, are also useful for evaluating the progress of BI. For example, if business executives enthusiastically volunteer to be lead users in a new BI project, it is reasonable to believe that BI efforts are progressing well. Finally, the extent to which the BI projects are aligned with the business strategy is a potentially useful indicator of how effectively the BI governance committee has prioritized BI investments (Larson and Matney, 2009).

In addition to internal benefits obtained from BI, sometimes the benefits from BI investments may be along external linkages. We discussed Air Canada earlier in Business Intelligence in Practice 8.3, where we focused on internal applications of BI at Air Canada. Air Canada's BI efforts have also helped its customers, as we examine in Business Intelligence in Practice 9.3.

Business Intelligence in Practice 9.3: Air Canada's Customers Benefit from Its BI Solution

Air Canada's use of WebFOCUS, which was discussed in Business Intelligence in Practice 8.3, has also helped the airline with its Corporate Pass program. Air Canada introduced the program in early 2006 to selected large corporations on a negotiated basis. The Corporate Pass system enables corporate customers who frequently fly their employees on Air Canada to earn credits for certain amounts of travel, and then divide the credits among various departments.

Air Canada wanted to make it easy for these corporate customers to book, manage, and track their flights and flight expenses, and also to view and analyze their travel data. This needed to be easy for customers to use, while handling sensitive corporate data in a secure, reliable way. According to Chantal Berthiaume, who has been in charge of BI at Air Canada since 1999, "Our managers wanted to find deals for corporate customers, but they didn't have the right reporting tools for the job. We had already proven that WebFOCUS is effective internally, so I suggested that we leverage our existing software assets and expertise for this application as well."

Two developers in the BI group were able to develop the needed externally oriented BI solution within a month, for a total cost of $25,000. "We delivered an innovative BI application in only a few weeks at an

(*continued*)

extremely low cost, proving that BI does not have to be an expensive or complex endeavor," Berthiaume remarked.

After receiving positive feedback from a small set of beta customers, the developers made needed modifications, and then rolled out this BI solution to members of Air Canada's loyalty program, Corporate Pass. The BI solution is now available to all Corporate Pass customers. Many of these customers use the BI tools embedded in this solution to manage their travel information, which makes the service more useful and compelling.

"Through a simple Web browser, our customers can access their travel data offline and drill down to certain categories within the system, such as types of travel, geography, time of day, date, and many other variables," explains Berthiaume. By integrating these BI capabilities into the Corporate Pass application, Air Canada has enabled corporations to manipulate their travel data in a variety of ways. For example, travel managers can determine how much travel was allocated to particular projects, departments, and employees. They can select certain types of travel and qualify data according to geography, time of day, and many other variables. The active reporting technology also lets them manipulate reports in various sort orders, filter data by their chosen criteria, and chart information for visual impact. According to Berthiaume, Corporate Pass provides Air Canada a competitive edge in the corporate travel market. "The ROI for this application is huge," she says. "The system has helped generate sales, improve customer satisfaction and solidify relationships with some of our key corporate customers."

Customers such as the Canadian telecommunications firm TELUS really appreciate the flexibility provided by Air Canada's BI solution. Instead of relying only on travel agencies or global distribution systems such as Sabre, TELUS now receives real-time access to its travel data through a corporate reporting portal, and thus has consequently been able to achieve significant cost savings. According to Geoff de Bruijn, director, Strategic Planning and Logistics Support at TELUS Enterprise Services, "Air Canada's robust self-service reporting interface allows us to extract and analyze our travel pass activity, providing us with the information we need to actively manage our air travel program." This might lead to a significant strategic return that exceeds benefits from internal BI efforts.

(Compiled from Corcoran, 2008; InformationBuilders, 2008; Smith, 2007; itbusiness.ca, 2006)

▶ 9.5 SUMMARY

In this chapter we examined the various actions related to management of BI. In doing so, we discussed three aspects—infrastructure, structures, and processes—that mutually affect each other. We examined several components of these three aspects, including data infrastructure, organizational culture, BI governance, BI competency center, centralization of BI, creating a business case for BI, building organizational support for BI, education regarding BI, and evaluation of BI. In addition, two other processes related to management of BI, sourcing and development of BI tools and solutions, were examined in Chapter 8. In Chapter 10, we discuss some of the future directions for BI.

► KEY TERMS

analytics culture
business case for business
  intelligence
business intelligence
  competency center
business intelligence
  steering committee

data infrastructure
data-driven decision
  making
education about business
  intelligence
evaluation of business
  intelligence

management of business
  intelligence
organizational support for
  business intelligence

► REVIEW QUESTIONS

1. Explain why data infrastructure is important for BI.

2. What do you understand by "analytics culture"? How does it affect BI?

3. Identify and briefly explain the three structural aspects that are important for BI. Why are they important?

4. What is BI governance? What are its main components?

5. What is a BI competency center? What specific roles does it serve in BI management?

6. What are two ways of viewing centralization in the context of the structure of BI? Briefly explain each view.

7. What is the relationship between building a business case for BI and building organizational support for BI? Are they mutually complementary, and if so, how? Or are they mutually conflicting, and if so, how?

► APPLICATION EXERCISES

1. Assume that you have been assigned the responsibility to form the BI steering committee for your organization (i.e., the organization you work at or the university at which you study). Based on your organization's structure, which individuals would you include on the committee? Why?

2. Visit http://www.sas.com/success/nedbankretail.html and review the case study on the use of a BI competency center at Nedbank Retail in South Africa. What specific benefits did the center provide in this case?

3. In what ways is the above BI competency center similar to the center in Business Intelligence in Practice 9.1? How are the two different?

4. Assume that you have been assigned the responsibility to develop a business case for BI for your organization (i.e., the organization you work at or the university at which you study). This business case could be for either starting BI efforts (if your organization does not have BI at present) or for increasing BI investments by 50% (if your organization already has BI). What would be the focal points of your business case? What benefits would you emphasize, and which of them would you be able to quantify? Would you be able to compute ROI for the proposal?

5. Based on Air Canada's experience with BI (according to Business Intelligence in Practice 8.3 and 9.3), which two benefits from BI do you consider to be the most important? Why? Which benefits might be useful for you to highlight in building a business case for BI for your organization?

▶ REFERENCES

Carte, T. A., Schwarzkopf, A. B., Shaft, T. M., and Zmud, R. W. 2005. "Advanced Business Intelligence at Cardinal Health." *MIS Quarterly Executive*, December, pp. 413–424.

Computerworld, 2007. "Honors Program: QlikTech International." *Computerworld*, August 22.

Corcoran, M. 2008. "The Value of BI in a Weak Economy." *Enterprise Systems*, http://esj. com/Articles/2008/12/03/The-Value-of-BI-in-a-Weak-Economy.aspx? (accessed April 5, 2009).

Davenport, T. H. 2006. "Competing on Analytics." *Harvard Business Review*, January.

Davenport, T. H., and Harris, J. G. 2007. *Competing on Analytics: The New Science of Winning* (Boston: Harvard Business School Publishing).

Duvall, M. 2008. "Business Intelligence at Your Service." *CIO Zone* http://www.ciozone. com/index.php/Business-Intelligence/Business-Intelligence-At-Your-Service.html (accessed June 27, 2009).

Glaser, J., and Stone, J. 2008. "Effective Use of Business Intelligence: Leveraging Your Organization's Business Data Could Improve Financial and Operational Performance— and Quality of Care." *Healthcare Financial Management*, February, pp. 68–72.

Gutierrez, N. 2006. Business Intelligence (BI) Governance. Infosys White Paper, October, http://www.infosys.com/industries/consumer-packaged-goods/white-papers/bi-govern- ance.pdf (accessed June 26, 2009).

Havenstein, H. 2007. "BI Tools Still Facing Use Push-back." *InformationWeek*, March 14.

Howson, C. 2008. *Successful Business Intelligence: Secrets to Making BI a Killer App* (McGraw-Hill Osborne).

InformationBuilders. 2008. Air Canada Soars with Web-Based Flight-Tracking Application, http://www.informationbuilders.com/applications/airCanada.html (accessed April 5, 2009).

itbusiness.ca. 2006. Air Canada Puts Browser-Based BI into Pilot Mode, http://www. itbusiness.ca/it/client/en/home/News.asp?id=39202 (accessed April 5, 2009).

Kelly, J. 2008. BI Competency Center Helps Italian Company Find Efficiencies, Share Solutions. SearchDataManagement.com, November 6, http://searchdatamanagement. techtarget.com/news/article/0,289142,sid91_gci1337943,00.html (accessed June 28, 2009).

Kelly, J. 2008. Gartner: Business intelligence ROI: Value a Matter of Mind Over Money. SearchDataManagement.com. March 13, http://searchdatamanagement.techtarget. com/news/article/0,289142,sid91_gci1305065,00.html (accessed June 25, 2009).

King, J. 2005. "Better BI Decisions." *ComputerWorld*, September 19.

King, R. 2009. "Business Intelligence Software's Time Is Now." *Business Week*, March 2.

Larson, D., and Matney, D. 2009. BI-BestPractices.com. http://www.bi-bestpractices.com/view-articles/4681 (accessed June 26, 2009).

Leonard, B. 2009. Framing Business Intelligence Governance. BI-BestPractices.com. http://www.bi-bestpractices.com/view-articles/4686 (accessed June 26, 2009).

Leproni, 2008. CSI-Piemonte and SAS: a Successful Partnership. SAS Global Forum 2008, Paper 057-2008.

LeVoyer, K. 2009. BI Competency Centers: The Brain of Your BI Strategy. sascom. http://www.bettermanagement.com/library/library.aspx?l=13561&pagenumber=2, (accessed June 28, 2009).

Lewis, L. 2007. "Your Data Is Served." *Teradata Magazine*, September. http://www.teradata.com/tdmo/v07n03/pdf/AR5377.pdf (accessed June 27, 2009).

McAfee, A., and Wagonfield, A. B. 2004. Business Intelligence at SYSCO. *Harvard Business School Publishing Case*, 9-604-080, July 19.

Miller, G. J., Brautigam, D., and Gerlach, S. V. 2006. *Business Intelligence Competency Centers: A Team Approach to Maximizing Competitive Advantage* (Hoboken, N. J.: John Wiley).

Mitchell, R. L. 2009. "Smart and Cheap: Business Intelligence on a Budget." *ComputerWorld*, May 14.

Pauli, D. 2009. "BI Projects Fail Due to a Lack of Training and Business Support." *ComputerWorld Australia*, February 23.

Preston, R. 2007. "Down to Business: Business Intelligence Still In Its Infancy." *InformationWeek*, January 6.

Sabherwal, R. 2007. "Succeeding with Business Intelligence: Some Insights and Recommendations." *Cutter Benchmark Review*, 7(9), 5–15.

Smith, B. 2007. "Air Canada Uses BI as Excel Exit Strategy." *IT World Canada*, July 25.

Swartz, N. 2007. "Gartner Warns Firms of 'Dirty Data'." *Information Management Journal*, May/June, p. 6.

Watson, H., Wixom, B. H., Hoffer, J. A., Anderson-Lehman, R., and Reynolds, A. M. 2006. "Real-Time Business Intelligence: Best Practices at Continental Airlines." *Information Systems Management*, Winter, pp. 7–18.

Weier, M. H. 2007. "Vendors Introduce 'Affordable' Business-Intelligence Systems." *InformationWeek*, March 14.

Weill, P., and Ross, J. W. 2004. *IT Governance: How Top Performers Manage IT Decision Rights for Superior Results* (Boston: Harvard Business School Press).

Williams, N., and Williams, S. 2004. "Capturing ROI through Business-Centric BI Development Methods." *Information Management Magazine*, August.

CHAPTER 10

THE FUTURE OF BUSINESS INTELLIGENCE

▶ 10.1 INTRODUCTION

In Chapter 9 we described issues related to managing BI over time, including cultural changes associated with BI, BI governance, approaches to managing BI, and how to build organizational support for BI. In this chapter we discuss some potential future directions for BI. As BI becomes widely accepted in corporate organizations, it will become increasingly critical for corporate managers to institute safeguards for insuring the security of internal and external information. In Section 10.2, we discuss some of the issues involved with creating security safeguards for corporate data. We also examine the future directions for BI, due to factors such as progress in information technology and the increased use of social networks, Web 2.0 and Enterprise 2.0, in Section 10.3. In Section 10.4 we describe what we call the Holy Grail in analytics: predicting what people want, using technologies such as collaborative filtering. In Section 10.5 we present the ways mobile applications for BI are increasing the pervasiveness of BI applications in the organization and stand to extend the value of BI by providing contextual cues. Finally, we conclude the chapter with a discussion in Section 10.6 of how new BI technologies, like those used for real-time data streaming analytics, could be used to minimize personal and organizational biases that often result in organizational disasters.

We begin with a discussion of the increasingly important role of security in protecting the enterprise data.

▶ 10.2 SECURITY STANDARDS FOR CORPORATE DATA

Data and information, both structured and unstructured and originating from within or outside the organization, are the building blocks for BI. However, as these critical sources have increasingly gone digital, data theft is increasingly becoming commonplace in organizations. Often the only way to detect that there has been a data breach is when banks that process credit card purchases detect unusual patterns among the transaction data, such as an unusually high number of credit card charges associated with customer purchases at a specific retailer. Essentially, banks use BI to find a correlation between cards with fraudulent activity and cards used to make purchases at a specific retailer. In this fashion, BI helps the banks to take proactive steps toward minimizing the impact of the data breach; otherwise the data breach will go on unrecognized, until the credit card customers gets the bill and complain about illegal activity on their statements.

Once a data breach has been discovered, the organization must report it to the appropriate authorities, which in the United States is the Secret Service. At this point the Secret Service recommends running background checks on everyone who could access the data, pulling personnel files on anyone that was let go it the past year, and triple-checking every system within the enterprise. The first step in remedying the situation is to understand the possible vulnerabilities in the data chain (McNulty et al., 2007):

1. The first vulnerable point is at the cash register, where the customer presents the payment card and it gets swiped by the card reader. At this point card readers could be hacked.

2. The information is then transmitted to the bank for approval. At this point the data lines between the store and the bank could be tapped.

3. The transaction data then may be stored on the company computers and appear in a number of reports, although credit card numbers should not be stored in the corporate computers. At this point the servers could be compromised or malicious code could reside within the company's software that diverts information to a remote computer.

In addition to fixing the organization's data security weakness, the CEO will need to launch a brand-restoration strategy, which includes quickly notifying the customers who were affected, setting up toll-free information hotlines, and offering credit-monitoring services to those affected. Often, customers many need to be offered extras such as discounts and sales in order to stay loyal, and companies may need to develop new policies and practices to prevent future recurrences.

Certain recommended safeguards in keeping the organization data secure include the following (McNulty et al., 2007):

1. Appoint a high-ranking corporate official in charge of information protection across the organization to manage and champion this area.

2. Develop a comprehensive strategy for risk management, including requiring each new initiative to identify the involved data, its value, and the appropriate safeguards to protect it.

3. Develop policies, procedures, and training protocols to reduce the likelihood that individuals make wrong choices due to a lack of understanding of the overall data standards.

4. Become fully PCI compliant. PCI, which stands for Payment Card Industry Data Security Standard, is a protocol created to help corporations that

PAYMENT CARD INDUSTRY SECURITY STANDARDS

Protection of Cardholder Payment Data

PCI Standards Include:

PCI Data Security Standard: The PCI DSS applies to any entity that stores, processes, and/or transmits cardholder data. It covers technical and operational system components included in or connected to cardholder data. If your business accepts or processes payment cards, it must comply with the PCI DSS.

PIN Entry Device Security Requirements: PCI PED applies to manufacturers who specify and implement device characteristics and management for personal identification number (PIN) entry terminals used for payment card financial transactions.

Payment Application Data Security Standard: The PA-DSS is for software developers and integrators of applications that store, process or transmit cardholder data as part of authorization or settlement. It also governs these applications that are sold, distributed or licensed to third parties.

FIGURE 10.1 Protection of Cardholder Payment Data
(Source: Adapted from PCI, 2009)

process credit card payments to prevent fraud through increased controls around the data that are designed to prevent its compromise. This protocol specified by the PCI Securities Council is the result of the aggregation of the payment devices standards (PIN Entry Device Security, PCI PED), the applications standards (Payment Application Data Security, PCI PA-DSS), and the infrastructure standards (Data Security Standard, PCI DSS), as depicted in Figure 10.1. Typically an organization's compliance is determined by an independent assessor. The standard, specified by the PCI Securities Council,[1] outlines the following principles and requirements, which are summarized in Figure 10.2:

a. Build and Maintain a Secure Network

    i. Requirement 1: Install and maintain a firewall configuration to protect cardholder data

    ii. Requirement 2: Do not use vendor-supplied defaults for system passwords and other security parameters

b. Protect Cardholder Data

    i. Requirement 3: Protect stored cardholder data

    ii. Requirement 4: Encrypt transmission of cardholder data across open, public networks

[1] https://www.pcisecuritystandards.org/security_standards/pci_dss.shtml

PRINCIPLES AND REQUIREMENTS

Build and Maintain a Secure Network
1. Install and maintain a firewall configuration to protect cardholder data.
2. Do not use vendor-supplied defaults for system passwords and other security parameters.

Protect Cardholder Data
3. Protect stored cardholder data.
4. Encrypt transmission of cardholder data across open, public networks.

Maintain a Vulnerability Management Program
5. Use and regularly update anti-virus software.
6. Develop and maintain secure systems and applications.

Implement Strong Access Control Measures
7. Restrict access to cardholder data by business need-to-know.
8. Assign a unique ID to each person with computer access.
9. Restrict physical access to cardholder data.

Regularly Monitor and Test Networks
10. Track and monitor all access to network resources and cardholder data.
11. Regularly test security systems and processes.

Maintain an Information Security Policy
12. Maintain a policy that addresses information security.

FIGURE 10.2 PCI Data Security Standard

   c. Maintain a Vulnerability Management Program

      i. Requirement 5: Use and regularly update anti-virus software

      ii. Requirement 6: Develop and maintain secure systems and applications

   d. Implement Strong Access Control Measures

      i. Requirement 7: Restrict access to cardholder data by business need-to-know

      ii. Requirement 8: Assign a unique ID to each person with computer access

      iii. Requirement 9: Restrict physical access to cardholder data

   e. Regularly Monitor and Test Networks

      i. Requirement 10: Track and monitor all access to network resources and cardholder data

      ii. Requirement 11: Regularly test security systems and processes

   f. Maintain an Information Security Policy

      i. Requirement 12: Maintain a policy that addresses information security

In case a breach occurs, organizations must have people on hand with digital expertise equal to that of cyber criminals, who are able to discern which systems are likely to be targeted. Also, it will be important to be familiar with privacy statutes and regulations and have the capability to gather and save the evidence necessary for the investigation.

As organizations continue to focus on BI as a competitive strategy, the amount of data stored throughout the firm will continue to increase. With this increasing growth of both structured and unstructured data, organizations are pressed to be vigilant stewards of the data to guarantee the privacy and security of this key resource. We continue with a discussion of social media in Section 10.3.

▶ 10.3 SOCIAL MEDIA: WEB 2.0 AND ENTERPRISE 2.0

We have discussed at length how BI applications provide decision makers with valuable information and knowledge by leveraging a variety of sources of data as well as structured and unstructured information; these sources of information and data could reside within or outside the organization. However, a new type of platform, Web 2.0, is giving rise to new forms of information collaboratively created through the Web, and represents the collective intelligence (also known as collective knowledge or collective wisdom). Collective intelligence is different from other forms of information in that gets better as more people contribute and use it. Emergent BI is increasingly utilizing not only data originating from transaction processing systems, text mining, and Web mining, but also data coming from collective intelligence via the increasingly popular Web 2.0.

The expression *Web 2.0* was originally coined in 2004 by Tim O'Reilly, who used it to describe the emergence of the Internet as a platform. **Web 2.0** is defined as "a living term describing changing trends in the use of World Wide Web technology and web design that aims to enhance creativity, information sharing, collaboration and functionality of the web. Web 2.0 concepts have led to the development and evolution of web-based communities and hosted services, such as social-networking sites, video sharing sites, wikis, blogs, and folksonomies."[2] One distinguishing characteristic of Web 2.0 application is that it is *democratic*, meaning the more people use it, the better it gets. Many people consider Web 2.0 as "the next big thing" due to its ability to exploit the collective intelligence, also known as "the wisdom of the crowds," meaning that these knowledge bases actually become more accurate the more people use them. As an example, consider eBay's ability to provide information about the seller's reputation. The more buyers that provide feedback to formulate this value, the more likely that this number will reflect an accurate picture of how reliable the seller might be. Figure 10.3 depicts the most significant social media applications in use today, and a definition of each social media application appears in Table 10.1.

---

[2] www.wikipedia.org according to Wikipedia, which is itself a Web 2.0 service and freely accessible Web-based encyclopedia, collaboratively written by its readers. Accessed on July 31, 2009.

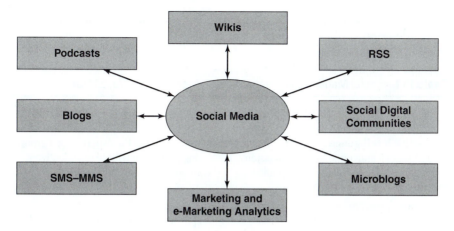

FIGURE 10.3 Social Media Applications
(Source: Adapted from Reichenstein, 2007)

Many organizations are similarly considering the implementation of Web 2.0 applications to support business objectives. A recent McKinsey survey confirms that 75% of the responding executives are sustaining or increasing their budgeted investments in Web 2.0 collaborative technologies, including blogging (32%), collective intelligence (48%), and peer-to-peer networking (47%) (Mc Kinsey, 2008).

The use of Web 2.0-like applications within the organization is known as **Enterprise 2.0** (McAfee, 2006). Typically, enterprise technologies used within the organization serve two purposes: either as *channels*, which create and distribute digital information that is visible by few people via technologies like e-mail and instant messaging; or as *platforms*, which enable content to be widely visible via technologies like intranets and information portals. The use of Enterprise 2.0 technologies in the organization includes (McAfee, 2006):

1. *Search and Links:* Users have become accustomed to search engines such as Google, and prefer to find information in corporate portals using keyword searches rather than navigational aids. Google was perhaps one of the first companies to understand the power of links in Web pages. Links provide structure to online content, and the "best pages" are those which are most often "linked to."

2. *Authoring, such as via wikis and blogs:* A *wiki*[3] is defined as *"a page or collection of Web pages designed to enable anyone who accesses it to contribute or modify content, using a simplified markup language. Wikis are often used to create collaborative Web sites and to power community Web sites."* A *blog* (a contraction between Web and log) is a form of online digital diary, and in essence is a Web site where a person makes regular

---

[3] www.wikipedia.org accessed on July 31, 2009.

written journal entries that form a statement of opinion, a story, an analysis, description of events, or other material.

Table 10.1 Social Media Applications (Source McKinsey, 2007a, 2007b)

Blogs (short for Web logs) are online journals or diaries hosted on a Web site and often distributed to other sites or readers using RSS.

Collective intelligence refers to any system that attempts to tap the expertise of a group rather than an individual to make decisions. Technologies that contribute to collective intelligence include collaborative publishing and common databases for sharing knowledge.

Mash-ups are aggregations of content from different online sources to create a new service. An example would be a program that pulls apartment listings from one site and displays them on a Google map to show where the apartments are located.

Peer-to-peer networking (sometimes called P2P) is a technique for efficiently sharing files (music, videos, or text) either over the Internet or within a closed set of users. Unlike the traditional method of storing a file on one machine—which can become a bottleneck if many people try to access it at once—P2P distributes files across many machines, often those of the users themselves. Some systems retrieve files by gathering and assembling pieces of them from many machines.

Online games include both games played on dedicated game consoles that can be networked and "massively multiplayer" games, which involve thousands of people who interact simultaneously through personal avatars in online worlds that exist independently of any single player's activity.

Podcasts are audio or video recordings—a multimedia form of a blog or other content. They are often distributed through an aggregator, such as iTunes.

RSS (Really Simple Syndication) allows people to subscribe to online distributions of news, blogs, podcasts, or other information.

Social networking refers to systems that allow members of a specific site to learn about other members' skills, talents, knowledge, or preferences. Commercial examples include Facebook, MySpace and LinkedIn. Some companies use these systems internally to help identify experts.

Virtual worlds, such as Second Life, are highly social, three-dimensional online environments shaped by users who interact with and receive instant feedback from other users through the use of avatars.

Web services are software systems that make it easier for different systems to communicate with one another automatically in order to pass information or conduct transactions. For example, a retailer and supplier might use Web services to communicate over the Internet and automatically update each other's inventory systems.

Widgets are programs that allow access from users' desktops to Web-based content.

Wikis, such as Wikipedia, are systems for collaborative publishing. They allow many authors to contribute to an online document or discussion.

---

3. *Tags, to categorize and share content:* User-generated tags serve to organize the portal contents. Examples of categorizing tags are the bookmark tags found in the site www.delicious.com. At this Web site, users save all their favorite Web page bookmarks online, share them with other people, and see what other people are bookmarking, also revealing the most popular bookmarks being saved across many areas of interest. The categorization system that emerges from this user collaboration is known as a *folksonomy* (developed by a group of people or "folks"). It serves the same purpose as a taxonomy, which is typically developed by an expert.

4. *Extensions:* Examples are *recommendations* matched to user preferences, much like the ones used by Amazon to alert potential buyers of new published titles related to a specific user preferences.

5. *Signals:* Examples are *RSS* (Real Simple Syndication) feeds and aggregators. An RSS feed is a data format used to provide users, who subscribe to a specific content, with periodic updates whenever this content is updated. For example, users who are particularly fond of a specific blog may subscribe to an RSS feed that alerts them whenever a new entry is published on the blog. Aggregators are used to periodically download information from specific Web sites that users find of interest.

Enterprise 2.0 technologies provide users with the potential to create corporate intranets built by distributed autonomous individuals, and the more that people participate in authoring, the better the content will get. Much like Web 2.0, Enterprise 2.0 provides a platform for gathering the collective organizational intelligence, and could be an equally important source of information for BI applications. In Business Intelligence in Practice 10.1 we explore how one innovative organization, Procter and Gamble, is exploiting the power of collective intelligence for its brand marketing campaigns.

Business Intelligence in Practice 10.1: Procter and Gamble Bets on Social Media

Value-driven emerging ventures such as Seventh Generation[4] were perhaps the early adopters of social media as a means to successfully communicate their ideals: that businesses should make sure their products are healthy and safe, their manufacturing processes cause as little pollution as possible, and their employment policies are humane and not harmful to local communities. Seventh Generation successfully

(continued)

---

[4] www.seventhgeneration.com offers a complete line of nontoxic household products, including nonchlorine bleached, 100% recycled paper towels, bathroom and facial tissues, and napkins; nontoxic, phosphate-free cleaning, dish, and laundry products; and others.

communicated its social values through blogs, forums, and Web 2.0 sites such as Facebook,[5] MySpace,[6] LinkedIn,[7] YouTube,[8] and even Twitter.[9]

But you know that social media has really arrived when you hear that consumer brand giants such as Procter and Gamble have made a strategic decision that "social media is the future of marketing" (Triplepundit, 2009).

P&G's entry into the social media marketing arena was a campaign they entitled "Loads of Hope," designed to promote the Tide brand while raising funds for the nonprofit organization Feeding America. The campaign offers a free laundry service to families who are victims of disasters, and encourages consumers to buy a Tide T-Shirt, with all the proceeds benefitting disaster relief victims. In order to design this innovative marketing campaign, P&G consulted with social media experts to kick off a fund-raising competition via Twitter, blogs, and other social networks to drive traffic to one of the four tracking sites (tide1.com, tide2.com, etc.). The goal of the competition was to raise $100,000 toward disaster relief and prove the value of social media.

The twist to the story is that those bloggers and "twitterers" involved in promoting the competition also had a stake in the competition, since by their participation they were also competing for a piece of P&G's $6.7 million advertising budget. How P&G spends its marketing budget has significantly changed over the last few years. The company used to spend about 85% of its marketing budget on 30-second television spots. The trend today, and over the last five years, is that the amount of TV advertising will continue to decrease. The company envisions being increasingly more fragmented in their spending, with increased spending on interactive social media, and more mobile, as they move their money to where the consumers are. P&G intends to follow its consumers and direct their marketing to the media at which these customers are spending most of their time (Colvin, 2008).

The Tide campaign garnered tremendous buzz for P&G, as key Web personalities endorsed the campaign through Twitter and the other afore-mentioned social media sites.

---

[5] www.facebook.com a social media site that lets users join networks and interact with other people, providing an integrated platform for users to maintain a profile and exchange messages, pictures, chat, and essentially stay connected with others.

[6] www.myspace.com is a social media site that lets users interconnect with networks of friends, maintain a personal profiles, and exchange blogs, groups, photos, music, and videos. MySpace is a competing platform to Facebook, but has established a niche in the music industry, as many musicians have selected it as the medium to release their new songs, recorded in MP3 format.

[7] www.linkedin.com is a business-oriented social networking site used mostly to stay connected with professional acquaintances.

[8] www.youtube.com is a social media site that lets users upload and share videos.

[9] www.twitter.com is a social media site that lets users post and share short updates, known as *tweets*. A tweet is a short (up to 140 characters) text-based status that is displayed on the user's profile and is delivered to all friends (or *followers*) who expressly subscribed to them.

New online tools, such as Twitter, enable users to microblog, which is posting frequent tiny (140 characters) updates of what they're doing. This innovative social media technology enables users to have an "online awareness," which means continual online contact with their friends (or even strangers) who may choose to *follow* them. For example, the 2008 Barack Obama U.S. presidential campaign has received much praise for its flawless use of social media, including Twitter, as a publicity mechanism. BI technologies can take advantage of this new information source to gather important information about their products. For example, BI technologies could be used in the P&G campaign described in Business Intelligence in Practice 10.1 to mine the content of customer tweets for the word TIDE to uncover how users are describing their experience with the product and the marketing campaign. Organizations that are first to understand how to mine the content of un-structured user-generated data in social media sites are poised to have a competitive advantage.

In Section 10.4 we discuss how innovative technologies are used to predict what people want.

▶ 10.4 HOW TO PREDICT WHAT PEOPLE WANT

Perhaps the Holy Grail in social media is learning how to predict what people really want. Figuring out what will constitute a blockbuster movie or who will be the winner of a political campaign is big business, and predicting consumer taste is a prominent feature of the entertainment and shopping landscape. The first attempts at predicting customer tastes were done by George Gallup, who in the 1930s developed the public opinion polls (Davenport and Harris, 2009a). However, it wouldn't be until the 1990s, when Amazon developed the first commercial use of predictions via collaborative filtering, that these efforts to generate useful consumer recommendations really began to pay off. Collaborative filtering uses the customer's past choices to create correlations with other products that the customer may like—the famous "daily recommendations, based on the items you own and more," which attempt to anticipate a sale by predicting what items consumers are likely to purchase, based on correlations between prior purchases and other products.

Much like other BI predictive technologies, collaborative filtering requires a substantial amount of data on past purchases to work effectively. Collaborative filtering can make correlations either *item by item* or *customer by customer*. In addition to collaborative filtering, other statistical and intelligent technologies (many which were already described in Chapters 4 and 5), are also used to predict customer online behavior and anticipate what they want. A summary of these technologies include (Davenport and Harris, 2009b):

1. *Collaborative filtering*, already discussed above, matches patterns in customer preferences and buying behaviors to other customers. It allows two types of filtering:

   a. Item to item: generates patterns such as that 90% of customers who bought product A also bought product B.

   b. User to user: creates a community of users with similar buying patterns, and makes recommendations to a user based on what other members of the community are also buying.

2. *Biological response analysis* uses biological and neurological responses to stimuli, such as eyeball tracking, to develop products that have an increasing appeal to specific user communities.

3. *Cluster analysis*, described in Chapter 5, is used to group specific product attributes that are attractive to particular customers and create new products based on those attributes.

4. *Attributized Bayesian analysis* is used to understand why customers behave as they do by examining the attributes of the products they like or dislike, and then finding other products with similar attributes.

5. *Content-based filtering*, described in Chapter 5, uses decision trees to create a tree-like path used to help customers select from a number of products, personalize video games, or identify cross-selling scripts for a given product.

6. *Neural networks*, described in Chapter 5, are used to predict creditworthiness and detect fraud, also to predict which movies will be successful based on characteristics of the script.

7. *Prediction or opinion markets* are aggregate bets on the likely success of a product such as a movie.

8. *Regression analysis*, described in Chapter 5, is a group of statistical techniques used to predict the value of a dependent value, such as how many copies of a book to produce, based on past results for a given author.

9. *Social network-based recommendation* uses social networks to encourage recommendation sharing among members, making the assumption that those who belong to a specific network are likely to have similar tastes in cultural products such as music.

10. *Textual analytics*, described in Chapter 4, is an analytical technique used to evaluate the frequency, semantic relation, and importance of specific textual terms in a document. The technique is used by search engines and some of the music recommending sites.

In Business Intelligence in Practice 10.2 we describe how collaborative filtering is creating an interesting viral phenomenon for Web-based retailers.

**Business Intelligence In Practice 10.2: Three Wolves Laugh
All the Way to the Bank**

Recommendations are credited to be producing some interesting buying patterns on the Web. An interesting phenomenon related to collaborative filtering happened last May 19, 2009 when Amazon retailer issued a recommendation to college students seeking to buy their college semester books: the purchase of a black T-shirt that featured the image of three wolves howling at the moon.

What followed when a student posted comment on Amazon on how the shirt had magical powers and helped him win the heart of a woman is hard to believe (Daum, 2009). Just a few days later, other content-sharing sites such as Digg picked it up, creating a viral marketing frenzy for the T-shirt. The shirt quickly became Amazon's top-selling apparel item, and sales for its manufacturer Mountain skyrocketed from two or three T-shirts a day to more than 100 a minute.

Enthusiasts of the Three Wolf Moon T-Shirt, the actual name of the T-shirt, have launched a Facebook group devoted to the shirt. It may not be clear exactly what it is that motivates would-be buyers to purchase the shirt, but the fact is that its manufacturer is making a lot of brick and mortar dollars out of the success of a perhaps completely lucky viral collaborative filtering marketing campaign.

In Section 10.5 we discuss the role of mobile technologies for BI.

▶ 10.5 MOBILE APPLICATIONS FOR BUSINESS INTELLIGENCE

Mobile applications have taken center stage over the last decade, including location-based services, mobile financial services, multiparty interactive games, mobile auctions, and software applications to support the mobile workforce, such as mobile enterprise resource planning extensions and personal information management (Varshney and Vetter, 2002). Increasingly, knowledge and business analytics are being discovered, created, and applied on the move by knowledge workers. **Nomadic computing** is defined as "the information systems support that provides computing and communication capabilities and services to users, as they move from place to place" (Becerra-Fernandez, Cousins, and Weber, 2007, p. 104). Figure 10.4 is a representation of what we mean by nomadic computing. Nomadic computing assumes that such support is provided in convenient and transparent fashion to the user, integrated with other relevant information artifacts, which are also adaptive to a set of changing environmental factors (Kleinrock, 2001). In nomadic computing environments, people on the move

FIGURE 10.4 Nomadic Computing

have access to diverse human and technological resources through a diversity of mobile devices such as mobile phones, personal digital assistants (PDAs), and handheld computers and laptops, via wireless Internet connectivity. Portable mobile devices are used to access services and applications that are integrated with the physical world. According to recent research, 56% of best-in-class companies characterize their BI solutions to be pervasive within the organization, and 83% of those firms deliver BI to mobile users within the same day the business events take place (O'Halloran, 2009).

In nomadic context-aware knowledge management systems and BI applications, computing becomes inseparable from the environment and work of the knowledge workers, and serves to support their knowledge-intensive activities as they move from one place to another. However, the significance of mobile remains to be not only on making BI applications pervasive for the user, but also on the fact that mobile applications allow defining additional internal and external dimensions of context, which help to develop the contextual model of the user.

A context-aware system relies on the contextual model to reason and recommend decisions by identifying from the repository of BI applications, such as those described in the preceding chapters, those that are in the same contextual domain as the user. The contextual model becomes the target situation used to compare analytics to, in order to complement their value. Based on this concept, the most relevant contextual components provide the cues, such as positioning, sensory, identity and informational components, that help identify the proper cognitive context within which the user is embedded, and thus improve the relevance of their knowledge management and BI applications. The contextual components that can be inferred through the mobile context-aware systems include the following (Becerra-Fernandez et al., 2007):

a. *Positioning component:* comprises factors such as positioning, sensing, location, spatial location and time, and environmental factors such as temperature (Gellersen, Schmidt, and Beigl, 2002).

b. *Sensory component:* involves both visual and auditory factors, including those specific contextual cues that can be inferred through technology such as video analysis and feature extraction. Vision could be used to determine location, navigate, and recognize situations as they would be seen from a camera (Gellersen et al., 2002).

c. *Identity component:* includes the users' identifiable information, social roles, and preferences that define their profiles.

d. *Informational component:* comprises information resources to support the analytics of the users' organizational context, such as the users' sequence of activities over time, work context, business processes, communications, computing devices and applications, as well as those of other users.

e. *Cognitive component:* represents "the reasoning capabilities used to derive relevant knowledge required to support a specific contextual model. The cognitive component relies on cues and information resources in the positioning, sensory, identity, and informational components as well as proactive actions by the user and the environment to recognize the changing cognitive context surrounding the user, and to build a contextual model" (Becerra-Fernandez et al., 2007, p. 109). For example, a first responder in a disaster moving from one demographic area to another would access a different contextual model as the mobile analytics system adapts to the specific demographics and the needs of the region; that is, problem solving and analytics activities would have shifted according to their respective contexts.

Recognizing the contextual model of a situation can enable a user to determine a specific course of action, and the identification of the cognitive context helps address potential ambiguities. In summary, nomadic computing environments can enhance current BI implementations not only by improving the pervasiveness of BI, but also by providing the contextual cues that can help overcome some of their existing limitations, therefore improving the usability of business analytics.

In Section 10.6 we discuss how BI could assist in making sense of weak signals.

▶ 10.6 THE ROLE OF BI IN MAKING SENSE OF WEAK SIGNALS

It is hard to believe that the economic tsunami that followed the collapse of the subprime markets in 2009 escaped the watchful eyes of so many brilliant minds in the financial industry. This disaster, much like other organizational disasters including the 9/11 terrorist attack of 2001, were long in the making before the inevitable emergency siren made their reality obvious, even to those who would rather ignore the impending signals. Many other examples of disasters stemming from tragic organizational oversights abound in the literature, including the *Challenger* accident, Pearl Harbor (Schoemaker and Day, 2009), and the Vioxx scandal at Merck (Bazerman and Chugh, 2006) (see Business Intelligence in Practice 10.3). Personal and organizational biases have been shown to impair decision-making abilities among managers. Specifically, personal biases filter information in order to confirm what we already "know" (Schoemaker and Day, 2009):

1. *Filtering:* What we pay attention to is determined by what we expect to see.
2. *Distorted inference:* We interpret evidence in a way that sustains our beliefs; moreover, **wishful thinking** makes us see the world in a pleasing way only.
3. *Bolstering:* We seek additional information to confirm our views, like confirming our beliefs with those who agree with us.

Organizational biases include what is known as **groupthink**, which may result in a group falling victim to a narrow-minded analysis or **tunnel vision**.

The obvious question that follows is: Could BI help overcome some of these biases? Consider the following example (*New York Times Editorial*, 2005, p. 30):

"Add to the painful postmortems of 9/11 this week's disclosure that federal aviation officials were more lulled than alarmed by a steady stream of intelligence warnings about Osama bin Laden in the months before the terrorist attacks. As with numerous other intelligence failures uncovered by the Sept. 11 commission, the warnings—dozens of them—were not deemed specific enough to provide adequate defenses at the nation's airports, according to Federal Aviation Administration officials. In 105 intelligence reports received during the five months preceding the attacks, Osama bin Laden or Al Qaeda were mentioned 52 times, according to the commission, which faulted the F.A.A. for not doing enough to heighten security."

As the above example shows, the streams of data flowing into the federal government failed to interconnect with the other pieces of the puzzle to reveal the face of terrorism, perhaps because the individual and organizational biases failed to aid the integration of the different perspectives, rendering the United States inefficient in recognizing the impending emergency. Efficient text-mining algorithms, as we described in Chapter 4, perhaps could have revealed this irregularity, much like the mining programs used by the banks processing credit card transactions in Section 10.2 successfully identified fraudulent activity.

In order to reveal weak signals, organizations are encouraged to, among other things, tap local intelligence (Schoemaker and Day, 2009). Relying on localized intelligence is said to be the key to success for terrorist groups. What does it mean to rely on local intelligence? In essence, "the key to safety and reliability is to spot problems early and share them among well-trained personnel. This requires procedures for real-time cognition and constrained improvisation to bring about flexibility and promptness in highly complex, volatile environments" (Schoemaker and Day, 2009, p. 84). Rewarding a culture of alertness, while providing support for knowledge sharing and localized real-time business intelligence, is perhaps the best first order of defense in overcoming biases and improved reasoning.

In the Business Intelligence in Practice 10.3, we discuss how one type of BI technology, **streaming data** software, can help gain intelligence from continuous, high-volume, real-time data feeds. In addition, video business intelligence can also be used to analyze feeds from standard video cameras to provide businesses with the necessary insights about people and vehicle flow information, ways to secure critical infrastructure, crowd detection, detecting unattended objects, and many other situational awareness applications.

Business Intelligence in Practice 10.3: Streaming Data for Real-Time BI

High-volume data feeds, like those involved in automated financial-market trading, use analytically discovered patterns to generate predictions, but the usefulness of these predictions is tied to how quickly they can be generated. For example, securities-trading data "consists of streams of ticker symbols and prices, lot sizes, times of the last trade, and bids and offers. NASDAQ alone hosts trading in 3,300 companies with billions of daily price quotes and trades" (Grimes, 2005). New BI technologies are offering systems to filter, join, and analyze trading data using a host of approaches. These new systems range from supporting "algorithmic" securities trading through the application of complex, adaptive market models, to assimilating operational data into warehouses that host many simultaneous, diverse data analyses, or, alternatively, into smaller marts refined for narrower analyses (Grimes, 2005).

Extracting intelligence from streaming data offers its own set of challenges, since the data are irregular, unpredictable, and the important data patterns embedded in them may only be uncovered by analyzing "time windows" rather than points, and only by correlating data from multiple information sources. For example, in the securities industry, the interesting trends may be uncovered only when the data in question is compared to prior historic patterns that may point out to anomalies or opportunities to

(continued)

either hedge or exploit. Furthermore, most of the data may include noise, which will need to be filtered from the analysis data.

While many of these technologies may be just stepping out of the university and industrial research labs, streaming-data technology is likely to continue to be well-received by the market, due to organizations' needs to increasingly be proactive when taking advantage of real-time, data-intensive, operational business analytics.

BI could play a role in providing an unbiased voice that could help warn managers of their own personal and organizational biases. In Section 10.7, we present a case study that describes the role that organizational biases at NASA played in the *Columbia* accident.

The benefits from business intelligence are considerable, and progress in BI technologies, in addition to new forms of information, is expected to increase the impact that analytics will continue to have in the organization. However, launching successful BI initiatives is not easy, and they face numerous challenges related to the adoption of technologies and the integration of data and information, technologies, and people within the BI processes. In this book we have tried to provide the reader with a comprehensive overview of the foundations of BI, the opportunities and challenges, as well as some of the important emerging and future directions.

In conclusion, even though interesting challenges may lie ahead for organizations, the future of BI is indeed an exciting one due to the opportunities it will bring to future generations.

CASE STUDY 10-7

ORGANIZATIONAL BIASES AS DECISION BLINDERS AT NASA

On February 1, 2003, the whole world watched in disbelief the loss of the space shuttle *Columbia* and its seven-member crew. Shuttle launches and landings had become such commonplace events that the media had stopped much of their coverage, other than the short mention and segment in the evening news. At once following the accident, a team of 13 was elected to serve in the **Columbia Accident Investigation Board (CAIB)**, supported by over 120 staff members and 400 NASA engineers. The CAIB team would examine more than 30,000 documents, conduct more than 200 formal interviews, hear testimony from dozens of expert witnesses, review more than 3,000 inputs from the general public, and conduct over 25,000 searches over the Western United States to recover and analyze the spacecraft debris (NASA CAIB Report, 2003).

One of the most troubling findings by the CAIB was that the accident "was probably an anomalous, random event, but rather likely rooted to some degree in NASA's history and the

(*continued*)

human space flight program's culture" (NASA CAIB Report, 2003, p. 9). In essence, the CAIB report found two probable causes for the accident, one "physical" and the other "organizational." The physical causes were the sequence of events on Shuttle Mission STS-107 that destroyed the Orbiter: a breach in the Thermal Protection System on the leading edge of the left wing, caused by a piece of insulating foam that separated just a few seconds after launch. During reentry this breach allowed superheated air to penetrate, causing a weakening of the structure and subsequent failure of the wing and breakup of the Orbiter (NASA CAIB Report, 2003).

However, the organizational causes were perhaps more incipient: "the mistakes made on STS-107 were not isolated failures, but rather were indicative of systemic flaws that existed prior to the accident" (NASA CAIB Assessment, 2004, p. 1); in other words, organizational causes were "precursors to the physical cause, in essence organizational conditions that allowed the technical failures to take place and eventually lead to the accident (NASA CAIB Assessment, 2004, p. 5). Organizational causes included resource constraints, schedule pressures, reliance on past successes, organizational barriers that prevented effective communication of critical safety information, lack of integrated management across programs, and the evolution of an informal chain of command and decision-making processes operating outside the organization's rules. What followed the *Columbia* accident was a concerted organizational effort focused on seven categories: establishing leadership, creating a learning organization with a strong commitment to knowledge management, improving the flow of communication including the fostering of diverse views, following its own processes and rules, strengthening in-house technical capabilities, empowering the safety and engineering organizational structures, establishing a consistent set of risk assessment tools, and not accepting increasing levels of risk. All of these measures are focused on minimizing organizational biases.

Could BI help minimize personal and organizational biases and thus prevent these organizational disasters in the future?

► 10.8 SUMMARY

In this chapter we described what social networks are and how they provide important external information that can be mined to make organizations increasingly competitive. Social networking technologies can have an important impact in the organization, when used both on the Internet, in what is known as Web 2.0, and within organizations, known as Enterprise 2.0. We included in the discussion how emerging technologies such as wikis and blogs are used in the organization, and how organizations are redefining their marketing strategy to increasingly incorporate the social media technologies that users are spending more of their time with. We presented the ways BI can be used to predict what people want. We also described the role that mobile applications play in BI, not only to increase the pervasiveness of these applications but also to improve their context awareness. Finally, we discussed how BI can be used to minimize personal and organizational biases, in particular via real-time data streaming.

► KEY TERMS

bolstering	distorted inference	filtering
CAIB	Enterprise 2.0	groupthink

mobile context-aware	social media	weak ties
systems	streaming data	Web 2.0
nomadic computing	tunnel vision	wishful thinking

▶ REVIEW QUESTIONS

1. What is the difference between Web 2.0 and Enterprise 2.0?

2. What is the difference between wikis, blogs, and microblogs?

3. Read the paper "Decisions without Blinders" by Bazerman and Chugh (2006). Describe the Vioxx scandal at Merck. How did personal biases contribute to this corporate disaster?

4. How do personal biases filter information in order to confirm what we already know?

5. Describe how streaming data is used in real-time BI.

6. What are the contextual components that can be inferred through mobile context-aware systems?

▶ APPLICATION EXERCISES

1. Could social networking redefine collaboration within organizations? How?

2. Research the practitioner literature to identify how some top organizations are deploying an Enterprise 2.0 architecture.

3. Research and describe the policies and guidelines for contributing to Wikipedia. Who developed these guidelines? How does Wikipedia reward contributions?

4. Post an entry in Wikipedia, either by a new contribution or by editing an existing article. How do the current contribution guidelines at Wikipedia support the ideals of collective wisdom?

5. How can extracting intelligence from streaming data help overcome personal biases in decision making?

▶ REFERENCES

Bazerman, M., and Chugh, D. 2006. "Decisions without Blinders." *Harvard Business Review*, January, pp. 88–97.

Becerra-Fernandez, I., Cousins, K., and Weber, R. 2007. "Nomadic Context-Aware Knowledge Management Systems: Applications, Challenges, and Research Problems." *International Journal of Mobile Learning and Organisation*, 1(2) 103–121.

Colvin. 2008. "Selling P&G: How Do You Sell $76 Billion of Consumer Goods? One Brand at a Time." *Fortune*, June 17.

Davenport, T., and Harris, J. 2009a. "What People Want (and How to Predict It)." *Sloan Management Review*, 50(2), 23–31.

Davenport, T., and Harris, J. 2009b. "The Prediction Lover's Handbook." *Sloan Management Review*, 50(2), 32–34.

Daum, M. 2009. "Three Wolves T-shirt Goes Viral on Internet." *Herald Online*, June 1. Last accessed at http://www.heraldonline.com/opinions/story/1293978.html on June 21, 2009.

Gellersen, H., Schmidt, A., and Beigl, M. 2002. "Multi-Sensor Context-Awareness in Mobile Devices and Smart Artifacts." *Mobile Networks and Applications*, 7, pp. 341–351.

Grimes, S. 2005. "Keeping Up With Streaming Data–Technology Proven in Stock Trading Can Tap the Details in the Flood of Streaming Data Coming Your Way." *Intelligent Enterprise*, May 1.

Kleinrock, L. Breaking Loose. 2001. *Communications of the ACM*, 44(4), 43–48.

McAfee, A. 2006. "Enterprise 2.0: The Dawn of Emergent Collaboration." *MIT Sloan Management Review*, 47(3), 21–28.

McKinsey. 2007a. How Businesses Are Using Web 2.0: A McKinsey Global Survey. www.mckinseyquarterly.com (September). Retrieved on September 12, 2008.

McKinsey. 2007b. How Companies Are Marketing Online: A McKinsey Global Survey. www.mckinseyquarterly.com (September). Retrieved on September 12, 2008.

McKinsey. 2008. How Businesses Are Using Web 2.0: A McKinsey Global Survey. www.mckinseyquarterly.com (September). Retrieved on September 12, 2008.

McNulty, E., Lee, J., Boni, B., Coghlan, J., and Foley, J. 2007. "Boss, I. Think Someone Stole Our Customer Data." Harvard Business Review Case Study and Commentary R0709Z, September.

NASA CAIB Report. 2003. National Aeronautics and Space Administration Columbia Accident Investigation Board (CAIB) Report, August.

NASA CAIB Assessment. 2004. National Aeronautics and Space Administration—A Renewed Commitment to Excellence: An Assessment of the NASA Agency-wide applicability of the Columbia Accident Investigation Board Report, January.

New York Times Editorial. 2005. "A Vital Job Goes Begging." *New York Times*, February 12.

O'Halloran, J. 2009. "Mobility Solutions for SMEs Business Intelligence Leaders Move to Mobile Computing." *ComputerWeekly*. January 7.

PCI. 2009. Payment Card Industry (PCI) Security Standard Council Payment Card Industry Security Standards, at a glance standards overview, https://www.pcisecurity-standards.org/security_standards/pci_dss.shtml (last accessed on August 19, 2009).

Reichenstein, O. 2007. The Future of News, How to Survive the New Media Shift. Manuscript V 0.5, Information Architects K.K., Tokyo.

Schoemaker, P., and Day, G. 2009. "How to Make Sense of Weak Signals." *MIT Sloan Management Review*, 50(3), 81–89.

Triplepundit. 2009. Twitter for T-shirts: Procter & Gamble Tests Social Media with Tide Loads of Hope, May 12. Accessed from the Web at http://www.triplepundit.com/pages/twitter-for-tshirts-proctor-and-gamble-t.php on June 20, 2009.

Varshney, U., and Vetter, R. 2002. "Mobile Commerce: Framework, Applications and Networking Support." *Mobile Networks and Applications*, 7(3), 185–198.

INDEX

tools and solutions for, 6
volume of data for, 9
windows of opportunity for, 9–10
Decision areas, 247
Decision makers:
KPIs for, 164
presentations for, 166
providing information to, 6, 7, 10, 14, 15, 17
Decision-making bodies, 246–247
Decision rights, 247
Decision Sciences, vi
Decision search trees, 129
Decision support systems (DSS), 11–12
BI vs., 12, 13
vertically-integrated, 131–132
Decision trees, 89, 129–132, 272
Declarative design, 184
Dedicated resources, 250
Dedication, of team members, 54
Deep Web, 97
Deficiencies, meeting, 160
Delicious.com, 269
Deliverables, in BI development, 234
Delivery of information, 83, 247
Delta Airlines, 66–67
Demographic data, 114
Demonstrating value, 140
Departmental-level BI, 249–250
Deployment:
of analytics, 139
of balanced scorecards, 162–163
as BI development step, 237
of data mining, 120
of data mining technologies, 139–140
of ERP, 75–77
Derived data, 57
Describing what happened, business analytics for, 121–124
Descriptive techniques (DM), 122
Design iteration, 230
Design specifications, 235–236
Desktop computers, 138
Desktop development, 32
Development:
agile, 230–233
of BI, 224–225, 234–237
desktop, 32
of enterprise architecture, 140
external, 224
in-house, 224, 225
joint, 224
planning for, 233–235
Dicing data (OLAP), 150

Digital content management systems, 30
Digital dashboards, 41–43, 154, 179, 187. *See also* Performance dashboards
Digital data storage, 138
Digital expertise, 266
Digitized platform, 66
Dimensions (OLAP), 149
Dimensional modeling, 59, 60
Diplomacy programs, 177–178
Director of BI, 247, 253
Discipline, 161
Discrete data, 121
Discriminant analysis, 126
Discussion groups, 28
Disparate sources, 28, 57
Dissemination, visual analytics for, 152, 153
Distorted inference, 276
Diversification operating model, 64, 65
DM, *see* Data mining
DMG (Data Mining Group), 121
DM Review magazine, 238
Document management systems, 30, 68–69
Dow Chemical Company, 19, 66
Drivers of BI, 8–10, 112–113
DSS, *see* Decision support systems
Duby, Sally, 39
Dunkin' Donuts, 20, 42
DWs, *see* Data warehouses
Dynamic environment, 223
Dynamic requirements, 231

E
EA, *see* Enterprise architecture
EA (environmental analyzability), 84
EAI, *see* Enterprise application integration
eBags, 114
eBay, 266
e-commerce, 114
Economic uncertainty, 19, 87
Economies of scale, 161
eCourier.co.uk, 17–18
Edelstein, H., 92
Education:
in BI, 256
for ERP deployment, 75
Effective communication, 54
Efficiency:
organizational, 15
from standardization, 64
EIS business performance dashboards, 169, 170
Elective courses, vi
Electric Power Research Institute, 133

Electronic data, 9
ELS, *see* Expertise locator systems
e-mail, 29, 34
e-marketing analytics, 166
Embedded business processes, 52
EMC Documentum, 68
Emergency response, visual analytics in, 152–153
Enacting mode (environmental scanning), 84, 85
End-user education, for ERP deployment, 75
Energizer Holdings, Inc., 252
Enterprise 2.0, 267–269
Enterprise application integration (EAI), 55, 95
Enterprise architecture (EA), 63–67, 140
Enterprise content management, 32, 34
Enterprise content management systems, 68
Enterprise data, 9. *See also* Data warehouses
Enterprise-level BI, 249, 250
Enterprise resource planning systems (ERP), 29, 30, 52–56
critical success factors for, 54
criticisms of, 54–55
defined, 52
at IBM Personal Systems Group, 71–77
for organizational memory capability, 181
Enterprise solution (DWs), 59
Enterprise-wide content searches, 29, 34
Entity-relational (ER) modeling, 59
Environments:
for data warehouses, 56–57
dynamic, 223
production, 61
regulatory, 87
social, 87
Environmental analyzability (EA), 84
Environmental scanning, 23, 85–88, 183
Environmental uncertainty, 84, 86–87
ER (entity-relational) modeling, 59
ERP, *see* Enterprise resource planning systems
e-tailers, 113, 114
ETL software, *see* Extract/transform (or transfer)/load software
Evaluation of BI, 256–257
Evelson, Boris, 234